I0616557

Evelyn Annuß, Raz Weiner (eds.)
Facing Drag

Evelyn Annuß, Professor of Gender Studies, heads the International Research Center Gender and Performativity (IGCP) at the University of Music and Performing Arts Vienna. Her work is dedicated to the flight lines of aesthetics, theories of performativity, and the critique of politics. As a cultural studies scholar of theatre and literature, she focuses, among other things, on political spectacles—their historicity and mediality—in the context of National Socialism, colonial racisms, and processes of (re-)fascization. Her new book *Dirty Dragging. Performative Transpositions* is being published simultaneously in German and in English by mdwPress.

Raz Weiner (Dr.) is a scholar of performance studies, politics, and embodiment. His work focuses on traditions, archives and contemporary forms of colonialism, racialization and queerness, the production of bodies and knowledge, and the co-constitution of human societies and digital worlds. Before becoming a guest lecturer (2024) and research fellow (2023) at mdw, he was based in the School of Politics and IR at Queen Mary University in London (2020—2022) and the Faculty of Architecture and Town Planning at The Technion in Haifa (2021—2023).

Evelyn Annuß, Raz Weiner (eds.)

Facing Drag

Gender Bending and Racialized Masking
in Performing Arts and Popular Culture

 [transcript]

Bibliographic information published by the Deutsche Nationalbibliothek
The Deutsche Nationalbibliothek lists this publication in the Deutsche Nationalbibliografie; detailed bibliographic data are available in the Internet at https://dnb.dnb.de

First published in 2025 by mdwPress, Vienna and Bielefeld
© Evelyn Annuß, Raz Weiner

transcript Verlag | Hermannstraße 26 | D-33602 Bielefeld | live@transcript-verlag.de

Cover design: Oliver Brentzel in cooperation with Evelyn Annuß
Copyediting: Michael Thomas Taylor
Layout: Auer Grafik Buch Web, Vienna
Printing: Druckhaus Bechstein GmbH, Wetzlar
https://doi.org/10.14361/9783839471708
Print-ISBN: 978-3-8376-8118-5
PDF-ISBN: 978-3-8394-7170-8
ePUB-ISBN: 978-3-7328-0015-5

This publication received financial support from the Open Access Fund of mdw – University of Music and Performing Arts Vienna.

Contents

Opening

Temporal Drag and Queering Fabulations

Performing along "the" Color Line

Facing Contemporary Commodification

Staging (Post)Colonial Relations

Epilogue

OPENING

Notes on Facing Drag

Evelyn Annuß

How do we connect the manifold carnivalesque articulations of colonialism and racism to a queer understanding of drag in the sense of exaggerated display (Lorber 2004)? In what ways are these articulations reinvoked and commodified within new media assemblages and differentiated within diverse geographical contexts and varied trajectories of racialization and Othering? How might they be conceived from a global perspective that also questions the reification of *the* putative color line through the lens of the Global South?[1] And how might we foreground existing forms of performing societal alternatives? *Facing Drag* is dedicated to exploring these questions by critically engaging with the paradigm of performativity as a key concept in gender studies (Parker and Sedgwick 1995): drag was theorized in the 1990s as a transgressive performative practice that exposes difference in repetition—reflecting the possibility of (re)signification and the change of norms (Butler 1990, Muñoz 1999). Against the backdrop of the ongoing resurgence of attempts to theorize critical drag in both recent and forthcoming publications, it seems timely to face—to address, confront—transgressive practices through the questions posed above (Heller 2020, Khubchandani 2023, McGlotten 2021, Schroedl 2025).

However, performativity itself has been resignified over the last decades. Once understood as a figure of critical thinking, it has also been absorbed into management rhetoric, where it affirmatively promotes successful self-presentations (Cabantous et al. 2016). The deconstructive turn from expressivity to performativity has been co-opted as a tool for neoliberalization and the political spectacles accompanying it. Today, the term is increasingly associated with the dragging—that is, with the gravitational, depressing, advent of new modes of governmentality that seem to bury not only the phantasm of an authentic inner self, but the dream of alternatives to capitalist relations—of alternative *Beziehungsweisen*, to cite Bini Adamczak (Adamczak 2017). Over the

---

1   See Erasmus in this volume; on the critique of Afro-pessimist US exceptionalism and its ahistoricity see—from within US academia—Thomas 2018, Reed 2018.

last decades, something already appears to have been lost in the translation of performativity into the celebration of individualized competitiveness under liberal economic regimes. This resignification, which undermines performativity's critical potential, may have gradually indicated the limitations of 1990s happy queer theory readings of performativity as gender-bending drag.

We are living in dragging times indeed—a historical shift in which the deconstructive force of earlier queer theoretical interventions has been overtaken by a new form of neoliberal dismantling: what was predominantly associated with the undoing of a (hetero)normative matrix has been superseded by the libertarian far right's systematic destruction of institutions—infrastructures and material conditions whose relevance was often sidelined in the wake of the performative turn of the 1990s (Annuß 1998, originally published in 1996). Contemporary assaults on queer, reproductive, and trans rights—manifestations of so-called antigenderism (Butler 2024, Sauer and Penz 2023)—are only one dimension of a broader neoauthoritarian turn and the potential fascization of economic liberalism on a global scale. While dismantling may resonate as an anarchic rallying cry,[2] undoing now risks becoming a new normal of unregulated racket ruling—a mode of organized destabilization performed as the destruction of "the establishment" (Bröckling 2024; Žižek 2024). Foucault identified queer liberties as the flipside of a new control society (Foucault 2008, 239—266), but that may already be water under the collapsing bridge. In the mid-1980s, he could still stress the ambivalences of neoliberalism—economic deregulation alongside the recognition of minority liberties. Decades later, in the wake of economic liberalization, populist politics of resentment have hit full scale to accompany what Naomi Klein termed *disaster capitalism* and what Alberto Toscano more recently calls *late fascism* (Klein 2007, Toscano 2023). As DEI initiatives and poverty relief programs are systematically defunded, antigenderism needs to be contextualized not as an isolated backlash, but as integral to this broader shift. Today, hegemonic appropriations of minority rights discourses in service of majoritarian rule (Farris 2017, Puar 2007) not only reinforce exclusionary politics, but also fuel a form of *belligerent accumulation*[3]—one whose targets are volatile, shifting with geopolitical, class, or

---

2   See Jack Halberstam's opening keynote "Dereliction: On Feminist Violence" at the 2025 opening of the International Research Center Gender and Performativity at the University of Music and Performing Arts Vienna, www.mdw.ac.at/icgp/events/international-research-center-gender-and-performativity-icgp-opening/, accessed July 25, 2025.

3   See Katja Diefenbach, Ruth Sonderegger and Pablo Valdivia Orozco at https://accumulation-race-aesthetics.org/, accessed September 25, 2024.

cultural location. In this very context, drag needs to be rethought as a situated practice (Annuß 2025).

This is especially pertinent given that the global right-wing backlash is increasingly accompanied by carnivalesque performances that celebrate the destruction of infrastructure and the destitution of law (Annuß 2019, 2024). Performative transgressions from the right—such as the costumed storming of government buildings during the COVID-19 pandemic in Berlin or in Washington, DC, or the chainsaw theatrics of figures like Javier Milei and Elon Musk—compel us to reconsider the biopolitical environments in which transgressive bodily appearances gain significance. Where some of us within gender studies used to conceptualize the carnivalesque primarily through the lens of queer subversion, as in gender-bending drag, it may now be necessary to critically reassess our research designs and the habitual use of certain figures of thought. This includes historicizing our analytical categories and recognizing their (geographical, often privilege-based) embeddedness.

Our understanding of drag as a paradigm in theorizing queer performativity may thus need expansion. We ought to account for destructive forms of mimesis, for stagings of excess referentiality that weaponize performative spectacle rather than parody hegemonic culture. And in this broader sense, drag has long been part of the spectacles of the right. If understood as a situated practice of transgressive public appearance, it might be reactivated as a tool for critical thinking on the specificity of particular political environments. Rather than confining drag to the domains of queer performance and disidentification, this book reconceptualizes it as an allegory of the ambivalent messiness of mimesis—with all its potential for both subversion and instrumentalization. *Facing Drag* thus interrogates the divergent affordances of situatedness in order to understand how mimetic practices can function across, and sometimes against, societal conditions and political imaginaries.

In light of today's appropriation of performative transgressions by the political right, studies of drag may be shifting—from a predominant focus on gender play to an expanded analysis that incorporates its historical and structural entanglement with performative practices of racialization: as early as the 2000s, Katrin Sieg proposed such a move, shifting the analysis of queer drag toward racialized forms of theatrical appearance (Sieg 2002). This implied a critical turn from the liberatory connotations of "dirty" bodily stagings to the invective exposure of "dirty" faces—exemplified by blackface as a form of racialized drag in the wake of colonial entanglements and overexploitation. Such performative practices—marked by grotesque distortion and figurations of difference—have long weaponized the constitutive referential messiness of mimesis, predating queer theory's institutionalization (Balke and Linseisen 2022). Mimesis, then, is not inherently subversive, but can also be complicit with hegemonic culture and, at times, operate in the wake of eliminatory violence.[4] By extending our conception of drag beyond its semiotic and affective potential for queer subversion to its transgressive appeal within a politics of resentment and destruction, we can more thoroughly historicize its ambivalent forms and functions and reflect the right's current occupation of mimetic transgression in the context of its historic precedents, particularly in the racialized articulations of the carnivalesque (Mbembe 2001).[5] This, however, calls for reassessing its scope of reference—specifying its usages within the slippery terrain where libertarianism intersects with alt-right forms of transgression: What does it imply when it is not the subaltern, but the dystopian anarchism of the self-proclaimed fittest that sets about dismantling what once was called the *master's house* (Lorde 2018, originally published 1970)? How does today's "rebellious, anti-systemic theater" (Schuster 2020, 234) of the ruling class reshape calls to recognize representations of queerness as a means of disrupting normative interpellations? In light of these questions, how might we rethink drag?

Extending the concept to encompass color bending—that is, practices of racialized masking—broadens the analytic horizon to include the dynamics of political violence more thoroughly. In this expanded frame, drag's alleged etymology of "towing a stage costume" comes into play. We might thus "face"—in both senses of confronting and giving face—the act of dragging as the schlepping-along of social entanglements.[6] Rather than relegating performativity to a coaching ideology or reducing drag to representationalism and politics of recognition, this volume foregrounds the analytic relevance of queer theories' postdeconstructive, materialist conceptual contributions. Elizabeth Freeman's take on drag, for instance, underscores a "necessary referential vulgarity"—a desire to relate to Other(ed), queer bodies across time and space (Freeman 2010). Her approach moves beyond abstract notions of resignification to highlight drag's affective charge. Crucially, Freeman's theorizing of drag as a historical pullback also helps to understand the affective operations of right-wing politics—particularly the mobilizations of resentment (Vogl 2022). In this light, drag emerges as a *Gedankenfigur*, a figure of thought, not only of queer memory and longing, but also as a vehicle for the actual dismantling of material relations and societal infrastructures—hard-won policies and institutions aimed at redressing structural inequalities. To summarize, drag may have lost some of its appeal as a subversive, empowering, and liberatory mode

---

4   See Weiner in this volume.

5   On US blackface minstrelsy, see Lott in this volume.

6   See the companion monograph *Dirty Dragging* for a differentiation of heterogeneous modes of drag and a more extensive conceptualization of its relation to dragging as *schlepping* (Annuß 2025, 2026); see also McGlotten 2021, 7.

of staging our messy selves, particularly in the wake of neoliberalism's increasingly destructive materializations. Yet appearing in drag has been and remains to be contested. An extended notion of dragging, one attentive to its embeddedness in specific historical and sociopolitical contexts, may open up avenues for analyzing the collective trajectories of public appearance and for imagining multidirectional solidarities (Rothberg 2009) that counter the co-optation of the transgressive. This could contribute to a rethinking of what Meredith Heller has called *queering drag* (Heller 2020).

As theorists of creolization have emphasized (Glissant 1990, 1997; Erasmus 2011, 2012, 2020), reappropriations of colonial and exoticist modes of performing illustrate the uncontrollable entanglements of mimesis. These entanglements carry the potential for new agencies. Analyzing and bringing together diverse historical constellations and mimetic practices may expose the possibility of collective acts of microresistance. These performative practices may not offer direct solutions to today's political catastrophes. But they may give form to a desire for otherwise—to what Saidiya Hartman has called *performing (an) otherwise* (Hartman 2020). In a time marked by political defeatism, such performative modes of relating may allegorize a disposition to move beyond competitive self-fashioning, provoking us to imagine transversal flight lines—forms of solidarity not bound to groupism, a terrain successfully occupied by the political right.

How, then, might this concept of drag intersect with questions of temporality and fabulation? What tools can critical race studies and perspectives based in the Global South offer toward an expanded understanding of drag as a mimetic practice embedded in systems of power? Moreover, what is the biopolitical backdrop of drag's contemporary theorization—especially within today's media assemblages and commodified visual politics? How can we map the historical, geographical symptomatology of what we involuntarily drag along when we appear in public? And what are the (post)colonial implications of performing within different contexts—contexts shaped by asymmetrical histories of representation, violence, and resistance?

*

Engaging with these concerns, *Facing Drag* is the outcome of international conferences and a concomitant lecture series taking place between 2022 and 2024 at the University of Music and Performing Arts Vienna (mdw)—conceived at a time when the postpandemic transformations of neoliberalism were not yet as visible as today.[7] These events were organized by what has since become the International Research Center Gender and Performativity (ICGP).[8] The contributions assembled here are primarily grounded in theorizations of performativity and performing arts studies. As a collection ranging from theoretical approaches developed in the Global South to the analyses of premodern European court spectacles, modern minstrelsy, and contemporary popular culture, as well as transcultural entanglements in modern theater, *Facing Drag* spotlights racial masking, colonial mimicry, and digital performance in connection to questions of gendering. In its deliberate heterogeneity and openness, it complements a monograph on minor mimesis and the reconceptualization of dragging as schlepping-along, titled *Dirty Dragging* (Annuß 2025, 2026), which explores the transoceanic trajectories of performative transpositions with regard to apartheid, Nazism, and the Jim Crow era. This volume likewise aims to rethink drag—bringing together scholars and artists from different fields of study and parts of the globe to address, historicize, and contextualize—that is, to face—practices of Othering and of mimesis in the performing arts and in popular culture. Elaborating on aesthetic materials, the assembled contributions to *Facing Drag* analyze differing performative modes of appearing in public. Diverse as they may be, these contributions indicate together a shift in perspectives—a postintersectional, transversal reflection of colonial relations and their afterlife, a new emphasis in questions of societal environments (Hörl 2018), the drive to rethink what drag might mean against the backdrop of today's political affordances.

Overview

Facing Drag is framed by contributions from intellectuals who stress the relevance of the Global South for rethinking drag: sociologist **Zimitri Erasmus** and artist nora chipaumire in conversation with curator Jay Pather. Possible reformulations of dragging are addressed in four sections following Erasmus's **opening** essay, *Caribbean Critical Thought and "Drag" Performances of Indigenization*, in which she reflects on the distant kinship of theorizing creolization and creolized masking practices in the Archipelago as well as in Southern Africa, seeking to extend established perspectives on coloniality and race.

---

7   For more information on the conferences, see www.mdw.ac.at/ikm/facing-ethnic-drag/ and www.mdw.ac.at/ikm/?PageId=4744; for more information on the film and lecture series, see www.mdw.ac.at/ikm/facing-drag-film-and-lecture-series/, all accessed September 11, 2024.

8   For more information, see www.mdw.ac.at/icgp/, accessed July 25, 2025.

The book then offers four sections. It starts with issues of temporality in film studies, followed by case studies of racialized drag in the United States and a section on visual popular culture, and concludes with historical prefigurations of what an extended understanding of drag might imply. It does not seek to give a complete overview on phenomena related to these themes and questions, but rather to offer exemplary readings that resonate, however distantly, with one another.

Temporal Drag and Queering Fabulations (Section 1) opens with two case studies in film. These contributions aim to reconceptualize our understanding of drag in relation to cinema as a paradigmatic medium of transtemporality (Freeman 2010) and to explore the relational dimension of fabulation (Nyong'o 2018). **Sam Ehrentraut** analyzes Jessie Dunn Rovinelli's So Pretty and its instrumental quoting of Ronald M. Schernikau's 1980s novel So schön, which depicts the West Berlin drag scene before the fall of the Wall. The film transposes Schernikau's book into a contemporary transgender constellation in New York City during the Black Lives Matter protests. Revisiting Freeman's concept of temporal drag, Ehrentraut's essay Transtemporal Making-Out—On "Temporal Drag" in Jessie Dunn Rovinelli's "So Pretty" (2019) studies the film's aesthetics to envision entangled forms of relating. It explores nonappropriative encounters that stage a blurry portrait of collective queer becoming—beyond the representation of fixed queer identities and beyond a respective "faceism" (Weigel 2013, 11). **Nanna Heidenreich's** "Whose Portrait?" Fabulations and Triangulations in Shirley Clarke's "Portrait of Jason" (1967) likewise develops a relational understanding of dragging as a queering practice. Through an analysis of cinematic documentation, fluid appearances and their reception in the context of racialized projections and desires, Heidenreich examines the triangular dynamics within the production and the reception. Her reading explores the potentiality of the film portrait beyond its definition as a medium of self-representation and exemplifies the violence inherent in social and love relations—violence that is dragged along in the cinematic capture of "the Other." In terms of temporal drag and queering fabulations, both contributions move beyond representationalism and reductive notions of binary relations. Ehrentraut emphasizes the queer utopian potential of rethinking drag in temporal terms; Heidenreich, in turn, foregrounds its biopolitical embeddedness within a specific context haunted by racialized violence.

Performing along "the" Color Line (Section 2) further drags the notion of drag from its associations with empowerment into contexts of racist violence in the United States. By historicizing blackening-up in popular culture, this section reflects on the invective flipside of transgressive performativity in drag. Again working with the trope of temporal drag, **Eric Lott's** Blackface from Time to Time addresses the deployment of the minstrel mask coined in the nineteenth century and their *survie* in contemporary popular culture. He reads the ongoing reappearances of this form of racial drag as indicators of the "time-to-time-temporality" of unresolved racist relations haunting popular culture—in film, music, masquerade practices, and political performances. Blackface, Lott argues, has a specific "throwback quality" that goes beyond "cross-racial" appropriative desires and instead exposes how its afterlife can be mobilized within the political present to "theatricalize" and thus reinforce the US color line through a recursiveness out of joint. While Lott focuses on the contemporary afterlife of blackface, **Elaine S. Frantz's** *Reading the Blackened Faces of the Ku-Klux Klan in the Reconstruction-Era United States* studies its use as racial mimicry by vigilante white supremacists' performing carnivalesque terror in the wake of abolition. Drawing on a multiplicity of historical sources, Frantz contextualizes these terrorist masquerades of the first Klan of the late 1860s within the broader popular culture of the time—especially in racist caricatures of minstrel shows. As she demonstrates, however, blackening the face was not only a mode of cross-racial misrepresentation, but also a sensationalist tool entangled with other traditions of violence. It was associated with nocturnal crime and the return of the undead. In this reading, blackface becomes an empty signifier with multidirectional referentiality, yet within a context of racialized violence that demanded its spectacular promotion. Its referential excesses may thus be understood as prefigurations of today's right-wing carnival. The section concludes with an outlook on performing arts neglected by hegemonic receptions: on Black drag shows in the mid-twentieth-century "Big Easy." **Aurélie Godet's** *Gender Bending in the Southern Babylon: Black "Female Impersonators" in 1940s–1960s New Orleans* focuses on queer performances within the Black community of a Southern city long associated with vice. Drawing on photos, text sources and oral history, Godet revisits the paradigm of performativity theory by foregrounding a community whose drag history has rarely been documented. She sketches out how performing in drag challenged not only binary gender norms, but also a specifically sexualized color line. Focusing on pre-Civil Rights New Orleans, the essay dispels the myth of the Black community as uniformly antiqueer and instead highlights how stars of Black drag—from Patsy Vidalia to Little Richard and Roberta—along with the "cross-fertilizing" *longue durée* of their shows, can be read as embodied prefigurations of a societal otherwise: one that transcends intersecting binaries of race, gender and sexuality.

Facing Contemporary Commodification (Section 3) addresses contrary afterlives of blackface: (1) with regard to affect politics in meme culture, and (2) through representations of "the Other" beyond the US color line. Contemporary media assemblages, shaped by affective politics of resentment, have generated new forms of facial drag that circulate globally—targeted at distinct societal bubbles, increasingly detached from live appearances. Social media platforms facilitate parallel public spheres in which transgressive visualizations of "the Other" can circulate and go viral. However, as noted above, drag may also be mobilized in service of racist representational regimes. There is a plethora of ways to "give a face," to deface or reface. This is where performance and media analysis can help illuminate the workings of spectacular symbolic politics—including the ones we are currently confronted with. Analyzing a popular Oprah Winfrey meme, **Katrin Köppert's** *Digital Blackface and Memetic Ambiguity* reads today's meme culture as a continuation of the minstrel tradition's grotesque defacing of Black people—now instrumentalized as digital signifiers of affect. Focusing on its feminized stagings on social media, Köppert shifts the lens from minstrelsy's masculinism to a contemporary regendering of "the mask." She interprets meme culture as a performative appropriation of a specifically situated notion of Blackness in the sense of asignification, that is, as the racialized visualization of affect. **Raz Weiner's** *On Arab Masquerades and Necropolitics: Invisibilization and Hypervisibilization in Israeli Popular Culture* transposes the question of facing and othering to the Middle Eastern conflict zone. His essay compares strategies of invisibilization and hypervisibilization—and their political function—through representations of Arabness in Israeli popular culture. Through contextualizing and recontouring the broader political fantasies upon which these impersonations rely, the necropolitical dimension of ethnic mimicry or drag is exposed—after all evoking today's sociocidal war crimes.

Staging (Post)Colonial Relations (Section 4) further globalizes and historicizes perspectives. This section discusses manifold appropriations of theatrical performances within early colonialism and modern exoticism and outlines complex transcultural entanglements. **Karin Harrasser's** *Borrowed Plumes, Jesuit Drag, and Costumes as Uncontrollable Residuals* analyzes European performances of indigeneity in the sixteenth century—long before the nineteenth-century US fashion of *playing Indian* (Deloria 2022). Ranging from courtly cross-dressing allegorizations of America by Friedrich I, to Jesuit performative *conquista* in Latin America as a governmental tool accompanying colonial extractivism, and to the "indigenizing" of Christian rituals in the context of anticolonial resistance and satire, these historical enactments indicate layers of ambivalent cultural techniques. Their afterlife, Harrasser suggests, may bear witness to an uncontrollable dragging-along of violence—as well as to the enduring dream of social change within the postcolonial imaginary. **Julia Ostwald's** *Japonist Drag: Performing Entangled Exoticisms in Dance and Theater around 1900* interrogates differing modes of (self-)exoticization within European-Japanese cultural encounters. Bringing together performances of Japonisme by the Kawakami ensemble in fin-de-siècle Europe and its queer reception by Alexander Sakharoff—as well as their later straightening Westernization of

Japanese modern theater—Ostwald challenges the notion of drag as cultural appropriation. In a detailed analysis of complementary dance performances, her essay underscores how phantasms of exotic authenticity, their performative queering, and reversals of exoticism complicate retrospective projections of binary power relations. Harrasser's and Ostwald's essays thus transpose manifestations of exoticism into a broader quest for epistemologies beyond representation.

The **Epilogue** returns to the questions raised by Zimitri Erasmus in the opening section of *Facing Drag*. **Jay Pather's** artist talk with choreographer, performer, and filmmaker **nora chipaumire** addresses practices of drag within contemporary performing arts against the backdrop of colonialism and globalization, while rhetorically staging the shapeshifting dimension of drag itself. This shapeshifting is also reflected in the constellation of our volume—dedicated to research from differing, yet corresponding, angles.

Facing Drag thus brings together prominent thinkers from various disciplines to reconsider drag beyond its conventional reading as a performance of gender transgression. Through original contributions that engage with cinema, choreography, online media, and critical historiography, the volume examines how drag has transformed through figures of analysis such as temporal and ethnic drag, and how it intersects with legacies of colonial domination, social entanglements, and political spectacle. Amid a worldwide resurgence of hostility against queer and gender-nonconforming articulations, the essays in this volume engage with political implications of various forms of drag. Drawing on contributions from diverse fields of cultural studies and geographic contexts, *Facing Drag* aims to broaden the conversation beyond dominant Northern paradigms, and to provide a cross-cutting, transversal intervention into contemporary debates on performativity and power.

References

Adamczak, Bini. 2017. *Beziehungsweise Revolution: 1917, 1968 und kommende.* Berlin: Suhrkamp.

Annuß, Evelyn. 1998. "The Butler-Boom: Queer Theory's Impact on Women's/ Gender Studies." In *Queering the Canon: Defying Sights in German Literature and Culture*, edited by Christoph Lorey and John L. Plews, 73—86. Columbia: Camden House. German original, 1996: "Umbruch und Krise der Geschlechterforschung: Judith Butler als Symptom." *Das Argument* 216 (1996): 505—524.

Annuß, Evelyn. 2019. "Populismus und Theater." In *Was zu fürchten vorgegeben wird: Alterität und Xenophobie*, edited by Susanne Teutsch, 226—236. Vienna: Praesens.

Annuß, Evelyn. 2024. "Populismus und Kritik." In *Populismus kritisieren: Kunst—Politik—Geschlecht*, edited by Evelyn Annuß, Ralf von Appen, Sarah Chaker, Silke Felber, Andrea Glauser, Therese Kaufmann, Susanne Lettow, 23—39. Wien/Bielefeld: mdwPress.

Annuß, Evelyn. 2025. *Dirty Dragging: Performative Transpositionen*. Wien/Bielefeld: mdwPress.

Annuß, Evelyn. 2026. *Dirty Dragging: Performative Transpositions*. Wien/Bielefeld: mdwPress.

Balke, Friedrich and Elisa Linseisen, eds. 2022. *Mimesis Expanded: Die Ausweitung der mimetischen Zone*. Paderborn: Wilhelm Fink.

Bröckling, Ulrich, Susanne Krasmann, and Thomas Lemke, eds. 2024. *Glossar der Gegenwart*. Berlin: Suhrkamp.

Butler, Judith. 1990. *Gender Trouble: Feminism and the Subversion of Identity*. New York: Routledge.

Butler, Judith. 2024. *Who's Afraid of Gender?* London: Penguin Books.

Cabantous, Laure, Jean-Pascal Gond, Nancy Harding, and Mark Learmonth. 2016. "Critical Essay: Reconsidering Critical Performativity." *Human Relations* 69, no. 2: 197—213. doi.org/10.1177/0018726715584690.

Deloria, Philip J. 2022. *Playing Indian*. New Haven: Yale University Press.

Erasmus, Zimitri. 2011. "Creolization, Colonial Citizenship(s) and Degeneracy: A Critique of Selected Histories of Sierra Leone and South Africa." *Current Sociology* 59, no. 5: 635—654.

Erasmus, Zimitri. 2012. "Apartheid Race Categories: Daring to Question Their Continued Use." *Transformation* 79: 1—11.

Erasmus, Zimitri. 2020. "'Who Was Here First?' or 'Who Lives Here Now?': Indigeneity, a Difference Like No Other." In *Persistence of Race*, edited by Nina G. Jablonski, 155—165. Stellenbosch: African Sun Media.

Farris, Sara R. 2017. *In the Name of Women's Rights: The Rise of Femonationalism*. Durham, NC: Duke University Press.

Foucault, Michel. 2008: *The Birth of Biopolitics: Lectures at the Collège de France 1978—79*, edited by Michel Senellart, translated by Graham Burchell. Basingstoke: Palgrave Macmillan.

Freeman, Elizabeth. 2010. *Time Binds: Queer Temporalities, Queer Histories*. Durham, NC: Duke University Press.

Glissant, Édouard. 1990. *Poétique de la relation*. Paris: Galimard.

Glissant, Édouard. 1997. *Poetics of Relation*. Ann Arbor: University of Michigan Press.

Hartman, Saidiya. 2020. *Wayward Lives, Beautiful Experiments: Intimate Histories of Riotous Black Girls, Troublesome Women, and Queer Radicals*. New York: W.W. Norton.

Heller, Meredith. 2020. *Queering Drag: Redefining the Discourse of Gender-Bending*. Bloomington: Indiana University Press.

Hörl, Erich. 2018. "The Environmentalitarian Situation." Translated by Nils F. Schott. *Cultural Politics* 14, no. 2: 153—173.

Khubchandani, Kareem. 2023. *Decolonize Drag (Decolonize That!)*. New York: QR Books.

Klein, Naomi. 2007. *The Shock Doctrine: The Rise of Disaster Capitalism*. New York: Metropolitan Books, Henry Holt and Company.

Lorber, Judith. 2004. "Preface." In *The Drag Queen Anthology: The Absolutely Fabulous but Flawlessly Customary World of Female Impersonators*, edited by Steven P. Schacht and Lisa Underwood, xv—xvi. New York: Harrington Park Press.

Lorde, Audre. 2018. *The Master's Tools Will Never Dismantle the Master's House*. London: Penguin Books.

Mbembe, Achille. 2001. *On the Postcolony*. Berkeley: University of California Press.

McGlotten, Shaka. 2021. *Dragging: Or, in the Drag of a Queer Life*. New York: Routledge.

Muñoz, José Esteban. 1999. *Disidentifications: Queers of Color and the Performance of Politics*. Minneapolis: University of Minnesota Press.

Nyong'o, Tavia. 2018. *Afro-fabulations: The Queer Drama of Black Life*. New York: New York University Press.

Parker, Andrew and Eve Kosofsky Sedgwick. 1995. *Performativity and Performance*. New York, London: Routledge.

Puar, Jasbir K. 2007. *Terrorist Assemblages: Homonationalism in Queer Times*. Durham, NC: Duke University Press.

Reed, Adolph. 2018. "Antiracism: A Neoliberal Alternative to a Left." *Dialectical Anthropology* 42: 105—115.

Reed, Adolph. 2022. *The South: Jim Crow and Its Afterlive*. London: Verso.

Rothberg, Michael. 2009. *Multidirectional Memory: Remembering the Holocaust in the Age of Decolonization*. Stanford: Stanford University Press.

Sauer, Birgit and Otto Penz. 2023. *Konjunktur der Männlichkeit: Affektive Strategien der autoritären Rechten*. Frankfurt: Campus Verlag.

Schroedl, Jenny and Samu/elle Striewski, eds. 2025. *Drag hier und heute! Theoretische und ästhetische Positionen zu einer queeren Praxis der Gegenwart*. Berlin: Neofelis.

Schuster, Aaron. 2020. "Beyond Satire: The Political Comedy of the Present and the Paradoxes of Authority." In *Sovereignty, Inc.: Three Inquiries in Politics and Enjoyment,* edited by William Mozzarella, Eric Santner, and Aaron Schuster, 161—250. Chicago: University of Chicago Press.

Sieg, Katrin. 2002. *Ethnic Drag: Performing Race, Nation, Sexuality in West Germany.* Ann Arbor: University of Michigan Press.

Thomas, Greg. 2018. "Afro-Blue Notes: The Death of Afro-pessimism (2.0)?" *Theory & Event* 21, no. 1: 282—317.

Toscano, Alberto. 2023. *Late Fascism: Race, Capitalism, and the Politics of Crisis.* London: Verso.

Vogl, Joseph. 2022: *Capital and Ressentiment: A short Theory of the Present.* Cambridge: Polity.

Weigel, Sigrid. 2013. "Das Gesicht als Artefakt: Zu einer Kulturgeschichte des menschlichen Bildnisses." In *Gesichter: Kulturgeschichtliche Szenen aus der Arbeit am Bildnis des Menschen,* edited by Sigrid Weigel, in collaboration with Tine Kutschbach, 7—29. Munich: Wilhelm Fink.

Žižek, Slavoj. 2024. "After Trump's Victory: From MAGA to MEGA." *e-flux.* November 13, 2024. www.e-flux.com/notes/641013/after-trump-s-victory-from-maga-to-mega. Accessed December 10, 2024.

Caribbean Critical Thought and "Drag" Performances of Indigenization

Zimitri Erasmus

> *The rigid nature of the plantation encouraged forms of resistance, two of which*
> *have a shaping force on our cultures: the camouflaged escape of the carnival,*
> *which I feel constitutes a desperate way out of the confining world of the plan-*
> *tation, and the armed flight of marronage, which is the most widespread act of*
> *defiance in that area of civilisation that concerns us.*
> Édouard Glissant, Caribbean Discourse

In this introduction I lean more towards offering a bricolage of ideas than a coherent argument.[1] My aim is to invite readers to expand and modify, and to keep or discard them as they think and play with these fragments. I hope this format enables thinking anew, and that these bits of ideas provoke more generative thought when brought together than they might when apart.

Caribbean Critical Theory

This fragment invites thinking with critical theory that engages the limits and exclusionary violence of the European canon. Such critical theory is concerned with the ways in which relations and practices that coconstitute modernity/ coloniality (Quijano 2000) shape histories, ecologies, the production of know-ledges, and the making of cultural formations. It problematizes meanings of "the human," of justice, and of freedom. As critical praxis, it challenges dominant ways of seeing and doing. To this end, it draws on a genealogy of radical anti-colonial and decolonial thought and related creative and political practices. It reworks these for the present with a view to form a more humane, ecologically

---

1   This contribution is an expanded version of my keynote address at the conference
     Facing Drag at the University of Music and Performing Arts Vienna in 2022 that gave
     birth to this volume. My gratitude extends to the conference organizers, presenters,
     and attendees. Special thanks to Evelyn Annuß for including me in this conversation.

conscious, and just world. This corpus includes the performing arts, literature, thinking behind and contestations within anticolonial political struggles—and more.

As a South African scholar shaped by histories of bricolage, I do not claim expertise in Caribbean critical thought. I am learning, too. That said, two historical features of the Caribbean archipelago shape its sustained and substantive contribution to critical theory. The first is its location as a key node of eighteenth- and nineteenth-century slave plantocracies and the second, its subjugated inhabitants' persistent struggles against these architectures of dehumanizing dominance. Against the backdrop of post-1994 South Africa and the afterlife of its specific colonial history, hegemonic and binary North American ideas about "race" are of little value as I attempt to make sense of the worlds that shape me and those that try to place me in ways that suit their arrangements. Instead, I find resonance in Caribbean Critical Theory[2] of both the archipelago and its diaspora. This sonorous mutuality emerged before I learned about histories of connection between radical anticolonial Caribbean intellectuals on the one hand, and on the other, such thinkers of the 1930s and 1940s in South Africa.[3]

This resonance is embedded in five key praxes. First, vehement contestation of the European idea of "race." Second, a conception of this idea of "race" as intricately linked to bounded conceptions of culture and to hierarchical class relations. Third, a conception of sociocultural worlds as imbued with power relations and at the same time as intertwined, not pure. Fourth, a carefully deliberate demystification of white worlds which includes illustration that European thought and practice is situated, not universal. And fifth, attentiveness to the cosmological worlds of the subjugated and the ways in which these shape historical and political processes. These synchronicities are testimony to

---

2   Among the key theorists are Jean Price-Mars (1876—1969), C. L. R. James (1901—1989), Aimé Césaire (1913—2008), Frantz Fanon (1925—1961), Édouard Glissant (1928—2011), Edward Brathwaite (1930—2020), Sylvia Wynter (b. 1928), Anthony Bogues, Paget Henry, and scholars of the Caribbean Philosophical Society as well as its journal, *The CLR James Journal*.

3   Among these are Isaac Bangani Tabata, author of *The Awakening of a People* (1950) and other texts; Ben Kies who wrote the essay, "The Contribution of the Non-European Peoples to World Civilisation" (1953); and Dora Taylor, writing as Nosipho Majeke, author of *The Role of Missionaries in Conquest* (1952). In addition to her critical political and cultural essays, Dora Taylor is also the author of two posthumously published novels, *Rage of Life* (2009) and *Kathie* (2008), and of a collection of short stories, *Don't Tread on My Dreams* (2008), among other creative works. For an analysis of these authors' contributions, see Soudien 2019.

the global circulation of ideas among anticolonial intellectuals and to questions of cultural and political entanglements.

However, unlike the Caribbean archipelago's slave plantocracies, the Cape Colony—which emerged from Dutch colonists' establishment of a refreshment station at the Cape—was characterized by household slavery and various forms of indentured and unfree labor. It was a key thoroughfare between two significant nodes of the global slave trade: to the west, St. Helena Island in the South Atlantic (Yon 2007); and to the east, the Indian Ocean islands (Hofmeyr 2007) and the East African coast. Without negating the specificities of each context, Caribbean Critical Theory remains valuable for understanding the ways that the history of the Cape Colony tacks migrations—forced and voluntary—to cultural formations as continuous processes forged in contexts of inequality. Caribbean Critical Theory is concerned with these among other significant processes.

Indigenization

In her unpublished monograph, *Black Metamorphosis*, Sylvia Wynter draws on Jean Price-Mars (1876—1969) to theorize Black experiences historically formed on slave plantations in the "New World." Price-Mars is remembered as a leading Haitian anticolonial intellectual and diplomat of the early twentieth century. He trained as a physician and served as professor of history and geography at the prestigious Lycée Alexander Pétion for twelve years. While Price-Mars's thought was understandably influenced by aspects of a key discourse of the early-twentieth century, namely, the relationship between "levels of civilisation" and the environment (Price-Mars 1983, 55—71), he nevertheless contested the European idea of "race" and fought against racism. He was among the first to emphasize the significance of the syncretic sociocultural worlds made by the enslaved in the "New World," and to see these social formations as "indigenized," the second fragment offered in this introduction. Despite challenges from his peers for his lack of attention to the political economy of Haiti, he remained a highly respected scholar and a leading political figure (ibid., ix—xxviii).

Reading Price-Mars, Wynter posits that experiences formed on plantations are best located within two interconnected historical processes. The first is Europe's violent socioeconomic conversion of people of the African continent *from* members of polities that drew material subsistence from the earth and from various forms of bartering *into* commodities to be bought, broken by labor and violence, sold, and disposed. She writes about this process as the transformation of African peoples "from the human subject[s] of [their] own cultures into the inhuman object of the European culture" (Wynter n.d., 10), and into the homogenized and commodified "negro" (ibid. 2—10; 24).

The second is African people's generative responses, amid suffering, to being ripped out of the worlds in which their subjectivities were in formation; to being unwillingly "planted" in the "New World" in which they were forced to live; and to Europe's dehumanizing forcible conversion. For Wynter, these responses are about the enslaved transforming themselves from "negro" into "native" of the "New World" through the process of "indigenization" (ibid., 2, 7, 63). This entails making oneself part of "the new soil" and of making "the new soil" part of oneself, by weaving symbolisms of belonging, remembrance, and resistance *out of* and *into* the landscape (ibid., 18, 46). Thus, "indigenization" as a process of (re)making place is qualitatively distinct from the concept "indigenous" which commonly refers to inhabitants of a place *before* the arrival of colonists.

For Sylvia Wynter, "indigenization" is shaped by the double-existence of the enslaved: existence as close-to-fully-human on the plot, provision ground, or the commons cultivated for mutual subsistence and as a symbolic place of rehumaning; and existence on the plantation as commodities, machines, as lesser humans to be owned and exploited. In this context, making "the plot" a place both for shared material survival and of symbolic significance reveals cultural creation as a practice of freedom—albeit limited and precarious. This practice is part of sociality with an ethos that challenges the forms of exploitation and alienation of the plantation. "The plot" offered the enslaved grounds for making sense of their "new" world ("new" by force, not by choice) in ways that enabled a hold onto freedom both in the moment, and for the future. Their relation to their "new" world as grounding inhabitants stands in contrast to the white creole's occupant relation which often meant a transient or absentee relation to the "New World" (ibid., 61). And, later, it stands in contrast to the Black creole elite's identification with the metropole and their distancing relation from the everyday practices of the "low people." For the most part, this elite saw themselves as "civilized," "westernized" fully assimilated into the "high culture" of the metropoles and therefore worthy of the privileges reserved for their colonizers. For this elite the "low people" engaged in "low cultures" from their "primitive" and "superstitious" African pasts, a "condition" from which the elite saw themselves as freed. They saw the carnival as part of "low culture."

My contribution deals with the "camouflaged escape of the carnival" (Glissant 1992, 248), as Glissant puts it, as a form of dragging. This reading underlines connections between South African and Caribbean cultural practices and concomitant critical thought that goes beyond theorizations situated in the Global North. My focus on the carnival as the masked public face of the enslaved, formerly enslaved, and their descendants complements questions of *marronage*—the flight of enslaved peoples from plantations to set up free, self-governing communities, of maroon societies, in proximate mountainous regions and on land that is not occupied by planters. My emphasis, however, is on theoretical entanglements that emerge from practices of camouflage in the wake of (post)colonial violence, not on the politics of militant fugitivity.

The Middle Passage, Masks, and Masquerades

Masks, masquerades, and their meanings constitute the third fragment offered in this introduction. In one of her earlier essays, Wynter (1970) conceptualizes Jonkunnu in Jamaica as a popular cultural performance in the form of a masquerade or dragging that emerges from and enacts a process of "indigenization." This performance was one among ceremonies and forms of communication that involved the use of music and masks. She suggests that reworked memories of the use of various masks—in parts of Africa with which they had become distantly familiar—in their efforts to rearticulate an inhabitant knowledge from which to make a Black counterworld. This knowledge enabled enslaved people to rehuman their "new," unfamiliar, and wounding environment in the wake of the Middle Passage, i. e., the forced transoceanic transportation of Africans and various island populations—who were captured by slavers along the circuit of maritime trade routes—across the Indian Ocean and the North, South, and East Atlantic Oceans (Lewis 2024).

With this counterknowledge enslaved people subverted dominant norms and during carnivals they used masks to disguise such subversion. They also used masks to embody different gendered modes of being and to embody animal and ancestral spirits in rituals that supported living, and that integrated dying into living (Henry 2013, 67). Such embodiment engenders and compresses the symbolic powers of a performer. It also facilitates passing on such powers among performers and between performers and their receptive viewers. Moreover, preparations for the masquerade—costume designs, choreography, musical composition, mask-making, and devising subversive ways with language and performance—constitute forms of intellect, ways of obfuscating political resistance, ways of coming to know, ways of imagining and of interpreting (Wynter 1970). These ways of coming to know stitch together, and into the new place, mindbody and memory; pain and joy; body and technology; the senses and the emotions; human and nonhuman forms of life; and members of a community. They weave different contexts into a tapestry of torn-away place, slave-ship place, plantation place, plot place, spiritual place, and the place of masquerade. They suture different times: before time, abyss time, plantation time, plot time, ancestral time, and masquerade time.

In Wynter's 1973 play titled *Maskarade* (2012), masquerade-place-and-time is ordinary-place-and-time, in other words, the normative social order, momentarily "reversed" or turned on its head. Such turning upside-down of norms is especially apparent in enslaved communities' use of their intimate knowledge of goings on in the masters' houses to mock planters' power. In this masked procession participants walk history into the present, walk the present into futures, walk the political into the personal, walk the human with other life forms, and breathe life into archives.

Wynter's conception of "indigenization" as a rehumanizing process by the enslaved and of Jonkunnu in Jamaica as its public enactment, does not engender a romanticization of slavery. On the contrary, it challenges Afro-pessimist notions of slavery and of Black living as social death by highlighting the agency of slaves as political beings who actively struggle for freedom amid catastrophes. Similarly, drawing on nineteenth-century court records of the Cape Colony, Yvette Christiaansë's (2006) historical novel *Unconfessed* offers a literary rendition of the political agency of the enslaved in that context, and of their conception of freedom as an ongoing process of struggle, not a static state enshrined in law. In this vein, the central character of this novel, Sila van Mozambiek, tells us: "Freedom is looking and looking" (Christiansë 2006, 321). These conceptions resonate with Price-Mars's argument that nighttime *Voodoo* assemblies among the enslaved in Haiti (from the sixteenth through the nineteenth century) were both ritualistic and political in character (Price-Mars 1983, 50). He posits that religious rituals inspired among the enslaved a "confidence in the correction of things [in the material world] that form[ed] the potential for action" (ibid., 174).

Return and Opening

I return briefly to the resonances noted at the beginning between Caribbean Critical Theory and understanding the history of the Cape Colony as central to slave trade routes across the Indian Ocean, the South Atlantic and from East Africa. These echoes may assist analyses of the Cape Town Carnival which, historically, was criticized for its use of grotesque blackface. The political work of *this* form of masquerade—its obscured subversion, rehumaning, and remaking of place—is distinct from that of nineteenth-century blackface minstrelsy of the urban north of the United States.

As Wynter writes, US blackface minstrelsy makes the Black person "the object of rather than the mechanism of satire" (Wynter n. d., 759). Masquerades by white men in blackface appropriate Black cultural forms and use these to reinscribe always insecure racial boundaries to their own and their audiences' benefit. Moreover, this form of blackface minstrelsy "depended on the material relations of slavery, and obscured these relations [from viewers], by pretending that slavery was amusing, right, and natural" (Lott 1992, 28). The racialization of "the human," of property, and of sexuality underpins these dominant depictions of Black people and reveals white Americans' racial fears and fantasies (Lott 1992) as well as projections of their tabooed desires onto Black people's bodies (Wynter, 1979).

This racialization of "the human" is echoed in the use of blackface in South Africa in the twenty-first century. On August 9, 2014, a South African national broadsheet, the *Mail and Guardian*, reported that two white female students at the University of Pretoria dressed in what is seen in this context as domestic workers' clothing, smeared their faces and arms with black paint, wore headscarves, and padded their bottoms, in my view, in a way reminiscent of eighteenth-century misrepresentations of Sara Baartman. The two students were suspended from university residence, but not from the institution.[4] On September 30 of that same year, this broadsheet reported that two white male students at the University of Stellenbosch who claimed to impersonate the tennis stars Serena and Venus Williams, blackened their faces and wore wigs and attire meant to represent these two Black American women. In this case the university opted for a "teaching moment" as a form of dialogic intervention, not disciplinary action. In both instances, the students had dressed up for a party and had photographs taken of themselves which were circulated on social media.[5] The debate about whether and in which ways *individuals* should be held accountable for such actions in a context where *systemic* racism persists despite the formal end of apartheid, continues in South Africa.

However, this is a very different form of blackface than the one used in the context of the Cape Town Minstrel Carnival. In her early work, Nadia Davids explores its history and contemporary reimaginings (Davids 2007). This is a masquerade of somewhat similar register to Wynter's conception of Jonkunnu in Jamaica, and to more recent scholarly interpretations of contemporary reimaginings of various such masquerades in the Caribbean (Innes, Rutherford, and Bogar 2013). Davids locates the Cape Town Minstrel Carnival in the context of slavery at the Cape in the eighteenth century and "Emancipation Day" in 1834, and contemporaneously, in the institutionalized racialization of space in colonial and apartheid South Africa in the nineteenth, twentieth, and twen-ty-first centuries. She conceives of this carnival as a "walking" and "moving" performance of resistance, and an enactment of reclaiming and memorializing

---

4   https://mg.co.za/article/2014-08-09-blackface-students-suspended-from-resi-dences/, accessed December 19, 2024.

5   www.aljazeera.com/news/2014/9/27/south-african-college-in-blackface-scan-dal, accessed December 19, 2024. See also www.politicsweb.co.za/documents/report-of-the-su-purpleface-inquiry#google_vignette, accessed December 19, 2024.

place on the part of subjugated communities from inner city District Six and in the wake of similar twentieth-century forced removals by the apartheid state. Like many other neighborhoods across South Africa whose residents were subjected to forced removals, District Six was racially and culturally heterogeneous and situated close to the center of Cape Town. The apartheid state bulldozed residents' homes to rubble and displaced them to townships far away from the city center. Today, this history is memorialized in various ways.[6] The carnival as a practice of indigenization and memorialization is an example of the resonance between Caribbean Critical Theory and theorizations of specific aspects of South African history.

References

Christiansë, Yvette. 2006. *Unconfessed: A Novel*. Cape Town: Kwela Books.

Davids, Nadia. 2007. "Inherited Memories: Performing the Archive." PhD dissertation, University of Cape Town.

Glissant, Edouard. 1992. *Caribbean Discourse: Selected Essays*. Translated by Michael Dash. Charlottesville: University Press of Virginia.

Henry, Jeff. 2013. "Carnival/Masquerade in Trinidad: Resistance through Performance." In *Carnival: Theory and Practice*, edited by Christopher Innes, Annabel Rutherford, and Brigitte Bogar, 65—77. New Jersey: Africa World Press.

Hofmeyr, Isabel. 2007. "The Black Atlantic Meets the Indian Ocean: Forging New Paradigms of Transnationalism for the Global South—Literary and Cultural Perspectives." *Social Dynamics* 33, no. 2: 3—32.

Innes, Christopher, Annabel Rutherford, and Brigitte Bogar. 2013. *Carnival: Theory and Practice*. New Jersey: Africa World Press.

Lewis, Thomas. 2024. "Transatlantic Slave Trade." *Brittanica*. www.britannica.com/topic/transatlantic-slave-trade. Accessed December 15, 2024.

Lott, Eric. 1992. "Love and Theft: The Racial Unconscious of Blackface Minstrelsy." *Representations* 39: 23—50.

Price-Mars, Jean. 1983. *So Spoke the Uncle*. Washington, DC: Three Continents Press.

---

6   One is reinvented forms of annual carnival organized under the auspices of the District Six Museum. The museum opened in December 1994 and is shaped by the former residents' contributions of photographs, oral histories, and remnants from the remains of what were once their homes. In line with such memorialization, South End Museum in Gqeberha, formerly Port Elizabeth, was opened in 2001.

Quijano, Anibal. 2000. "Coloniality of Power, Eurocentrism, and Latin America." *Nepantla: Views from South* 1, no. 3: 533—580.

Soudien, Crain. 2019. *The Cape Radicals: Intellectual and Political Thought of the New Era Fellowship 1930s—1960s.* Johannesburg: Wits University Press.

Wynter, Sylvia. n. d. "Black Metamorphosis: New Natives in a New World." Institute for the Black World Records, Sylvia Wynter Papers. New York: Schomburg Centre for Research in Black Culture (NYPL).

Wynter, Sylvia. 1970. "Jonkonnu in Jamaica: Towards the Interpretation of Folk Dance as a Cultural Process." *Jamaica Journal* 4, no. 2: 34—48.

Wynter, Sylvia. 1979. "Sambos and Minstrels." *Social Text* 1: 149—156.

Wynter, Sylvia. 2012. "Maskarade: A 'Jonkunnu' Musical Play." In *Mixed Company: Three Early Jamaican Plays*, edited by Yvonne Brewster, 17—132. London: Oberon Books.

Yon, Daniel A. 2007. "Race-Making/Race-Mixing: St. Helena and the South Atlantic World." *Social Dynamics* 33, no. 2: 144—163.

TEMPORAL DRAG AND QUEERING FABULATIONS

Transtemporal Making-Out—On "Temporal Drag" in Jessica Dunn Rovinelli's *So Pretty* (2019)

Sam Ehrentraut

> "*im anfang, wenn wir uns in der küche trafen nicht zu zweit, guckten wir uns geheimnisvoll an. dann brauchten wir auch das nicht mehr. wenn einer nicht ausgelastet ist, belästigt er den andern. wenn wir zu zweit sind, sind wir zu mehreren. oder: wir sind immer auch zu zweit. es geht, weil es mit den andern geht.*"[1]
>
> Ronald M. Schernikau (2012, 63)

Jessica Dunn Rovinelli's feature film *So Pretty* (2019) invites us into the shared living sphere of a polycule of individuals in their mid-twenties, set in contemporary Brooklyn, New York. Through camera maneuvers that seem almost reluctant, the viewer is introduced to a group of gender-deviant[2] people, who meet, interact, and separate, their relationships shifting in closeness throughout the film. The various genders and sexual orientations of the characters remain ambiguous—some of them might be genderqueer, some of them transgender, but clear identification is unspecified, a move which I will further elaborate as aligning with Rovinelli's overall aesthetic motive. *So Pretty* tells the story of Tonio/Tonia and Franz, Paul and Erika, sharing daily life, cooking, chatting, meeting friends, having sex, fighting, and being politically active together. Rather than following a tightly knit plot, the film's blurry narrative unfolds through the evolving and shifting

---

* The work on this publication was fully funded by the Austrian Science Fund (FWF) (P 35728-G).

1 "In the beginning, when we met in the kitchen not just the two of us, we looked at each other mysteriously. Then, we didn't even need this anymore. When one of us isn't occupied, he bothers the other. When it's just the two of us, we are more than two. Or: we are always two as well. It works because it works with the others" (author's translation).

2 To avoid an intrusive classification of genders and bodies that would override the film's intention, I follow Jessica Dunn Rovinelli's own descriptive language for her character constellation here. The phrase "gender deviant" and other terms are traceable for example in a *Scene Report* podcast episode (Dunlea 2019).

relationships within this central constellation. *So Pretty* seeks to create a cinematic space for queer and trans bodies, exploring ways of relating beyond conventional regimes of representation. Through its focus on interior spaces, fluid camera movements, and an evocative soundscape, the film evokes an ephemeral in-between space that reimagines relationality. The analysis will follow *So Pretty* into its social microcosmos and trace the ways in which the film deploys a form of temporal dragging to imagine a community that holds multiple layers of time present.

Figure 1. Jessica Dunn Rovinelli, "So Pretty," 2019, Screenshot, 00:31:25, © Jessica Dunn Rovinelli.

So Pretty is a blurry portrait of four friends and lovers and their social environment that lets the viewer witness a queer constellation without handing over their intimacy to the spectator's eye. However, the film is also composed as an intermedial transposition of German writer Ronald M. Schernikau's text *So Schön* from 1982, a then unpublished text with the subtitle "a utopian film." Schernikau's text, characterized by its laconic language, can be read as a literary testimony of the gay communist movement in West Berlin a few years before the fall of the Berlin Wall. In its particularly casual language, *So Schön* tells fragmentary stories from the lives of a circle of gay men, some of whom bend gender norms, who find each other in shifting relationships oscillating between coupledom, casual sexual relations, and extended friendship structures. The text captures their political engagement, disoriented daily life, and changing intimate relations as entangled and closely interrelated aspects of their gay existence.

Rovinelli not only adapts Schernikau's script for her film in a modified form; she transposes Schernikau's *So Schön* from 1980s Berlin to contemporary New

York, translating it into a different gender matrix and creating a cinematic realm in which strands of the past and the present constantly layer and intermingle in a shared gesture of utopian longing.[3] By implementing Schernikau's text as a script, Rovinelli uses the text as a mirroring field of reference, and, at the same time, as a subject of discussion and discourse. Her reading of Schernikau's text is loving, even as it reorganizes its structures and forms. From her predecessor's literary script Rovinelli molds a contemporary story of a community struggling with singularization, heteronormative coupledom, a political context of racist oppression and the increase of neofascist movements, showing how these political struggles materialize in the entangled daily life of its inhabitants.

In this text, I am most interested in how *So Pretty* engages with Schernikau's text in order to generate a particularly transtemporal narrative. I will also explore how the image production in Rovinelli's film allows for a form of community to unfold on screen which materializes in the interstices of the created images and is built through the entanglement of people, times and media brought into touch. The shared space imagined by the film emerges in the small cracks within the cinematic tissue and the intentionally created gaps between scenes, events, and people that in many cases show their temporal dynamics. Following the different reformulations of "drag" as a theoretical figure and as a multifaceted aesthetic practice presented in this anthology, I will use Elizabeth Freeman's concept of "temporal drag" to trace the ways in which the film constructs itself as a multidimensional, interrupted citation of Schernikau's text, and thus operates through an intermedial form of temporal entanglement. By conceptualizing the specific forms of community and coexistence the film displays, I will trace how *So Pretty* deals with the political weight of community building in a nonprogrammatic way and centers the topic of nonhomogeneous relationality in its formal language and image politics. I follow the film in its modes of parenthetic political dreaming and longing for a space alleviated from the heaviness of clear readability and unambiguous identification. By looking at how *So Pretty* introduces a specific form of transtemporal cohabitation, I want to reconstruct the aesthetics of withdrawal and the countering of visual representation. I consider that to be Rovinelli's contribution to a search for a modified form of nonintrusive imaging of communal existence that also carves out space for modes of queer and trans existence without pursuing an agenda of exclusionary and self-contained identity politics.

---

3   For an extensive reading of the concept of the utopian *So Pretty* articulates, see McKenzie Wark's essay "Femme as in Fuck You" (2019), published on *e-flux*. See also the recorded conversation between her and Jessica Dunn Rovinelli "More Pretty: Jessie Jeffrey Dunn Rovinelli and McKenzie Wark in Conversation" (2019), published on *e-flux*.

I am not searching for presumably better or genuine forms of representation of trans or gender-nonconforming people and their ways of community building—and neither is *So Pretty*. In my encounter with Rovinelli's film, I am rather interested in the aesthetic strategies that allow collective figurations to appear in and in between the images, while at the same time defying gestures of gender reveal and literal modes of representation. As I will try to show, the reflective work with and against representation enables a more substantial form of performing community longing for an alternate form of being with one another, a vision of community that implies a transtemporal form of relating. Before I turn to *So Pretty*, I first want to tread a path into a concept crucial for my understanding of temporal layering: what is created, when dragging different layers of time onto and into each other?

Temporal Drag

In her seminal book *Time Binds* (2010), Elizabeth Freeman introduced a trope of queer temporality that is characterized by a specific form of anachronistic interrelation between the past and the present.[4] In her analysis of mostly film and video works, Freeman traced encounters between past and present which exceed both the practice of critical historical reference—the present addressing the past with methodological skepticism—and harmonious coexistence of different temporal layers—the present welcoming the past without contention. Her concept of "temporal drag" describes a layering of queer temporalities which manifests as a conflictual and heterogeneous relation between the past and the present: "I'd like to call this 'temporal drag,' with all the associations that the word 'drag' has with retrogression, delay, and the pull of the past on the present" (Freeman 2010, 62). "Temporal drag," in this understanding, does not simply signify a past making itself present. In the movement of temporal *dragging*, the past and the present are exerting pressure on each other, forcing themselves into a complex relation.[5] "Temporal drag" thus implies a reemergence of the past *as* a past element and as a temporal clashing that marks itself as nonfitting, heterogeneous, and, in many cases, incompatible. The movement of temporal dragging displaces the present, making porous the present and the past alike. Freeman conceptualizes temporal drag as an interactional dynamic, an adhesive getting-in-relation between the past and the present that

---

4   See Freeman 2010, xvi.
5   See Freeman 2010, 63f.

interrupts a chronological order and creates a pierced and perforated next-to-each-other of temporal layers.[6]

In the queer film and video works that Freeman is reading, this tension-filled imbrication of temporalities appears as an attempt to get in touch with a queer past that is unredeemed, problematic and hard to integrate.[7] But "temporal drag" is more than just a trope of queer art, and more than the staging of an encounter with queer precedents that do not smoothly fit into the frames of queer bonding through time and a reparative approach of cross-temporal queer history-making. Temporal drag is the movement of a discomforting and unsolvable rubbing of the past and the present against each other—a temporal alteration that inflicts both past and present exerting an anachronistic effect on all temporal layers involved. It goes beyond a citational reiteration and reactualization of a past life, embodiment, and (queer) practice.[8] According to Freeman, "temporal drag" opens a transtemporal space of rewriting history and reembodying an altered kind of relating to the past. In her reading of Frankenstein's monster she explains that temporal drag, in some contexts, can be read as "a historiographic practice wherein the past takes the form of something already fragmented, 'split,' and decaying, to which the present and future are somehow porous in an analog way, and for which bodies are both metaphor and medium" (ibid., 116).

Freeman assigns a historiographic potential to the movement of temporal drag, an embodied form of writing history she coins "erotohistoriography."[9] This historiographic potential renders temporal drag as a mediated practice of negotiating and reshaping history that admits and gives space to the mutual incommensurability of past and present. This form of writing or redoing history is not bound to entirely close the gaps and mitigate the fissures between the layers brought in touch. Rather it is a form of historiography that makes the irreducible cracks and fissures feasible and activates the generative and

---

6   For the *topos* of stickiness, see Freeman 2010, 112f., 122f.

7   She exemplifies this multiple times in the clashing of different strands of feminism and emphasizes that the effect of this temporal drag is not a distancing from the anachronistic other, but its haunting presence and the reemergence of its lost and compromised potential in the present that cannot simply integrate the past elements in its fabric and discourse. See Freeman 2010, 62ff., 130f. and Freeman 2000, 728f.

8   For Freeman's juxtaposition of "temporal drag" with Judith Butler's concept of citationality, see Freeman 2000, 732f.

9   Expanding on the definition of this term, Freeman writes: "Erotohistoriography is distinct from the desire for a fully present past, a restoration of bygone times. Erotohistoriography does not write the lost object into the present so much as encounter it already in the present, by treating the present itself as hybrid" (2010, 95).

persisting possibilities at play in the transtemporal rubbing of queer historical fragments.

There are two key features that I wish to borrow from Freeman's concept of "temporal drag" and its potential for a historiography that does not rely on chronological progression and teleological narrations. First, her conception holds space for heterogeneous, nonappropriative forms of temporal encounter. This encounter is fundamentally tense: Freeman's focus on the differing temporalities that come in touch and clash with one another enables a rethinking of how historical referencing operates and how a transformative influence and leaking of times into one another can be conceptualized beyond an affirmative genealogy.

The second aspect I will apply in my reflection on *So Pretty* is the potential for the creation of an altered, nonhomogeneous narrative through the performative labor of "temporal drag." I transpose Freeman's concept of an embodied historiography into my analysis of transtemporal dialogue in Rovinelli's film to grasp how the encounter of two different time frames is structured, and to understand what kind of renarration the interactional temporal dynamics between Schernikau's *So Schön* and *So Pretty* generate.

In the clashing of a literary text that captures traces of a gay Berlin in the 1980s and the cinematic depiction of a gender-deviant social world in present-day New York, the film articulates an intermedial encounter that relates one geographically and temporally distant fragment of queer life to another. In bringing together these diffuse contexts, the film creates a temporal tension from which a mutual redefinition and reshaping of the respective temporal frames result. As I will show, this transtemporal movement also goes beyond a historical and historiographical dynamic. It longs simultaneously for an alteration of the cinematic present and a possible future that cannot be outlined. In the rest of the essay, I will explore the performative, aesthetically constituted practices of transtemporal relationality that are central to the narrative and the formal tissue of *So Pretty*. First, let's look at the imagery of *So Pretty* to better understand how the film creates a delicate space for a transtemporal form of relating while taming an investigative gaze.

Transtemporal Making-Out

So Pretty is episodic and sparsely narrative, reflecting the situations and events that the central characters and their surrounding community live through in an anecdotal, almost accidental manner. The film's enclosed world contains four characters who are tied together through changing relationships of friendship, romantic love, and connections which oscillate across coupledom and nonmonogamy. The film rejects any classification of the characters' identities, and this rejection is central to the gaze and form of viewership *So Pretty* prefigures.

For the film script, Rovinelli transposed Ronald M. Schernikau's main character constellation of four gay men into a gender-deviant group of friends and lovers in a North American context involved in antifascist activism and the Black Lives Matter movement: Schernikau's character constellation of Tonio, Franz, Erika, and Paul reappear and get remodeled in Rovinelli's translation of the text into a film script: some of them get different gender markers (Tonia), feminine characters switch from a marginal position in the text to a central role (Erika), and the refiguration of the cast generally breaks with the more exclusively gay male microcosmos Schernikau depicts in *So Schön*. Rovinelli's adaptation alters the language and codes of gender via transposition. It actualizes the gender-blurring potential of *So Schön*, present through a range of deviant masculinities and explicit references to *Tunenästhetik*.[10] Through the contemporary transposition into a different language and a different context, the character constellation becomes modular material for the film that softly undermines the male- and gay-centered focus of Schernikau's text and models a contemporary set of gender modes and presentations.

So Pretty uses *So Schön* as a matrix for its script, selectively renarrating events taken from the literary text and building an intertextual zone between the textual past and the blurry present of the film time. But beyond using Schernikau's literary film as an actual film script, *So Schön* is also present *as* a text and as a subject of translation. We see multiple scenes of readings of text passages in a park, listen to conversations about translation on the way to a club, and study close-ups of faces and interiors while parts of *So Schön* are spoken over the resting or slowly moving images. The use of Schernikau's utopian film text constantly shifts between script template, object of transposition, and body of text that is read, heard, and perceived as an external element

---

10   *Tuntenästhetik* can be understood as a spectrum of performative and embodied expressions of nonconforming femininities, often characterized by theatrical, grotesque, and "trashy" elements. Typically (self-)ascribed and closely associated with gay identities, being a *Tunte* involves mirroring, exaggerating, and transgressing normative concepts of femininity. The category of *Tunte* intersects with, but is not fully encompassed by cross-dressing and drag, and overlaps with broader notions of transgender identities.

Historically, *Tunte* is a reappropriated and politically charged term rooted in the German gay movement of the 1970s and 1980s, with a particular concentration in Berlin. For a more detailed contextualization of the *Tuntenbewegung* within the contested heterogeneity of the gay movement, see Griffiths 2012. For distinctions between drag queens and *Tunten* as subcultural spheres in Berlin, see Balzer 2004.

in the diegetic realm of the film. In this oscillation between embodiment and exposition of the text as text, an intermedial dynamics of levels of narratives and their temporal layers occurs.

Through the constant back and forth between the rereading of Schernikau and its cinematic reinterpretation, So Pretty creates a specific temporal blurring. The intermedial staging leads to an entanglement of two temporally distant queer worlds—Schernikau's literary mirroring of splinters of communist gay West Berlin and a presumably contemporary US gender-deviant conglomerate of friends and lovers. The world of So Pretty, however, becomes porous and opens up as a fabric of reference and queer correspondence that brings two languages, two different media, and two temporal spheres of queer existence in touch with each other. Watching the film, I experienced this blurring as a suspension of temporal and spatial exactness. Entering the world the film creates, I lost grip of time and location while witnessing a permeable but self-contained social cosmos.

Coming back to Elizabeth Freeman's concept of "temporal drag" outlined above, one can understand how the bringing together of two temporal frames becomes an encounter of past and present queer life that creates a constant tension and transitioning between multiple layers. The touching and merging of the two time spaces facilitate a dragging that holds both elements present and next to each other without engaging in hierarchization or mastering of past and present elements (Freeman 2010, 64—65). This movement induced by the rubbing of differently time-coded frames and narratives permeates the present of the film narrative and exposes its constructedness (Gemachtheit). In the intermedial and transtemporal entanglement, So Pretty spatializes a specific form of interrelated queer performativity. While still being recognizable as separate elements and staged as a transtemporal dialogue between text and film, both spaces start to bleed into each other, alter each other, and generate a continuous movement of distinctiveness and hybridization of contexts.

This heterogeneous coexistence of two space times that come with very different vocabularies and codes of queerness destabilizes a chronological and progress-oriented conception of cinematic time. We intentionally never see the context or a chronological cause of an event; instead, we glide through the cinematic space witnessing glimpses and cut-outs from the line of events, being denied what has taken place before or after. In one scene, for example, a small evening get-together unfolds in the shared apartment. Helmut, a transmasculine character, is seen playfully spanking Tonia and Franz, while Paul takes photos of them, and Erika is sitting next to them, distracted by her phone. Their laughter and chatter, the music and the spanking sounds blend into an indistinct soundscape. As the interaction unfolds, the camera slowly, but consistently moves in and out of the sexually charged, playful situation, slipping away from the vivid scene and seamlessly continuing the tracking shot that is then interrupted by the next scene fragment.

The derooting effect of these aesthetic means of film cut, editing, and montaging allows the images to evoke a temporally permeable space that is not representational. What emerges at the margins of visual representation is a historically deunitized and dynamized space for a less controlled form of becoming. So Schön enters the fabric of the film as a text from the past and as an anachronistic constellation and vocabulary of gender from elsewhere, from West Berlin before the fall of the wall. Through this transposition, So Pretty opens itself to an alteration by its literary sibling, continuously generating its narrative from the text while taking distance from the text, interweaving new realities into it that exceed So Schön without assuming a position of critical judgment, dismissal, or discarding the nonintegrable elements tied to it. So Pretty leaves space for incompleteness. Instead of focusing on a correcting and replacing approach, the film emphasizes the space opening up in between the space times it collides. In between the images and in the entanglement of gay and gender-deviant times, So Pretty materializes a nonspace for a queer becoming not yet articulated and it does so by letting itself be haunted and informed by a past space. By allowing this nonspace to become visible in the gaps of its imagery, So Pretty partakes in a form of aesthetic dreaming for a transtemporally connected and resistant form of transgenerational encounter that accepts the incompatible, uncatchable, and unredeemable element of the historical encounter.

So Pretty's aesthetic language further supports this effect of temporal entanglement by engaging tropes of leftist essayistic filmmaking of the twentieth century that detach the camera's perspective from the representation of individualized gazes and instead focus on situational settings and collective figurations. Also, the color grading of So Pretty, the rough film grain of its image aesthetics, and its sometimes-analog vernacular constantly oppose the temporal markers the digital format entails. The different layers of mediality and the copresence of multiple historically connotated imageries subvert a clear localization of the film's events in the present. Also on the formal level, So Pretty is using the effect of temporal dragging for its own purposes. Aesthetically, the adhesive potential of the temporal layering is multiplied and the anachronistic elements are emphasized in a way that impacts the temporal signature of its cinematic space. Both the narrative and the formal language embrace the transtemporal dynamic of their multilayered structure. They are informed by a past that is not enclosed in history but takes effect within the time-crossing dialogue So Pretty is concerned with. While temporal dragging is a central mechanism in the intermedial and transtemporal dynamics of the film, So Pretty's strategies of imaging further support the vision of community building that is specific to the film's aesthetic agenda. I will further pursue these strategies in the following paragraphs to get closer to the construction of a gaze that avoids a scrutinizing approach to gender, embodiment, and relationships.

Imaging beyond Intrusion

We follow the camera's gliding eye through the spaces of the main characters' daily life—workplaces, demonstrations, clubs, public transport. However, the majority of the scenes take place in the apartment all four share, which also functions as a space for gatherings and meet-ups with a wider circle of friends, as a community space. The gaze offered to us by the film through its specific camera work is nonintrusive. Extensive dolly shots (a specific kind of tracking shot characterized by smooth and controlled camera movements) and the play with distancing and approaching simulate an experience for the viewer that they are constantly passing by.

In its continuous movement through So Pretty's world—the rooms of the apartment, the park, occasional walks on the streets—the camera acts as a nonhierarchizing tool, unfazed by the differing intensities and emotional states its protagonists may live through. The shots do not put the main focus on the interactions between the human actors. Instead of embodying an individualized perspective, the camera—and by extension the viewer—wanders through rooms, situations, and encounters, following its own slow pace with a constant acknowledgment of the environment and contextual setting rather than a focus on the conversations or specific interactions between the protagonists. The camera's presence never controls the beginning or the end of a scene. The imaging is presented as an accidental act of noticing, always on the edge of fading out. If bodies or faces are centered, they barely move or they rest, and so does the camera for the time it spends with them.

This effect of accidental and uninterested registering is further supported by the atmospheric sound recording characteristic of So Pretty. We hear chatter, conversations we can barely follow as they are partially drowned out by traffic noise, ambient sound, music, and other voices. There is—beyond the reading of the passages from So Schön that are spoken into a microphone or used as commentary voice—no consistent recording of the individual voices. The soundtrack follows the camera's movement, getting closer and becoming more distant in accordance with its gliding path. The atmospheric capture of sound encompasses the viewer and listener in the cinematic world without creating the impression of a close partaking in the scenes.

The listening experience resembles a time and space of sharing and accidental witnessing. It is in itself a mode of passing by, an adjacent copresence that is fostered also through the sonic arrangement. The soundscapes and occasional conversation scenes create a nonpsychologizing approach to the events and people in the film, an aesthetic effect of sensory implication that corresponds to the visual nonintrusiveness. This massively contributes to the sliding, dehierarchizing effect of the camera work. Viewing and listening are always slightly suspended, at a distance to the narrative content and its medial layers. One is left with feelings of boredom and of disorientation in the situational fabric of the depicted world—several times I tried to bridge the gaps left by the editing by rewatching and relistening to passages, before I ultimately let go of the desire to capture the discursive interactions, instead giving in to the cinematic dynamics of fragmentation. The detachment of sound and camera movement from a rhythm dictated by the plot creates a space for an intensified reflection on the media dynamics and its different aesthetic registers. The camera does not invite us to enter into the psyche of the protagonists, nor does it give access to their motivations, inner conflicts, or desires. The aesthetic arrangement of sound and image defies the embodiment of a personalized way of looking and works towards a disengagement from an objectifying and penetrating gaze.

In her essay on *So Pretty*, which is partially based on conversations with Rovinelli, the theorist McKenzie Wark describes this cinematic language as an inversion of a violently intrusive film aesthetics which she refers to as "meta-rape cinema." "So Pretty attempts to invert the genre of the meta-rape film. … She [Jessica Dunn Rovinelli] is not investigating, exposing, revealing" (Wark 2019, n. p.). Wark's argument and the usage of rape as a media-specific formal trope is based on Rovinelli's claim that film—in its structural manifestation of a penetrating and nonconsensually objectifying gaze—is a medium of violence.[11]

Film as a hierarchized arrangement of looking forces filmmakers, those depicted on screen, and viewers into an interpretative order of visibility and exposition. In its appropriation of bodies, narratives, and topics, the cinematic *dispositif* imposes a hierarchical and often exploitative regime of depiction. Wark reads the movie as consciously dealing with this form of structural epistemic violence, as drafting a utopian cinematic countervision that materializes as disruptively structured image production and provides spaces for the tender presentation of trans existence and relationality. "This is a utopian cinema,

---

11 See Wark 2019, n. p. For a further discussion on the interrelation of film and violence, see also Nanna Heidenreich's contribution "'Whose Portrait?' Fabulations and Triangulations in Shirley Clarke's *Portrait of Jason*" in this volume. In her critical analysis of the film and its reception, Heidenreich discusses the exploitative dynamics at play in the speculative relation between filmmaker, protagonist and audience, tracing the currents of desire informing the film along the structuring axes of sex and race.

then. To the extent that this is possible. The first principle of utopia as a genre is the exclusion of violence. That means that the violence is contained and neutralized, but still there. This is a place or a time, a constructed situation, where it is kept at bay, so something else might flower" (Wark 2019, n.p.).

So Pretty works towards an aesthetic articulation of imaging that seeks to escape the objectifying and appropriating gaze as well as the manifestations of the cisnormative order that deeply informs seeing, and the positionalities of doing film. The gesture of the camera avoids "clocking"—the uninvited recognition of a trans person as trans—and a clear readability of nonconforming embodiments and identities. Sound and image let the bodies be, let them move, let them rest and fail in the interrelatedness of their becoming and maintaining. For the time being, we are allowed to witness them, but without intruding into their fluidly and collectively organized intimate space.

By rejecting an explanatory and revealing mode, So Pretty longs for a form of cinematic aesthetics at the margins of the codes of representation dominated by the cisnormative visual and auditory regimes. So Pretty sidesteps expectations in the categorization of gender and queerness and the construction of clearly identifiable identities. It is not a movie about transitioning; it is not a film that makes space for the gender-deviant body as a primary site for visual representation. Rovinelli's film rather makes space for being-in-movement, for the figuration of bodies and their fluid reconstellation in order to create a communal and community-based depiction of being together and for each other. In between the images and as the performative undercurrent of the episodic film, a negatively spaced sphere of a possible world is articulated, which is—according to Wark's analysis of the trans femme aesthetics the film unfolds—not beautiful, but radically pretty.[12] It allows trans existence to take space and flourish without being in the scrutinizing focus. So Pretty's indirect imaging of the utopian does not exclude conflict—identity issues, structural violence, clashing positionalities, and emotional harm are present throughout the whole film. We see couples losing connection, falling apart and forming new intimate relations, we witness Erika letting down Paul in the streets. But Rovinelli implements the conflicts emerging between the protagonists as a genuine part of creating and negotiating shared life in a present that is

---

12   See Wark 2019, n.p. In her collaborative reading of So Pretty, Wark conceptualizes prettiness as the dominant aesthetic category in the film, an aesthetic register often considered minor but with a potential to hint towards the utopian. Wark's engagement with the film centers on the presence of trans-femininity in the film and its trans femme aesthetic. For an extension of Wark's thoughts on the interrelation between trans-feminine aesthetics and prettiness, and a critique of cuteness as a politics of the surface, see her essay "The Politics of Cuteness" (2024).

constantly subverted and haunted by past gender-deviant experiences, tropes, and histories. The irreducible contradictions and multilayered hardships of community building are a material part of the utopian longing for another way of being, not a mere obstacle to an otherwise purified vision of a (potentially) alternative future.

So *Pretty* lovingly repositions the receptive gaze as a visiting one. The aesthetic decisions that inform the viewership clearly communicate the gaps and the incompleteness of what is depicted—leaving the imaged world and its inhabitants the right to nonvisibility and nonexposure. Between the split scenes and in the echo of the events and occurrences the camera leaves behind on its way through the scenes, an undefined zone of becoming enfolds that lets itself be haunted by temporal entanglements. It is reaching out for potentially comforting and unrepresentable folds in the fields of visibility.

Desiring Community

Being trans implies multiple ways of being in community: finding form through and in each other, creating spaces for survival and the livability of trans existence, sharing bits of a mostly forgotten and buried history. In many cases, contemporary trans artists deal with the questions of community building and struggle for sustainable trans spaces through their work. The aesthetic modes deployed in their artistic production do not necessarily have to make transness a main topic. Mirroring a desire for an extended shared space that makes possible the formation of nonhegemonic forms of living—and among them, trans lives—informs the ways trans artists fashion layers of media, opt for the gaps between images, and play with references from a not-always consistent communal sphere. Working in a mostly cisnormative world—i.e., a world in which the identification with one's gender assigned at birth is instituted as the norm—trans artists work towards an extension and protection of spaces that allow for trans becoming to happen, to be embodied, to become readable.

So *Pretty* joins this contemporary struggle for alternate forms of visibility beyond representation—an endeavor that is shared by different fields of artistic production and theory. The ambivalent dynamics of representation remain a pressing and ongoing question, especially for cultural productions of minoritized and marginalized communities. Trans and queer artists continue to develop changing approaches that work towards a disruption and modification of distorting regimes of readability and recognizability. They reflect on the competing and interacting temporalities in forms of performativity and embodiment—a sensitivity for temporal complexities that equally informs queer theories focused on modes of performance and time-based visual media.[13]

Adding her voice and gaze to this pressing discussion, Rovinelli searches for a way of producing images that gives space for a nonexploitative circulation of relations rather than determining a fixed frame for gender-deviant representation. In the tender and consciously distant depiction of community, Rovinelli deploys an aesthetic strategy of the parenthetic that disinvites the curiosity-driven normative cis-gaze in favor of a nonexposure and a collectively structured form of resisting representation. The way the film performs community—and forges a corresponding space for it through its intermedial and transtemporal engagement—opts for a shared practice of collective world-building located in daily life. So Pretty actively dreams of a protected but structurally open body of becoming with one another. It presents a blurring vision of a utopian constellation that does not fall into an exceptionalist idealization of trans community. In its distancing mode that gives not only the protagonists but also the viewer space for the slowness of the everyday political struggle, and collective privacy of nonsurveillance, it offers a possibility for becoming and meaning-making. It distances itself from the framing epistemic registers of queerphobia, trans misogyny and racialization without naively excluding their existence and impact.

The protagonists of So Pretty come together, touch and diverge on the basis of their partly shared, partly segregating positionalities. The film marks the epistemic violence the inhabitants are confronted with and that constantly influences the embodiments and the ways in which these bodies become readable within the order of the visible. Despite the failures in solidarity and connection that are also depicted as part of this desired community, it nevertheless manages to articulate a search for an aesthetics that allows for a different vision of life. In doing so, the film turns against the classificatory oppression of bodies, systemic discrimination, and enforced segregation and individualization. On the surface of the imaging dynamics of So Pretty, a glimpse of a historically permeated counterspace can be perceived—a space of diffusely located, structurally impossible breathing, a space emerging from within the ordinary that might not be glorious or beautiful, but pretty.[14]

It is also in this longing for a different form of shared life and a politically altered reality where Schernikau's So Schön and Rovinelli's transformative take

---

13   See for example Keeling 2019, Muñoz 1999, and Nyong'o 2018, who might stand in here for the quite extensive literature on queer temporalities the field of queer studies has produced in interdisciplinary encounters with other disciplines.

14   For the distinctions between the aesthetic value of the pretty and the beautiful, see Wark 2019.

on the text meet. *So Schön* is also a story about a communist utopia dreamt within the interstices of the daily in the capitalist West Berlin of the 1980s. It is a story about failure, about comrades who love, fight for, and also betray each other. Schernikau, who wrote the text before becoming a citizen of the GDR in its latest stage in 1989, i.e., just before the fall of the Berlin Wall, traces the marginalized communist organizing and its entanglement with the gay and *Tunten*-scene in the western part of the city, depicting how political longing is not equivalent, but inseparable from personal and sexual desire. In grasping the potential for a future that is at odds with the present but might become imaginable Schernikau offered a literary vision of another existence in the cut-off city he lived in. Rovinelli's reactualization of *So Schön* explicitly touches this strong dimension of political longing in the text, picking up the—by definition—not actualized part of Schernikau's depicted daily life utopia and letting it become a layer of her search for articulations of the (im)possible. Amid the temporal dragging that the encounter creates, the shared—and at the same time not shared—time and space of what is longed for, of a possibly different life, constitutes a strongly interacting layer in the film. Letting *So Pretty* get dragged by the unfulfilled utopian void *So Schön* captured and left behind for future reading, creates a transtemporal correspondence in the undefinable time-space of the not yet realized. But it is in this formally and narratively sketched sphere of the not yet there and in the folds of the consequently pragmatic and daily life fabric of both frames where a further transtemporal correspondence, a further rewriting and writing forth next to each other happen.

When Freeman points towards the historiographic potential in "temporal drag" and emphasizes the bodily dimension in this form of historicizing queer performativity, we are made aware of the historiographic potential that lies in conflictual and heterogeneous forms of transtemporal encounters. In her transposition of Schernikau's text and its narrative constellation of characters, Rovinelli's film manages to reactivate an impossible history of the utopian buried in the novel. The transtemporal dialogue is not merely a contemporary restaging of a lost piece of what has retrospectively been labeled queer life, it also opens the *So Schön*'s texture to a generative form of historiography that operates through the reanimation of questions of communal existence and the survival of marginalized perspectives within a persistently hostile and oppressive environment. *So Pretty* is unhinging *So Schön* from its localization in the past by asking the text's questions anew, letting them take an altered form, and trigger an open conversation with a present not anticipated. The form of historiography the transtemporal encounter evokes is an act of imaging and reembodiment that gives the presumably historically and contextually distant text a new existence—altered by the present.

Retrospectively, the text can be experienced in its persistent anachronistic features. Historiography, in this sense, means releasing the unfulfilled desires for a different being. It means looking at Schernikau's *So Schön* again, with a different gaze formed by a different time and place—and making it present again in its unresolved utopian potential while reconsidering the traces of its pastness. Following Freeman's thoughts, this historiographic effect advocates for an imagining of the future that does not affirm or discard the past, but creates conditions for actively engaging with it. But it also means to account for the pastness of the past and to not fall into the simplistic approach of a reactualization that tends to smooth out the not-compatible, resistant, sometimes problematic aspects of points of reference.[15] So *Pretty* can be read as an attempt of holding exactly this complexity present and making it viral for its gender-deviant inhabitants and their tenderly alluded life worlds. Though *So Pretty* does not claim to give answers, it carves the space to let questions of community building emerge—dragging them along as unresolved tasks for a transtemporally informed community.[16]

References

Balzer, Carsten. 2004. "The Beauty and the Beast." *Journal of Homosexuality* 46, no. 3—4: 55—71.

Dunlea, Reed, host. 2019. "Jessie Jeffrey Dunn Rovinelli of 'So Pretty' on Gender Deviant Film." *Scene Report*, podcast. September 3, 2019.

Freeman, Elizabeth. 2000. "Packing History, Count(er)ing Generations." *New Literary History* 31, no. 4: 727—744.

Freeman, Elizabeth. 2010. *Time Binds: Queer Temporalities, Queer Histories.* Durham, NC: Duke University Press.

Griffiths, Craig. 2012. "Konkurrierende Pfade der Emanzipation: Der Tuntenstreit (1973—1975) und die Frage des 'respektablen Auftretens.'" In *Rosa Radikale: Die Schwulenbewegung der 1970er Jahre*, edited by Andreas Pretzel and Volker Weiß, 143—159. Hamburg: Männerschwarm.

Keeling, Kara. 2019. *Queer Times, Black Futures.* New York: New York University Press.

---

15   On past's pastness, see Freeman 2000, 728f.

16   I would like to thank Jessica Dunn Rovinelli for taking the time to engage in a written conversation with me, which reshaped and deepened my interpretation of *So Pretty*. I am also profoundly grateful to Evelyn Annuß, Adam Czirak, Julia Ostwald, and May Vajt, whose insights and feedback were invaluable in helping this text reach its final form.

Muñoz, José Esteban. 1999. *Disidentifications: Queers of Color and the Performance of Politics*. Minneapolis: University of Minnesota Press.

Nyong'o, Tavia. 2018. *Afro-fabulations: The Queer Drama of Black Life*. New York: New York University Press.

Rovinelli, Jessie Jeffrey Dunn and McKenzie Wark. 2019. "More Pretty: Jessie Jeffrey Dunn Rovinelli and McKenzie Wark in Conversation." *e-flux Events*. November 25, 2019. www.e-flux.com/events/298067/more-pretty-jessie-jeffrey-dunn-rovinelli-and-mckenzie-wark-in-conversation/. Accessed September 1, 2024.

Rovinelli, Jessie Jeffrey Dunn, director. 2019. *So Pretty*. Paris/New York: Les Films du Balibari/100 Year Films. https://vimeo.com/ondemand/sopretty?autoplay=1. Accessed September 1, 2024.

Schernikau, Ronald M. 2012. *So Schön: Und als der Prinz mit dem Kutscher tanzte, waren sie so schön, dass der ganze Hof in Ohnmacht fiel*. Edited by Thomas Keck. Berlin: Verbrecher Verlag.

Wark, McKenzie. 2019. "Femme as in Fuck You." *e-flux Journal* 102 (September 2019). www.e-flux.com/journal/102/282888/femme-as-in-fuck-you/. Accessed September 1, 2024.

Wark, McKenzie. 2024. "The Politics of Cuteness." *Frieze Magazine* 246 (October 2024). www.frieze.com/article/mckenzie-wark-politics-cuteness-246. Accessed: October 30, 2024.

"Whose Portrait?" Fabulations and Triangulations in Shirley Clarke's *Portrait of Jason* (1967)

Nanna Heidenreich

Portrait of Jason, the fourth feature-length film by American filmmaker Shirley Clarke, was released in 1967. It is a white heterosexual female filmmaker's film about and with a Black gay man, the self-professed "hustler" and performer Jason Holliday. After *The Connection* (1961) and *A Cool World* (1963), *Portrait of Jason* was Clarke's third film about/with Black protagonists, a series if you will,[1] which she concluded in 1985 with her last film, *Ornette Made in America*. All of Shirley Clarke's films were restored by Milestone Films in New York between 2012 and 2016. Each time a film's restoration was completed, it was shown in the Forum section of the Berlinale, the International Film Festival Berlin. This was my introduction to *Portrait of Jason*. In 2013, I was asked to write a short text for the Forum catalog that, despite its brevity, was supposed to address the complex and critical reception of the film.[2] This critical reception mainly revolves around the relation between the filmmaker and the film's protagonist. Is this film, made out of material from a nonstop twelve-hour shoot at Shirley Clarke's penthouse suite at Hotel Chelsea in New York City, with Jason Holliday increasingly drunk and stoned and presumably on heroin, a display of exploitation? How do we understand the constellation of white, heterosexual, middle-class, avant-garde filmmaker and Black, gay protagonist, at least temporarily homeless, addicted, and dreaming of stardom? Whose portrait is it actually? What is this film a portrait of?

The soundtrack of the film contains numerous requests for Jason Holliday to tell "the truth" and to be "honest," and the critical reception to the film for the most part appears troubled by the tension expressed in this directive. The two poles (truth/lie) thus have been transferred into constellations of two,

---

1   In Irene Gustafson's words a "series of films in the 1960s that centrally explore issues of Black masculinity" (2011, 26n1).

2   Some of the ideas developed here began to take shape in that catalogue contribution and I have taken up some of the formulations used there to develop them further in this article. See Heidenreich 2013.

such as Gilles Deleuze's analysis of the relation between the "film-maker" and the "character," the "white camera" and the "black forger," or, in Rachel Brown's words, "the duality of fantasy and reality" (Brown 2017)—a longtime fascination of Clarke's. In a footnote however, Brown describes the troubling uncertainty of the film with the phrase "the audience's unanswered questions" (ibid.). Instead of relegating the audience to a footnote, in what follows I propose to think it as a third party that demands consideration. Instead of asking whose truth the film reveals or hides—that of Shirley Clarke or her protagonist, Jason Holliday—I would like to leave this duality, these "questions of two," behind and consider the film as a set of triangulations. I loosely borrow this term from Haile Gerima's concept of triangular cinema, which he presented at the Edinburgh Film Festival's Third Cinema Conference in 1986, and which insists on the necessity of creating a relationship between audience/community, film-makers/storytellers, and critics/activists. For Gerima, the political potential of cinema, especially in the confrontation with racism and through the lens of an Afro-diasporic perspective, must be thought of as triangular (Gerima 1989). I would like to expand from this and consider triangulation as a queer mode of reading (and filmmaking); as that-which-is-not/beyond/more than-binary. These triangulations serve to complicate the truth/lie constellation that seeps into literal understandings of drag, and they also address the entanglements of race and sex that inform every aspect of the film, its making and its reception.

In relation to *Portrait of Jason*, some of these triangulations involve additional actants in the (making of the) film, some concern the film's materiality, in other words its (un)availability, some follow along the line of critical reception, of scholarship and film criticism as well as less formal forms of writing and engagement, while some connect to other works—films—that expand the notion of what *Portrait of Jason* actually *is*. In following these triangulations, I take my lead from what Marc Siegel has called the "porousness of the cinematic text," which makes it possible to "open onto a cinematic experience beyond that of the moment of projection" (Siegel 2017, 196). Siegel argues against the tendency to fix "both images and identities" in an "originating textual system" and instead shifts his attention to "the dynamic, speculative relationship between them" (ibid.). He theorizes this as "a gossip of images," as a queer practice "apposite of cinema." Gossip always requires more than two— *you didn't hear it from me!*—to come into being. Gossip is always about an absent other, or several others, and it covers its tracks by refusing authorship, or taking credit, yet gossip is based on its own version of credibility, trust, and of fact-checking. Its scene is that of intimacy (as opposed to rumor, as Siegel argues)—in other words, it is not speaking from a distance, but from a position involved. In this sense, I also think of triangulations of/with/in/around the film as vectors of desire, expanding *Portrait of Jason* in numerous directions.

Like Marc Siegel, I want to look at the circulation of images and "intel," or words, in relation to *Portrait of Jason*, joining a queer cinema practice that does not aim at a "conclusive truth claim" (ibid., 200) but (with Marc Siegel taking a theoretical lead from the late Douglas Crimp's writing about queerness as fabulousness) as "non-normative possibility" (ibid.). This not least as Jason Holliday himself claims to be fabulous, but also because his performance has been described as a form of fabulation. Fabulation, following Marc Siegel reading Deleuze, effects a transformative movement, destabilizing the positions in front of and behind the camera.[3] In this sense, fabulation has to be understood as a form of *drag*; here specifically not only in relation to gender, but also in terms of race and class. Or, as Tavia Nyong'o succinctly argues, *Portrait of Jason* should be understood as a form of "afro-fabulation" (2019). Before going into this in more detail, first let me introduce the film and the people involved in its making—and its remaking.

Shirley Clarke was born in New York in 1919 to a wealthy Jewish family of inventors and engineers. She first studied dance, including with Martha Graham, and in the 1950s went on to study film at the City College of New York with Hans Richter and others. Clarke made numerous short experimental films—first dance-related, then an architectural film nominated for an Oscar—joined the New York Independent Film Makers' Association, and soon became one of the leading figures on the American avant-garde film scene.[4] She won an Oscar for Best Documentary Feature in 1964 for her portrait of Robert Frost. Her first feature-length film, *The Connection* (1961), was banned in the US for many years as obscene, since the term "shit" was constantly used in the film, which in this case was actually a slang term for heroin. Beginning in the mid-1970s, Clarke taught film and video at the University of California. In parallel, she experimented with live video, thus returning to her roots as a dancer. Shirley Clarke died in 1997 in Boston, Massachusetts.

Milestone Films, the company that restored Clarke's films, was founded in 1990 by husband and wife team Amy Heller and Dennis Doros, who called their work with and on Clarke's films *Project Shirley*. The intimacy suggested by this title—just the first name—is essential here.

---

3   Marc Siegel argues this in his forthcoming book *A Gossip of Images*. In all of my thinking about and with *Portrait of Jason* Marc's work and input and his generous sharing of ideas as well as bibliographical references and of course, gossip, has been constitutive. This text would basically not exist without his work.

4   For biographical references see, for instance, Milestone Film's press kit "Portrait of Jason" (n. d., a), the Berlinale Forum 2013 catalogue ("Portrait of Jason" 2013), but also Nyong'o 2019 and Siegel (forthcoming).

What is known about the film's protagonist, Jason Holliday, is much sparser, not least because he himself provided various different biographical narratives. He was born as Aaron Payne, and his parents owned a restaurant in Trenton, New Jersey, where they had moved to from the South. He apparently contributed to the family's finances as a child performer, attended but did not finish college, went on to study acting and dance (also with Martha Graham among others), performed on stage and in nightclubs, and died in 1998 in Flushing, in New York. Milestone Films's press release for the restoration of *Portrait of Jason* provides further information.[5] However, they are a very involved player with interests of their own, and their narrative does little to reveal "the truth" either—not least as they appear only to follow the tracks of written accounts and documents, and most of which speak the language of whiteness in twentieth-century USA.

"*Okay, Jason, go!*" This call goes to Jason Holliday at the beginning of *Portrait of Jason*. The image is blurred at first, then comes into focus and Jason answers to the camera: "*my name is Jason Holliday, my name is Jason Holliday ... laughter, pause ... my name is Aaron Payne.*" Aaron Payne is Jason's birth name, but Jason—that is the name that best expresses his personality, as he states in the film. Jason's decision to introduce himself not just once, but three times, sets the tone of his *portrait* right from the start: "*What I really want to do is what I am doing now: perform.*" And that is what he does: he stages himself, is staged, narrates, invents, confesses, asserts. He challenges first and foremost the 16mm Auricon camera that records him and that is handled by Shirley Clarke and her longtime lover and collaborator Carl Lee, son of the legendary African American actor Canada Lee. It was Carl and Canada Lee who introduced Clarke to Jason Holliday. Clarke had also worked with Carl Lee on *The Connection* and *The Cool World*, films in which he also starred as actor. Also present was Jeri Sopanen, the Finnish-born cinematographer who had previously worked with luminaries such as Jean-Jacques Cousteau. But Jason Holliday not only challenges the camera and the team; he also challenges us viewers and our ideas of identity, identification, and truth.

---

5   See Milestone Film's press kit "Portrait of Jason" (n.d., a). I use Jason Holliday without the much used addendum "né Aaron Payne," as he claims in the film that Jason is the name, that he chose for himself and that best suits his personality. The use of the prefix "né" is used in the frame of the patriarchal logic of name changing in marriage for women (née). From today's perspective of naming politics within queer, trans, and nonbinary communities, I refrain from using "né" because I cannot ascribe this formulation to Jason Holliday himself, but to a logic of origin and truth that both the film and my (as well as others') critical thinking seek to defy.

Portrait of Jason defies categories: documentary, fiction film, casting reel, interview. It may well be all of these things, as well as a "critical test of reality," in Irene Gustafson's words (Gustafson 2011). The film was enthusiastically received immediately after its release. To this day, many texts about the film quote Ingmar Bergman, who was among the first to see it as part of a carefully curated sneak preview audience,[6] who allegedly had called it "the most extraordinary film I've seen in my life."[7] Despite its fame, the film has barely been available for decades. With remaining film prints in utterly poor condition, it circulated mostly on VHS, and since 2006 also as a first restoration attempt on a DVD by the British company Second Run Features, accompanied by a booklet containing a speculative note by Tom Sutpen: "It's been described as so many things that one possible explanation for the persistent unavailability through the years of a film so exceptional has been its unusual way of eliding all categorization."[8] Then in 2013, Portrait of Jason was restored by Milestone Films and released on DVD and Blue-ray (and for cinematic distribution as DCP); an event that seems to echo Jason Holliday's own words, "This is a picture I can save forever."

In the course of the film, Holliday talks about drugs, about the almost exclusively white women he works for (as a domestic servant—"a houseboy," in his words), his big nightclub show project, the sex he no longer wants to have, but talks about, the doctors he consults and his white "head shrinks," presumably psychiatrists ... and he also talks about racism (without using the word)—for instance when he calls these white doctors cops. He talks about props and uses them to reenact scenes from the movies and musicals he performs, many of which could be called "classic" drag performances, such as a Barbra Streisand musical number from the stage version of Funny Girl, and impersonations of Mae West, whom he calls a female faggot. He distances himself from the concept of gay marriage understood as a long-term monogamous relationship: "I have better taste," he says. He identifies as a lesbian, he tells us about his childhood, about his violent father, about his mother, and he tells us about feeling lost and being homeless. He tells us that he has to tell, that he will better not tell: "I'll never tell—I have to tell. I AM HERE ON THE THRONE. I get to tell whatever I want. THIS IS MY CHANCE TO REALLY FEEL MYSELF AND SAY—I'M THE BITCH." In between, he is asked by Clarke to tell more: "what else have you got?" The picture becomes blurry time and again, the sound continues,

---

6   Including luminaries such as Amos Vogel, Arthur Miller, Tennessee Williams, Norman Mailer, Elia Kazan, Andy Warhol, Geraldine Page and Ruby Dee, see Milestone Films's website "Portrait of Jason" (n. d., b).

7   Milestone Films press release uses the attributed quote as epigraph without referencing a source.

8   As quoted in Gustafson 2011, 2.

even when the camera is off and we see a black screen. The only person we do see in the film is Jason Holliday—but off-screen, on the soundtrack, we hear the voices of the other crew members, including Carl Lee, who in the last part of the film begins to berate Jason Holliday: *"be honest, motherfucker," "you're just full of shit."* Holliday responds with, among other things, a declaration of love and a request for attention: *"Please turn around and smile at me."*

Since the release of the restored version on DVD and Blue-ray by Milestone Films, additional layers have been added to the film, its restoration, and its reception, expanding the film in several directions. These new layers include, in the words of Tavia Nyong'o, "another chapter" added to a "saga that began almost a half century ago" (Nyong'o 2015), namely, Stephen Winter's 2015 film *Jason and Shirley*. It is a fictional reenactment of the twelve-hour film shoot, starring Sarah Schulman, who cowrote the script, as Shirley and Jack Waters as Jason. Like Rebecca Brown, who connects her wording of "the audience's unanswered questions around Portrait of Jason," to Winter's film (Brown 2017), Nyong'o too understands *Jason and Shirley* as a response to the viewing experience of *Portrait of Jason*: as "an attempt to dig a little deeper into the dynamic of attraction and repulsion between the auteur and her star, and offers one plausible answer to the question that has bedeviled viewers of the confrontation" (Nyong'o 2015).

Stephen Winter, who himself is both gay and Black and probably best known for his film *Chocolate Babies* (1996), said of *Jason and Shirley*, or rather regarding his motivations for making it, that *Portrait of Jason's* years-long unique selling point—the only American film with an openly gay Black protagonist—had been both extraordinarily relevant to him and, especially as a cinema-loving kid, utterly disturbing. The film stayed with him for decades:

> My take after over 20 years of viewing is that Jason is not only complicit in his exploitation but ultimately the film's primary engineer of narrative and characterization. Remember, Jason's profession was hustling and part of the hustle is to take more for your service than what was originally offered, and hold your liquor longer than the mark. Shirley is the one who seems to give up and say, "End, end, end," when she can't stand to film anymore. (Winter in Kohn 2015)

I will come back to Winter's film and its relationship to Milestone Film's restoration project. Before I do so, however, I would like to address Tavia Nyong'o's concept of afro-fabulation, that is, a "theory and practice of black time and temporality" (Nyong'o 2019, 5), which he develops in resonance with Saidiya Hartman's concept of critical fabulation in his 2019 book *Afro-fabulations: The Queer Drama of Black Life*. I am particularly interested here in the chapter

"Crushed Black: On Archival Opacity," in which Nyong'o discusses *Portrait of Jason*. Nyong'o's focus is the impossibility of repair, and a critical reading of restoration and/or as reparation. The history of racism and violence, he argues, cannot be repaired, especially not in a present that is equally, albeit differently, marked by it. The restoration of *Portrait of Jason* by Milestone Film incorporates the release of additional material—including the fifty-four-minute comedy act recorded by Jason Holliday sometime after the film shoot, but in the same year, 1967, as well as a scene that was present in the first cut of the film, the preview version, but which Clarke then edited out. In this scene, she confronts Holliday with accusations concerning Carl Lee—what Holliday did or didn't do with him, revealing the centrality of Lee to her relation to Holliday. By including these extras, we might concede, Milestone Film also wanted to give Holliday space, to give him credit, not only to Clarke. In a sense they tried to restore him too.

Nyong'o asks what happens when practical restoration and historical reparation collide. His argument expands on the photographic term "crushed blacks": "These are the 'shadow areas that lack detail and texture due to underexposure' and are thus called 'blocked up' or 'crushed,' according to the Illustrated Dictionary of Photography" (ibid., 47). Crushed blacks need to be "improved" in postproduction or, as with *Portrait of Jason*, in digitization:

> To link the phenomenon of blocked-up shadows to the question of African American representation in cinema, theater, and visual culture might appear to overburden a technical detail with symbolic and cultural weight. If I persist in drawing these connections, it is because I am persuaded that representations must be treated as immanent to the technical apparatus that construct them, especially if we would wish to unburden ourselves of their oppressive weight. (Ibid., 49)

Nyong'o suggests considering technical imperfections for their queer antiracist potential and he links these to, in Gavin Butt's words, the "imperfect and troublesome relations" (Butt quoted in ibid., 54), within the film and in the production of the film:

> That is to say, if *Portrait of Jason* was from its inception troublingly imperfect, then the best that restoration or recovery could hope for might be to amplify those imperfections. The tangled relationships in the film would need to grapple with the feelings of shame, delight, exposure, and anger that *Portrait* both depicts and evokes, complications that strike at the heart of all we risk when we claim both life and art for performance. (ibid., 55)

By looking at the restoration of the film, the question of who owns (or controls) the story—Holliday, or Clarke, or Lee—begins to shift. The same goes for the question of who—or whose truth, if any—the film actually shows: Aaron Payne, Jason Holliday, or Shirley Clarke? I would suggest that the film both shows and embodies constellations—including power structures and contradictions—because the film is thoroughly embedded in desire. Desire is multivectorial, yet its existence does not require reciprocation. On the contrary, it lays claims, can become possessive, violent even. At the same time, it makes the desirer dependent. Desire is also key to cinema, it makes cinema come into being, driving performers, filmmakers, audience, and critics alike. Desire is a messy, at times violent, potentiality.

I would like to return here to Stephen Winter's film *Jason and Shirley*, the reenactment of the making of *Portrait of Jason*. The film's release led to a remarkable backlash by Milestone Films founders, Amy Heller and Dennis Doros, who publicly denounced the film (and were on the verge of suing Winter) under the headline "The Cruelty and Irresponsibility of Satire" (Heller 2015). They claimed that, while they believed in freedom of speech, they felt: "we must go on the record about the film's inaccurate and simplistic portrayals of a brilliant filmmaker and her charismatic subject" (ibid.). Heller and Doros called the film "bad cinema and worse ethics—that cynically appropriates and parodies the identities of real people" (ibid.). Winter responded with astonishing calm to this public accusation, insisting that his point was not to set the record straight—or to misrepresent it, as Doros and Heller had claimed. Instead:

> It was never my intention to replicate that day, but rather to reimagine its historical and emotional significance from Jason's point of view. So contacting people whom I don't know wouldn't help me get to the film I wanted to make. I wasn't crafting a documentary, or biopic, or a remake. I needed to go deep into the archive of my own life to find the emotional truth of Jason. I had to get to the Jason within me so I could reveal the Jason within us all. (Winter in Kohn 2015)

The argument of Doros and Heller vs. Winter once again revolves around questions of truth, and realness. In reference to *Portrait of Jason* both parties miss the point: The film is not a "true portrait," but it is also not a "false" one, it is *cinema vérité* in the sense of Deleuze: not a cinema of truth, but the truth of cinema. In his second cinema book, *Cinema 2: The Time-Image*, Deleuze reflects on fabulation as a form of storytelling in which the character and the author/director are mutually dependent, each invented by the other:

> What cinema must grasp is not the identity of a character, whether real or fictional, through his objective and subjective aspects. It is the

becoming of the real character when he himself starts to "make fiction," when he enters into "the flagrant offence of making up legends" and so contributes to the invention of his people. The character is inseparable from a before and an after, but he reunites these in the passage from one state to the other. He himself becomes another, when he begins to tell stories without ever being fictional. And the film-maker for his part becomes another when there are "interposed," in this way, real characters, who wholly replace his own fictions by their own story-telling. (Deleuze 1989, 150)

A few pages later Deleuze directly addresses *Portrait of Jason*, a film in which "it is the passage which must be grasped in all its possible "distances," in relation to the character and to his roles, but always internal distances, as if the white camera had slid into the great black forger" (ibid., 154).[9]

What Deleuze is missing here however, is that the camera is not only white. It was not only Shirley Clarke who directed the camera (and Jeri Sopanen), but also Carl Lee, who is the key presence in the much-discussed disturbing final sequence of the film. In this scene, he throws accusations at Jason Holliday and argues with him, audibly giving directions, speaking from the off space, from "behind the camera." The camera is, in this sense, also Black. And what the film shows is not just a relationship of, in Deleuze's words, black forger and white camera, but a constellation with several agents.

Portrait of Jason is a film that was supposed to explore cinema's potential as a medium of the "self," and had therefore initially been planned as a self-portrait, as Clarke later stressed in various interviews, only to declare herself too camera-savvy to be suitable for the project.[10] So it became a film about Jason Holliday. However, Milestone Films' furious response to Winter's *Jason and Shirley* seems to suggest that *Portrait of Jason* is in fact a self-portrait of Shirley Clarke. Doros and Heller took issue with what they thought was an attack on Clarke's reputation, and not on Holliday's.

The vehemence of their reaction, however, speaks also to a different relation. I have already pointed out the strange name they chose for the restoration project of Clarke's feature-length films: *Project Shirley*. The use of her name

---

9   See also Marc Siegel's thinking about fabulation and his complex reading of Deleuze in his forthcoming book *A Gossip of Images*.

10   Clarke talks about this in Burch's and Labarthe's film (1970): "The reason I didn't do me and did do Jason, is that I think it's very difficult for a person who is a filmmaker who is so aware of filmmaking to make a film about themselves. A person who that is done to ... can't be as au courrant as a filmmaker would be. I would have destroyed the film before the film is over."

indicates the intimacy Doros and Heller assumed with the subject of their work. In a public announcement after the completion of this project, Dennis Doros describes this moment as "the end of a long and happy marriage." He writes: "Amy liked to call Shirley Clarke the other woman in my life" (Doros 2016).[11] And as disturbing as this possessive cis-male claim to a polygyny marriage, in which one of the partners is dead and thus deprived of the possibility of giving consent, might be, it is one of the triangulations that I consider to be key to *Portrait of Jason*—and to the film's incommensurability, as Nyong'o puts it with reference to José Muñoz (see Nyong'o 2019, 49ff.).

Shirley Clarke is said to have made the film to outmaneuver Andy Warhol, who apparently had had his eyes on Jason Holliday too.[12] So, we also have a competitive triangle of Clarke, Warhol, and Holliday. Then, as Nyong'o points out, the restoration and work with Clarke's archive revealed that the film may actually be dealing with a love triangle between Shirley Clarke, Jason Holliday, and Carl Lee:

> As the night progressed, Holliday's increasingly belligerent audience derailed his intended performance and set the stage for the angry confrontation between Holliday and an off-screen Lee. The final edit of the film is elliptical about what those "lies" are, exactly. But notes left by Clarke in her log books now held in her archive refer to some of the topics Jason discussed on those other ten hours of film: "straight guys" who are "idiots waiting to be had"; "gigolos" who are "really fags-for-money"; and, most scandalously, a story "about stealing a guy from a girl." When this missing footage is included in the extended cinema of every night life, it is the bizarre love triangle between Lee, Holliday, and Clarke that emerges as the true subject of Clarke's portrait. (ibid., 64)

---

11   The article by Doros on the website of Milestone Films is framed by two photographs, one showing a woman in a bridal dress (Clarke? Heller?), the other a baby. This one has a caption: "Shirley Clarke in 1919." Doros's claim is also one of genealogy, of patrilineage, the project is his baby, as is Shirley Clarke, who is also his second wife...

12   See for instance the press by Milestone Films' press kit "Portrait of Jason" (n. d., a), in which she is quoted off record: "In a 1969 interview at the George Eastman House, Clarke said, off-the-record, that a month before shooting her film, Warhol coincidentally met Jason Holliday at a bar through Paul Morrissey. He then tried to shoot a film with Jason and Edie Sedgwick, which Clarke said, was in the wastebasket as far as she knew. 'They simply couldn't do it.'"

And this kind of archival gossip—the porousness of the cinematic text—continues in other directions too, complicating everything even further, as it includes heterosexism and racism expressed in or as desire.

When Nyong'o speaks of "crushed blacks," he is also addressing another layer of meaning of the term, namely, that of having a crush, being smitten, crushed out on someone or something. Nyong'o's theorization of the crush refuses any romantic notion of shared mutual desire. Instead, he looks at the emotional manipulation of the documentary camera turned into a hostile tool for interrogation, as in the final scene of *Portrait of Jason*, where Jason Holliday is verbally tackled and taken apart by Carl Lee, where he bursts into tears, only to abruptly recompose himself and declare that "I am happy about the whole thing." As Nyong'o puts it:

> To be crushed, after all is to be dejected, defeated, and abject in the face of another. But also: to "have a crush" is to construe love as a kind of defiant ownership of one's abjection: I may not have you, we crushed ones say, but I have the way you have me. (ibid., 56)

The "I have the way you have me," the desire for someone else's desire, can also become very icky, to say the least, as the next constellation of triangulations reveals, which entails racist, homophobic, and sexual violence. "I am not to my knowledge a homosexual," writes filmmaker James Toback in an article on Alain Delon.[13] Since 2017 hundreds of allegations of sexual harassment have been made against Toback by numerous women* (Whipp 2018). By claiming that he is not a homosexual, Toback expresses his desire for Delon by means of disavowal for this man he desperately wanted to work with, as he tells Roger Ebert in an interview, using the words "who is my most desired" (Ebert 2012). In addition to a number of comedies, Toback directed the film *Black and White* in 1999, a story of white middle-class teenagers fetishizing the "black" lifestyle of rap, guns, and big cars. This "semi-improvised piece of documentary fiction," as Michael Sragow writes in the introduction to his Toback interview (Sragow 2000)—featuring, among others, parts of the Wu Tang Clan, Mike Tyson, Claudia Schiffer, Ben Stiller, and Brooke Shields—is a difficult piece to watch and is not my subject here. I mention this film because, on the one hand, the film supposedly cross-references Shirley Clarke's 1963 film *The Cool World* in terms of content and form. On the other hand, in an interview following the release of *Black and White*, Toback talks about his desire for Black men, for

---

13   I could not find this article that Toback says he published in the paperback magazine *Projections* 41, no. 2. This quote is based on Toback's own self-referencing in various interviews, such as Sragow 2000 or Ebert 2012.

which Shirley Clarke again plays a crucial role. The interview is titled with the N-word, quoting Toback's claim in the interview that as a teenager he lived the life of a "White N" (Sragow 2000). To explain his motivations for making *Black and White*, Toback begins by locating its origins in his childhood. He recounts his obsessive interest in the sons of the domestic worker his parents had employed—in his words "the woman who worked in our apartment when I was growing up"—and nonchalantly interjects a violent episode: "I was keenly aware of them being a completely different kind of person because of race. I think I ended up doing something physically violent to one of them, but it was out of a competitive friendliness" (ibid.). In the interview, he immediately moves on from this creepy story to then talk about his best friend in high school, the only Black boy "in a purely white, liberal, upper-middle-class, largely Jewish private school in New York," with whom he was "quite close," to then switch to Clarke—more precisely to her partner/boyfriend/lover, to Lee:

> The real turning point came when I met and fell under the spell of Carl Lee. When I was 15 or 16 I saw Shirley Clarke's *The Cool World* [the 1963 urban underground classic] and was magnetized by Carl Lee. I went back to 72nd Street, where I lived, and down the block, there, two hours after seeing him play the lead on screen, was Carl Lee standing in front of his white Triumph TR6, smoking a cigarette in his navy-blue blazer and his white shirt, looking very debonair. I told him I'd just seen the movie and that he was great. He was effusively friendly, and by the end of the conversation I had lent him $20 and bought some marijuana for him. (ibid.)

James Toback moves on to praise Carl Lee, as "hip-black-actor icon ... He had a huge effect on everyone who knew him" (ibid.). Then he shifts to describe the relationship between Clarke and Lee, thereby claiming intimate knowledge:

> Shirley Clarke's whole life revolved around Carl Lee; they had this on-and-off 30-year relationship and she totally supported him the whole time. His influence was a combination of language, style, personality and psychology. ... The attraction was definitely physical, and stylistic and psychological. (ibid.)

This is also exactly the moment where he expresses his own desire for Lee, which he introduces with his "strange little thing" for Alain Delon: "In my first sentence I say, 'I am not to my knowledge a homosexual.' That would be the appropriate phrase to describe my response to Carl Lee" (ibid.). James Toback goes on to describe his relationship to Lee as a "very unusual, interesting friendship" (ibid.), which is said to have lasted until Lee's death—claiming more years than Lee's relationship with Clarke. His claim resembles the disturbing intimacy that Dennis Doros claims to have with Shirley Clarke beyond her death, and is further reinforced by his account of financial domination. Carl Lee played a small role in James Toback's 1983 film *Exposed*. Toback reports that Lee showed up to the set completely high and in urgent need of money, which he, Toback, provided: "He died of an overdose an hour later" (ibid.). However, Carl Lee died in 1986, so this too is a telling fable, a fabulation, revealing nothing about Lee, but a lot about Toback.

His claim to have supplied Carl Lee with money two times—first he "lends" him twenty dollars in exchange for weed, then he provides fifty dollars for the last fix—also hints at another triangular constellation, that of drugs, more precisely heroin. Both Lee and Holliday were addicts, and the intimacy of shared drug use also constitutes something of a love affair (in addition to Holliday's profession of love for Lee). This intimacy definitely played a big part in the legendary jealousy of Clarke that set the film project in motion in the first place.[14] Toback's "sugar daddy" act, however, simply means that he is trying to force himself violently into a constellation that he too is crushed out on. But Clarke herself is also caught in an abject kind of possessive crush. Between 1964 and 1972 Janine Bazin and Andre Labarthe produced a series of portraits, called *Cinéastes de Notre Temps*, filmmakers of our time. Clarke was included in the series in 1970 (*Rome Brule, portrait de Shirley Clarke*). In this film portrait, she fabulates about her films and filmmaking in the presence of an illustrious audience of mostly figures from the French film avant-garde, such as Jacques Rivette. Here, she delivers the very portrait of herself that then became that of Jason Holliday. Or in the words of Gilles Deleuze, who gossips about *Portrait of Jason*:

> The "I is another" of Shirley Clarke consists in this: that the film that she wanted to make about herself became the one she made about Jason. What has to be filmed is the frontier, on condition that this is equally crossed by the filmmaker in one direction and by the real character in the opposite direction." (Deleuze 1989, 154)

In her actual portrait—that is that of Burch and Labarthe—Clarke fabulates in style and tonality as "one of the boys," attempting to deflect the way those male colleagues of her tried to gender her by talking about "*ladies and cameras.*" She does her best to show that, in fact, she's got more balls and definitely a

---

14   See, for instance, Bob Fiore's comments in Wolfe 2010.

bigger dick than them. Her claim to rank among the (white straight) boys—her "holding court"[15]—leads to a bizarre homophobic denial of Holliday's gayness:

> Jason is very symbolic. Obviously, he is a real person, but what has happened to Jason, and what has made Jason who he is, is definitely the fault of American white society. And what intrigues me so much in the film is that Jason, without ever once saying this, you can't leave that film and not be aware of what has been done to him. Not only his de-emasculation [sic] because I'm absolutely convinced for instance that Jason is a made-up homosexual.

Clarke claims in this portrait, her own fabulation, that Holliday "screams at you I love you!," but that he could never truly love. Holliday does however declare his love—but for Lee, not for her. Nyong'o comments on this scene:

> Setting aside the question of what a "made-up" (as opposed to real?) homosexual might be, I am taken by Clarke's telling misremembering of her own film, the film that she claimed to have obsessively edited over months. In this quotation, she implies that Jason screamed "I love you" at her, when in point of fact, as she must know, he screamed it at Lee. So her insistence that he could never, never, really love must be read as overdetermined by her refusal to admit that her beloved Lee could ever have made a reciprocal "adjustment" to America, could ever have "de-emasculated" himself to a level where he could desire someone like Holliday, even for one night. (Nyong'o 2019, 66)

What speaks here, in this postscript portrait masked as prequel to *Portrait of Jason*, is Clarke's denial of her own feelings and desires, even if these are what set her film in motion in the first place. But what *Portrait of Jason*—"*this is a picture I can save forever*"—does, is continue to expose that very desire.

Shirley Clarke, in her "own" film portrait, calls for a specific coming together: "*the filmmaker, the audience and the film must all be part of something together. And I don't want them separated behind the screen anymore.*" A suggestion that in my mind resonates with Haile Gerima's triangular cinema:

> This triangular relationship best functions through constant critical and innovative deliberation that includes an analysis of the history and practice of conventional cinema. In this process, all inevitable,

---

15   See "Rome Is Burning" 2025.

spontaneous, aesthetic outbursts take motion, becoming organised, coherent, dynamic and vibrant cultural moments. (Gerima 1989, 69)

I do consider *Portrait of Jason* an aesthetic outburst, but one that defies becoming coherent or organized—because it is suffused with desire. This desire opens the film to constellations beyond "sets of two" and beyond the binaries of true/fake and revealed/hidden, beyond simplistic understandings of drag—to what I have described as triangulations. But this desire is not only "crushed out," it also potentially crushes that which it lays claim to with the violence that informs it.

References

Burch, Noël and André S. Labarthe, directors. 1970. *Rome brûle: Portrait de Shirley Clarke*. Paris: Audiovisuel Multimedia International Production.

Brown, Rachel. 2017. "Portrait of Jason (Shirley Clarke, 1967)." *Senses of Cinema* 82 (March 2017). www.sensesofcinema.com/2017/1967/portrait-of-jason/.

Deleuze, Gilles. 1989. *Cinema 2: The Time Image*. Translated by Hugh Tomlinson and Robert Galeta. Minneapolis: University of Minnesota Press.

Doros, Dennis. 2016. "The End of a Long and Happy Marriage." *Milestone Films*. June 21, 2016. https://milestonefilms.com/blogs/news/the-end-of-a-long-and-happy-marriage?srsltid=AfmBOorm3_BigOBx7CzJ6LtJchQP7ZWFTTagUqZGo60uxcIFSQIbjBJI.

Ebert, Roger. 2012. "Toback on Life, Death, Tyson and His Own Personal Hit List." *RogerEbert.com*. December 14, 2012. www.rogerebert.com/interviews/toback-on-life-death-tyson-and-his-own-personal-hit-list.

Gerima, Haile. 1989. "Triangular Cinema, Breaking Toys, and Dinknesh vs Lucy." In *Questions of Third Cinema*, edited by Jim Pines and Paul Willemen, 65—90. London: British Film Institute.

Gustafson, Irene. 2011. "Putting Things to Test: Reconsidering Portrait of Jason." *Camera Obscura* 26, no. 2 (77), 1—31. doi.org/10.1215/02705346-1301521.

Heidenreich, Nanna. 2013. "Portrait of Jason." In *Berlinale Forum 2013*, catalog. www.arsenal-berlin.de/assets/Legacy/user_upload/forum/pdf2013/forum_pdf/Portrait_of_Jason.pdf. Accessed November 4, 2024.

Heller, Amy. 2015. "'Jason and Shirley': The Cruelty and Irresponsibility of Satire." *SydneysBuzz The Blog*. June 23, 2015. https://blogs.sydneysbuzz.com/jason-and-shirley-the-cruelty-and-irresponsibility-of-satire-9037ffc84459.

Kohn, Eric. 2015. "Stephen Winter Explains the Challenges of Being a Gay Black Filmmaker and His Controversial Decision to Reimagine a Classic Film." *IndieWire*. July 10, 2015. www.indiewire.com/features/general/stephen-winter-explains-the-challenges-of-being-a-gay-black-filmmaker-and-his-controversial-decision-to-reimagine-a-classic-film-60423/. Accessed November 15, 2024.

"Portrait of Jason." 2013. Catalog. Berlinale Forum. www.arsenal-berlin.de/assets/Legacy/user_upload/forum/pdf2013/forum_pdf/Portrait_of_Jason.pdf. Accessed November 4, 2024.

"Portrait of Jason." N.d., a. Press kit. Milestone Films. http://www.projectshirley.com/press/portraitofjason.pdf. Accessed November 2, 2024.

"Portrait of Jason." N.d., b. Website. Milestone Films. https://milestonefilms.com/products/portrait-of-jason?_pos=1&_sid=abf3829ee&_ss=r. Accessed November 4, 2024.

Nyong'o, Tavia. 2015. "Jason and Shirley: Restoring an Underground Star's Lost Honour." *The Guardian*. September 19, 2015. www.theguardian.com/film/2015/sep/19/jason-and-shirley-restoring-an-underground-stars-lost-honour. Accessed November 2, 2024.

Nyong'o, Tavia. 2019. *Afro-fabulations: The Queer Drama of Black Life*. New York: New York University Press.

"Rome is Burning (Portrait of Shirley Clarke)." 2025. American Film Festival. November 6—11, 2024, Wrocław, Poland. https://www.americanfilmfestival.pl/film.do?lang=en&id=7075. Accessed November 15, 2024.

Siegel, Marc. 2017. "The Secret Lives of Images." In *The State of Post-cinema: Tracing the Moving Image in the Age of Digital Dissemination*, edited by Malte Hagener, Vinzenz Hediger, and Alena Strohmaier, 195—210. London: Palgrave Macmillan.

Siegel, Marc. Forthcoming. *A Gossip of Images*. Durham, NC: Duke University Press.

Sragow, Michael. 2000. "The Return of the White Negro: Filmmaker James Toback Talks about Race, Sex, Warren Beatty and His Explosive New Movie, 'Black and White.'" *Salon*. March 30, 2000. https://www.salon.com/2000/03/30/toback/. Accessed November 2, 2024.

Whipp, Glenn. 2018. "395: The Number of Women Who Have Contacted The Times with Allegations of Sexual Harassment against James Toback." *Los Angeles Times*. January 7, 2018. www.latimes.com/entertainment/la-et-mn-james-toback-women-sexual-harassment-breaking-silence-20180107-story.html. Accessed November 2, 2024.

Wolfe, Matt. 2010. *Another Portrait of Jason*. Commissioned by Triple Canopy. https://canopycanopycanopy.com/contents/another_portrait_of_jason. Accessed November 2, 2024.

PERFORMING ALONG "THE" COLOR LINE

Blackface from Time to Time

Eric Lott

Trigger warning, anyone? Blackface performance has always been both offensive and indelible. Why does it endure if it is so objectionable? It still surrounds us in many different forms, types of entertainment, and horizons of expectation. Racial "drag" in the form of white performers in blackface seems to exist in some kind of eternal present. Instances of its performance go back centuries (carnival, "primitive rebels," Shakespeare's *Othello*); come into commercial popularity in the US in the 1820s and 1830s; dominate popular entertainment on stage in the form of the "minstrel show" all across the nineteenth century; then migrate to Hollywood film as well as the music industry in the twentieth century and into the twenty-first. And it is a global phenomenon, extending from Great Britain to South Africa, Japan to Australia. The official censuring of blackface in the 1960s and after, which gave it a new but not altogether straightforward political complexion, coincided with its continual "vernacular" reappearance in Halloween costumes and Rotary Club functions and fraternity parties and college yearbooks to this day, where from time to time blackface makes its inevitable return. Then there are the recent cases of white North American activists, scholars, and writers passing for Other (Rachel Doležal, Jessica Krug, Andrea Smith, Sam Forster's *Seven Shoulders*) that only thicken the plot. I want to address the time-to-time temporality of blackface's ongoing present and the question of why US-American culture—my focus here—seems to require the racial, sexual, and gendered interventions of its eternal returns.

I mean "time-to-time" in two senses or registers. The first is occasional, as in, every now and then, or, there it is again—which is true to the lived reality of racial drag's sudden flare-ups, its inevitable reoccurrences in day-to-day life. No one is particularly shocked anymore when a skeleton shows up in some celebrity's or politician's closet or an ill-advised costume happens in the public eye. The other sense of time-to-time is allusive—the circuitry or shuttling from our time to *back then* (nineteenth-century minstrel shows, say), current blackface practice gesturing to more relaxed racist old-time performance ways, which measures an arc that is more like a jagged or even recursive line: the costume recalling other times or out-of-time costumes, or perhaps only willfully recalling times when it was still ok to do blackface! So time after time times two, one logic animating the other; as Ian Baucom (2005) remarks in *Specters of the Atlantic*, time piles up, accumulates, thickens rather than merely passing in progressive or linear fashion with the past bested and out of sight. If blackface or any racial drag is ongoing, it always carries other times in it, unsettling time, implying a temporality of race and a racing of time, a kind of mixing of historical signals.

In another context Jacques Derrida (1994) has termed this phenomenon "hauntologie"—say it in French—ontology haunted by a pun on haunting, "being" being no simple thing but rather an unsettled, out of joint, noncontemporaneous affair, prey to repetition and ghosted past acts (the past is not even past, per William Faulkner [1951]), the repressed that returns to consort uneasily with the present, no matter how conscious or informed we might be. What does it mean to be haunted by blackface, by racial drag?

The chief domains of this returning repressed are Hollywood, the pop music industry, Halloween rituals, the public political realm, and the odd inverse passing cases I will note later; they are reliable hosts of blackface reiteration and repetition in the time-to-time temporality of racial drag's eternal return. I say repetition because these instances are, as I say, often citational: a tacit historical resurrection, a remembering the time of minstrelsy's classic form. Anyone who puts on the blackface guise—see Al Jolson in *The Jazz Singer* (1927) or Bing Crosby in *Holiday Inn* (1942)—mimics or updates the canonical costume of black face paint, exaggerated lips, woolly hair, and shabby (or, conversely, overly elegant) clothes. These accoutrements enable the brutal caricature of African Americans for sport, so central to the hugely popular nineteenth-century commercial minstrel show. Very often, even if in updated form, there are vestiges of the North/South split on offer in the enduring stereotypes of carefree Southern rustic slave Jim Crow and buffoonish northern urban dandy Zip Coon (when Ted Danson roasted his then-girlfriend Whoopi Goldberg in blackface at the Friar's Club in 1993, he was outfitted as a Zip Coon dandy). Despite Spike Lee's *Bamboozled* (2000), the definitive takedown of the form, key elements continue to punctuate such examples—the watermelon in Katy Perry's pretend-Black *This Is How We Do* (2014), dance appropriations like Miley Cyrus twerking at the 2013 Video Music Awards (complete with Black backup dancers), and speech mimicry such as Meghan Trainor's "blaccent" and the song *All About That Bass* (2014). But mostly this kind of appropriation, mixing, transubstantiation, whatever you'd like to call it, happens without the mask, so it's more generalized, tricky, and submerged if unmistakably there once again.

To borrow from Elizabeth Freeman's study *Time Binds*, such recent performances are characterized by what Freeman calls "temporal drag" (Freeman 2010, 62), a sort of undertow or throwback quality that at the least qualifies the novelty of these new works.[1] This is a second order of drag to add to the idea of racial and ethnic drag, and, again, introduces the way in which linear or progressive time is unsettled or disordered by it as well as suggesting that we ought to consider race and racism's temporal dimension—complementary to what Freeman does with drag and queerness —alongside the rather more familiar and frankly easier critiques of cultural appropriation. The tug of the anterior is stubborn. As Stuart Hall (1988) has remarked, race and racism, while always operative, are not everywhere and always *the same*; there are conjunctural and contextual, and I would add temporal, pressures that affect their deployment, in performance or in social relations generally. That is why in addition to being citational, instances of blackface in the ongoing present are marked by their occasion: instances both congeal and create a buzz that speaks to the racial regime of their moment. When on Halloween 2013 *Dancing with the Stars* dancer Julianne Hough put on blackface to mimic "Crazy Eyes" Warren, the mentally unstable inmate played by Uzo Aduba in the show *Orange Is the New Black*, a controversy erupted regarding Hough's offensive choice of party gear, followed by the usual rites of apology and face-saving public self-abasement. In addition to its unconsciously summoning the racial-carceral regime currently contested by proponents of abolition of the prison-industrial complex, the costume's swift denunciation indicated a relatively new widespread intolerance of blackface. As a 2017 *Daily Show with Trevor Noah*[2] segment featuring comedian Roy Wood, Jr. had it, "Race Is Not a Costume" (see it on YouTube): the bit made it witheringly clear that blackface on Halloween is never a good idea.

Yet at the same time, as I have discussed elsewhere, there came a resurgence of *ironic* blackface deployments after the election of Barack Obama, one of them by Obama himself.[3] This development, in my view, complicates the

---

1   See also a number of the essays in the splendid collection by Colbert et al. 2020 as well as Lloyd 2019, 70—72.

2   www.youtube.com/watch?v=7Kl1cnGoQmY, accessed November 2, 2024.

3   I draw here on my analysis initially presented in my *Black Mirror: The Cultural Contradictions of American Racism* (2017), Chapter 1. There were other examples just before Obama's ascendancy, among them the variously raced characters played by Tracey Ullman in her Showtime mockumentary "State of the Union" (including a West Indian airport security guard called Chanel Monticello) and the revolting Shirley Q. Liquor stand-up act by comedian Chuck Knipp. Joshua Alston, "The Dark Side of "Corking Up," *Newsweek* (March 14, 2008); Neely Tucker, "Hollywood's About-Face on Blackface," *Washington Post* (March 16, 2008), M8. I have profited very much from the renewed attention to this tradition to be found in Nicholas Sammond's excellent *Birth of an Industry: Blackface Minstrelsy and the Rise of American Animation* (2015); also useful (by analogy) is Katrin Sieg's *Ethnic Drag: Performing Race, Nation, Sexuality in West Germany* (2009).

conjunctural and temporal drag of blackface's eternal return in the years before 2016. The general notion seemed to be that in our enlightened "postracial" age—a temporally tendentious assessment, one that has quickly dissipated—it was OK to play around with blackface, make fun of the very idea *by putting on the mask*. We were beyond all that now, and the best way to show it was to do it all over again! The election of the first African American president of the United States occasioned the apparently legitimate return of blackface comedy. The burnt cork snuck back, most notably in comedian Fred Armisen's many Obama impressions on television's *Saturday Night Live*. Armisen had already ventured his version of pop star Prince; his blackface (and "blindface") New York governor David Paterson was a big hit. Before you knew it, *Mad Men*'s Jon Hamm was cooning opposite a protesting Tracy Morgan in a spoof of *Amos 'n' Andy* on TV's *30 Rock*, Fox *NFL Sunday*'s Frank Caliendo blacked up *for a broadcast* as basketball star Charles Barkley, Billy Crystal resurrected his blackface Sammy Davis Jr. for the opening segment of the 2012 Academy Awards telecast, and the gang on *It's Always Sunny in Philadelphia* pursued more than one greasepaint remake of *Lethal Weapon*. Even Robert Downey Jr. got into the act, however ironically, using blackface to lampoon a white Method actor playing a hard-bitten Black GI in the Ben Stiller lark *Tropic Thunder* (2008). The kitchen heating up, SNL replaced Armisen's Obama during election season with that of African American Jay Pharoah, whose artificially lightened skin on top of the inevitable comparisons to his comedic predecessor only redoubled the minstrel quotient. Earlier in the decade, Dennis Haysbert had laid important representational track for Obama's advancement in his portrayal of Black president David Palmer on Fox's *24*, a more solemn version of comedian Chris Rock's conceit in the 2003 film *Head of State*. With Obama's actual triumph came the conscious restoration of what they used to call "negro minstrelsy," this time in a mode meant to mock the form but by definition stuck within its contours.

These contradictions descend from the nineteenth-century ones I tried to document in my study *Love and Theft: Blackface Minstrelsy and the American Working Class*, but public censure alongside self-consciously ironic uses of blackface, with a Black man in the White House, is obviously a whole new representational conjuncture. Consider the temporal drag afoot in two purposeful blackface displays in the teens. One of these was the mock movie (still on YouTube) produced for President Obama's April 2013 appearance at the yearly White House Correspondents' Dinner. The spoof opens with a deadpan Steven Spielberg recalling how it hit him to follow up his award-winning biopic of Lincoln with—Steven Spielberg's *Obama*. But who on earth to play him? "As it turns out," the director says, "the answer was right in front of me all along: Daniel Day-Lewis!" The actor so brilliant as Hawkeye in *Last of the Mohicans*, as Bill the Butcher in *Gangs of New York*, and most recently as Spielberg's Abraham

Lincoln, a quick montage of clips certifies, "becomes his characters." "And you know what?" crows Spielberg, "He *nailed* it." Cut to Barack Obama being interviewed with the large caption, "DANIEL DAY-LEWIS, Method Actor." The joke has arrived. "Was it hard playing Obama? I'll be honest, yeah it was," says Obama as Day-Lewis as Obama. Shots of Obama in the mirror practicing "his accent": "Hello Ohio! Hello Ohio! I love you back!" For one thing, the actor avers, "the cosmetics were challenging"—and almost 200 years of blacking-up roll into the picture. After a quick, almost obligatory bit with Tracy Morgan talking about his performance as (who else?) Joe Biden, we're back to "Day-Lewis." "The hardest part? Trying to understand his motivations ... What makes him tick? Why doesn't he get mad? If I were him [sic] I'd be mad *all the time*. But I'm not him. I'm Daniel Day-Lewis." Fade to black on "Obama" doing his hair and checking his hand gestures in the mirror. Subverting the color line by taking the White House, Obama attempts to subvert it doubly by making fun of racist blackface. This is far more playful and sanctioned than, say, the 2019 discovery of then-Governor of Virginia Ralph Northam's college yearbook with a picture of Northam in blackface standing next to someone in a Ku Klux Klan outfit, which produced public outcry and calls for him to resign (he managed to survive the incident politically). Obama as Day-Lewis as Obama seems delighted to exploit the joke that an actor in blackface could play him best. One wonders, however, whether the implication that there's a white man inside him kills the joy a little.[4]

A very different set of ironies attended a second instance from the teens. In 2015, Baltimore ex-cop Bobby "Al Jolson" Berger, who for decades performed as Al Jolson in blackface at local venues, which created tension within the police department and with other civil authorities and which likely cost him his job, offered to resurrect his Jolson act. The occasion was a fundraiser for the police officers charged in the death of Freddie Gray, a Black suspect who was thrown unsecured into the back of a police van and driven around intentionally roughly, leading to injuries that killed him. Cue Bobby Berger, who wanted to help raise funds for the cop perpetrators with a blackface act that reiterated the violence, a sort of exorcism of racist policing through representational legitimation. The fundraiser was canceled after public alarm—the officers themselves refused to accept any funds raised, and the venue disavowed the performance—though Berger remained unrepentant, claiming there was nothing racist about his act.[5] Here again the strange coexistence of knowing distanciation, outright endorsement, and public censure of racial drag, all of it underscored by a steady

---

4   See Roediger 2010; Sugrue 2010; Lipsitz 2011; Touré 2011; Jeffries 2013; Keller 2015; Dyson 2016.

5   See Contrera 2015.

drumbeat of police violence that by 2020 would lead to the Black Lives Matter movement and marches.

Just another moment, that is to say, in the time-to-time temporality of time immemorial. While the nineteenth-century minstrel show was organized around the quite explicit "borrowing" of African American cultural materials for white dissemination, a borrowing that depended on the material relations of slavery, such performance obscured these relations by pretending that slavery and racial oppression was amusing, right, and natural. This is still blackface's primary and primordial urgency, transposed in the present day to racial dominance more generally. Like minstrelsy of yore, blackface in the ongoing present is also a space for playing with or making theater out of white guilt, fear, desire, and other affects devoted to Black people, Black culture, and the political relations that govern discourse between the races. For all its ridicule, blackface in my view sublimates a secret envy of, even erotic desire for, "Blackness." The blackface mechanism of cultural control over "Blackness" and Black cultural forms has had a sadly lasting legacy, but it has also, perversely, provided a channel for the Black cultural "contamination" of and influence on the dominant culture. The dynamic I have called "love and theft" names the dialectic of white racial attraction and aversion, cultural appropriation born of cross-racial desire, that first arose commercially in the minstrel show but is plain today wherever you look (the NBA, boxing, the NFL). Only by beginning to inventory the racial deposits the minstrel show has paid forward can we hope to acknowledge the racial impulses, reckonings, and unconscious reactions that lie so deep as to feel inevitable and given.

That said, racial drag pivots less on appropriation or impersonation than on the "theatricalization" of race itself, the production of a kind of fantasy zone amenable to racial phantasmagoria. Not unlike cross-gender drag, Black mirroring results less in the reproduction of "Blackness" than an activation of it for white purposes, which always redound to social dominance and self-regard. What artist Kara Walker once called in a series of screen prints the Emancipation Approximation is that asymptotic vector of misrecognition and fetishism, a pure playing in the dark, whereby classic American literature, Hollywood film, pop musical artistry, concerned social commentary, and the performative commons of everyday life summon "Blackness" in acts, often unwitting, of supremacist redundancy.

Fifty years ago, Richard Slotkin (1973) published the classic volume *Regeneration Through Violence*, a study of the ways continuous settler extermination of indigenous peoples on the so-called frontier functioned continually to renew settler life. What I'm describing in the eternal return of blackface drag is something akin to *regeneration through ignorance*, the privilege of unknowing.[6] There seems a persistent desire on the part of whites in everyday blackface to forget or remain innocent of and clueless about racial dominance and indeed violence, including the violence of the mask itself; the mask, that vehicle of amnesia, is a brand (in many senses), a title of ownership to the "Blackness" it affixes in black skin, a threat, a mark of terror. How striking it is when a blackface perp cries out, once busted, "I didn't know it was offensive!" or "I didn't mean it racially!" This willed refusal to acknowledge one's power, or, what is the same thing, the privilege of remaining unaware of it, amounts to that blissed mix of stupidity and sublimity that Sianne Ngai terms "stuplimity" (2005).[7] Bathed in ignorance, reveling in regression, happily exposing repressed or unconscious matters they know not of, racial and ethnic drag kings and queens produce racial dominance in its most leisurely, casual, chill, and fun registers, an idiot's sublime. It is the consummate exhibit of blackface's offensiveness as forgotten but not gone.[8]

Which makes the white liberal attempts to make use of it across the last century so oddly compelling. Behind it all, whether in the projections of intellectuals or the entanglements among outsiders, is the white fascination with an imagined "Blackness" that Norman Mailer was in 1957 to call "The White Negro" (Mailer 1957): Harlem Renaissance broker Carl Van Vechten, jazzmen Mezz Mezzrow and Johnny Otis, Elvis, rapper Eminem. As Leslie Fiedler once trenchantly remarked, "born theoretically white, we are permitted to pass our childhood as imaginary Indians, our adolescence as imaginary Negroes, and only then are expected to settle down to being what we really are: white once more" (Fiedler 1972, 134). By the turn of the 1960s, this structure of feeling could be seen as a kind of cross-racial solidarity, and with John Howard Griffin's 1961 *Black Like Me* (remarkably still in print) the gesture was enshrined. Griffin famously went through various skin-altering treatments to go undercover for a six-week tour of the South to discern the answer to the question, as the cover of several paperback editions puts it, "What was it like, really like, to be a Black in the Deep South?"—intimating among other things that a host of Black authors addressing precisely this had failed the task. The book's longevity suggests how forceful a hold this putatively sympathetic crossing has had on the US imagination. *Black Like Me* took the available materials of white cross-racial interest and used them to new ends; it is the crucial historical switchpoint between a racist history of cooning and a new politics of antiracism. And while

---

6   See Sedgwick 1993, 23—51.

7   Ngai (2005, Chapter 6) uses the notion somewhat differently than my meaning here, though performative repetition is key to her concept.

8   See the keen insight of Joseph Roach in his *Cities of the Dead* (1996).

the cooning still hasn't gone away, the book instantiated an enduring civil rights template (updated in the form of today's white "ally" figure, one might argue) that captured the interest of (among many others) writer Grace Halsell, who a few years later did a mimic version of Griffin's stunt, published as *Soul Sister* in 1969. (The infinite regress of mimicry, a hauntological house of mirrors, comes with the territory: besting Halsell, Robert Bonazzi who wrote a 1997 study of John Howard Griffin called *Man in the Mirror* and married Griffin's widow.) While meant as sympathetic gestures of solidarity, these texts are complicitous with the racial designs they set out to expose.[9]

More than a little of this dynamic appears to be at work in the case of Rachel Doležal, the putatively Black president of the Spokane NAACP who in 2015 was revealed to be a white woman passing for Black, causing an international scandal. If whiteness performed in full ideological rectitude depends upon the renunciation of enjoyment, the body, and an aptitude for pleasure, with the Other seen as especially gifted in this line (with regard especially to food, music, bodily exhibition, and sexual appetite), Doležal's upbringing was by her account quite forcibly renunciatory. Her severely strict rearing by fundamentalist Christian parents put her in search of something better, which she found first in her adoptive Black siblings and then Black college friends and mentors, and later her (now ex-) husband; she went on to enroll in an MFA program at historically Black Howard University. Organizing her enjoyment and self-definition through the Other whose identity she herself assumed, Doležal not only accessed a new relation to the world but took it upon herself to push for African American civil rights, ultimately as head of the Spokane chapter of the NAACP, in all respects apparently earnest in the effort of demarcating her universe, disavowing with fervor her appropriation even while enacting it. This is rather precisely the mixed erotic economy of American whiteness, here turned to the account of a strange antiracist alchemy.[10]

This structure has no doubt meant that the dispossessed become bearers of the dominant classes' "folk" culture, their repository of joy and moral passion and general revivification; yet one of the less recognized shapes of that revivifying has come in instances of white identification with Black oppression. Whether it precedes or follows a dominative logic of pleasure, an identificatory white antiracism in blackface guise is in fact its twin. This perhaps explains Doležal's expressed feeling of being home at last upon racially crossing over, and her embrace of the rearranged kinship structure by which she has more or less adopted two of her parents' four adopted Black children as her own. According

---

9   See Gaines 2017, passim. My analysis of both Griffin and Doležal outlined in this text draws on Chapter 5 of my book *Black Mirror* (2017).

10   See Doležal 2017, Chapters 1—15; Sunderland 2015; Oluo 2017; Žižek 1990, 57.

to Doležal, interestingly enough, it all began with Black hair: braiding her Black sister's hair, then having hers done in various Black-styled braids and weaves, she pursued her inner "Blackness" through the pleasures of bodily expression. Much has been made of Doležal's having sued Howard while a student there for discriminating against her whiteness, which makes her turn to Black seem all the more opportunistic. To my mind, there is hardly any contradiction here: both moves are underwritten by white privilege, both seek recognition from her chosen people.[11]

Doležal's position on her adopted Blackness rather amusingly aligns with Walter Benn Michaels's (1997) arguments about the incoherence of racial identity, something that racial drag unwittingly illuminates. Michaels has long scored social-constructionist arguments for being tacitly biologistic; passing is logically impossible, according to Michaels, because you can't "secretly" be your former race once you pass if race is in fact a social construction: you just are your new racial definition, with no blood residue about it. Michaels would logically have to consider Doležal to be as Black as she regards herself. She is now known as Nkechi Amare Diallo. It is indeed essentialist to remind her she's white—which is why antiessentialism isn't really the point. Doležal and Michaels both disregard the desperately uneven historical pressures, the burdens and opportunities inequitably distributed to white and Black, in the formation of racial regimes, no matter how "false" the category of race may be; these pressures cannot be readily circumvented either by breezily casting off whiteness or by newly shouldering Blackness, nor can they be reduced to tidy syllogisms à la Michaels. True, Doležal crossed over not for fame or money but for inner peace as well as social justice and race leadership; in this, she suggests she is trans not unlike Caitlyn Jenner (though Doležal doesn't push the analogy); and such commentators as Melissa Harris-Perry (on MSNBC), Kareem Abdul-Jabbar (in *The New York Times*), and scholar of passing Allyson Hobbs (2014) (ditto) came variously to her defense. Doležal does ironically encapsulate in one body a long NAACP history of white patrons/allies and Black race leaders. But this performance of identity is not so easily decoupled from the legacy of blackface. In assuming the privilege to speak for and as a Black woman, she is nothing if not, at least in part, white once more.[12]

Other recent visible examples of such inverse passing follow a brassier logic than this model of care mixed with guilt. In September 2020, Jessica Krug, a professor of African and African American studies at George Washington University who had passed for years as one or another variant of Algerian/

---

11   See Doležal 2017, Chapters 10, 13, 15; Wilson 1994, 11—17, 47—55; Mercer 1994, 97—128.
12   See Doležal 2017, 246, 232f., 244.

Caribbean/East Harlem/Bronx Afro-Latina, confessed her own "napalm toxic soil of lies" in an essay on *Medium*: she grew up white and Jewish in suburban Kansas City. Describing her ploy as "the very epitome of violence," Krug was within days forced to resign from her job. For as long as it worked, Krug leaned into the persona, calling herself "Jess La Bombalera," using a cringy "barrio" accent, and testifying angrily and profanely before the New York City Council about East Harlem gentrifiers. Krug's insistent insiderism made references to "we" and "us" with friends and acquaintances of color and badgered light-skinned Black friends about their Blackness. Testimony since her self-outing suggests that people around her not infrequently suspected something fishy. Krug certainly outdid Griffin and Halsell in presumptuousness, her uber-Boricua osadía seeming to rather overdo it. What is striking is Krug's autocritique, which is useful in its severity (and seems to spring from the same source as her appropriative self-righteousness). Krug's story by her own admission amplifies the white entitlement, recursive repetition, and citational force in all racial drag.[13]

Indeed we might call on her analysis to take a closing look at the latest (but surely not last) entry in these annals. The author is quite aware of the history I have outlined but chooses to repeat it. As if to square racial drag's circle—confirming its eternal returns, producing to boot a time-to-time sense of temporal drag, a second- or even third-order mimicry—comes now Sam Forster's *Seven Shoulders* (2024). The author is a white Canadian journalist (not from the US and therefore *reliable* is the implication) bent on self-consciously redoing Griffin's *Black Like Me* or Halsell's *Soul Sister*, which Forster glosses in the first section of the book.[14] Placing himself in the line of these and other undercover racial travelogues, Forster hitchhikes as white on one day and then as Black on the next (Maybelline Mocha his makeup of choice) on seven different city roadside shoulders; he receives seven offers as a white hitcher and only one as a Black hitcher. Thus proving what hardly needed proof, the gambit has been roundly ridiculed. Touted on Amazon as "the most important book on American race relations that has ever been written," *Seven Shoulders* was defended against early haters on X by Forster himself in the most fulsome terms. This is

---

13   See Krug 2020; Flaherty 2020; Jackson 2020; Ziyad 2020; Daniels 2021, Chapter 4. A figure adjacent to Krug in the pop world is Ariana Grande, an Italian-American pop star who is often taken as some variety of Latina (with the help of certain racially ambiguous gestures by the performer herself, though she doesn't technically seek to pass); a good study of Grande's "off-whiteness" is Guterl 2023.

14   Alisha Gaines's article "The Strange History of Journalistic Blackface" (2024) conveys the findings of her book *Black for a Day* (2017) and offers the appropriate rebuttal to Forster's stunt and claims.

a masculinist right-wing departure in these already murky swamps, fitting for a moment that includes "hillbilly elegist" and Vice President J. D. Vance (2016).[15]

Hauntology rules Forster's world. "Griffin is possibly the most interesting son America bore in the twentieth century" (3), Forster implausibly suggests, overestimating the force and interest of Griffin's stunt: "Griffin was a mammoth. There are few people who had a greater impact on American race relations throughout the course of the Civil Rights movement, and fewer still who were White" (9). And so Forster determines as it were to take up Griffin's offer, producing a recursive temporality that is profoundly out of joint and yet in step with our times. Forster doesn't read the room. Sensing rightly that he would have a tough time finding a publisher for a twenty-first century Griffin, Forster launches his own publishing company, Slaughterhouse Media—first entry his own *Seven Shoulders*. "In addition to constituting a tremendous literary achievement, I believe that this book constitutes a tremendous achievement in the realm of civic progress" (16), he writes, and as Michael Jackson quipped to Paul McCartney in "The Girl Is Mine," you keep dreamin'. As with Krug, racial self-aggrandizement is key: it takes Forster to do this work, he claims with near-Trumpian temerity, because Blacks have "never been anything but Black" and so "have no experiential barometer with respect to race ... My barometer [wait for it] is better than anyone else's" (17). Yet the "taxonomy" of the book's subtitle is hopelessly muddled, its division between "institutional racism" (basically eradicated, it is here claimed) and "interpersonal racism" (still in effect, says the author), is no division at all, to say nothing of the incorrect judgments here; as the author himself admits, one by definition bleeds into the other (151). As for the decision to make hitchhiking the litmus for racial dominance in America, it is hard to know where to begin. Snap judgments at high rates of speed, the mix of motives for picking up *anybody* hitching, all kinds of circumstantial variables, the racial and gender and sexual quiddities in the decision to pull over or not (paternalist racialism, fear of rape, sexual calculation—Forster assumes that one driver stops because he "wanted to fuck me" [89]), and so on (68): not a problem here. Forster makes a case for the free, voluntarist, and therefore lab-certified nature of the privatized mobile theater that is the automobile.

Haunted by precursors of every stripe, as he knows, Forster is weirdly breezy about his undertaking. Pondering the thorny question of whether his excursion "counts" as blackface, he decides, well, that it doesn't—it's *journalistic* blackface, somehow different in kind (76). Forster has fits of defensiveness like this throughout the book; in a volume whose tone is never quite under control,

---

these bursts still come quite unexpectedly. Given the context, they seem racially overdetermined, and definitely New Model Army brutal. Dismissing potential critics of his undertaking, he takes up startlingly violent rhetorical arms in the defense of friends and family: "But if you use this book as a pretense to attack my friends or family, if you threaten them or go at them in any way, I will do everything in my power to ruin you. I will make destroying you my rabid obsession, and I won't stop until you're either dead or so fucked up that you wish you were" (18). Noted, Sam!

Sam Forster manages to expose how indefensible and yet irresistible is the impulse behind time-to-time blackface performances. His work is valuable in letting us see the wheels behind the impulse turn. The mix of amnesia with recall, blindness and unwitting insight, brutality with solidarity, trepidation and willfulness. Blackface blithely not a problem and very much a problem. A fitting stop in the saga of racial drag that is sure to go on. See you around the next bend.

References

Baucom, Ian. 2005. *Specters of the Atlantic: Finance Capital, Slavery, and the Philosophy of History*. Durham, NC: Duke University Press.

Bonazzi, Robert. 1997. *Man in the Mirror: John Howard Griffin and the Story of "Black Like Me."* Maryknoll, NY: Orbis Books.

Colbert, Soyica Diggs, Douglas A. Jones Jr., and Shane Vogel, eds. 2020. *Race and Performance after Repetition*. Durham, NC: Duke University Press.

Contrera, Jessica. 2015. "A Final Night in Blackface: Baltimore's Al Jolson Impersonator Calls It Quits." *Washington Post*. November 12, 2015.

The Daily Show. 2017. "Roy Wood, Jr.'s Advice for Costumes with Blackface." October 31. https://www.youtube.com/watch?v=7Kl1cnGoQmY. Accessed June 13, 2024.

Daniels, Jessie. 2021. *Nice White Ladies: The Truth About White Supremacy, Our Role in It, and How We Can Help Dismantle It*. New York: Seal Press.

Derrida, Jacques. 1994 (originally published 1993). *Specters of Marx: The State of the Debt, the Work of Mourning, and the New International*. Translated by Peggy Kamuf. New York: Routledge.

Doležal, Rachel (with Storms Reback). 2017. *In Full Color: Finding My Place in a Black and White World*. Dallas: BenBella Books.

Dyson, Michael Eric. 2016. *The Black Presidency: Barack Obama and the Politics of Race in America*. New York: Houghton Mifflin.

Faulkner, William. 1951. *Requiem for a Nun*. New York: Random House.

Fiedler, Leslie. 1972 (originally published 1966). *Waiting for the End*. New York: Stein and Day.

Flaherty, Colleen. 2020. "White Lies: Prominent Scholar Outs Hersel fas White Just as She Faced Exposure for Presenting Herself as Black." *Inside Higher Ed.* September 3, 2020. https://www.insidehighered.com/news/2020/09/04/prominent-scholar-outs-herself-white-just-she-faced-exposure-claiming-be-black. Accessed June 13, 2024.

Forster, Sam. 2024. *Seven Shoulders: Taxonomizing Racism in Modern America.* Austin: Slaughterhouse Media.

Freeman, Elizabeth. *Time Binds: Queer Temporalities, Queer Histories.* Durham, NC: Duke University Press.

Gaines, Alisha. 2017. *Black for a Day: White Fantasies of Race and Empathy.* Chapel Hill: University of North Carolina Press.

Gaines, Alisha. 2024. "The Strange History of Journalistic Blackface." *FlaglerLive. com.* June 27, 2024. https://flaglerlive.com/journalistic-blackface. Accessed June 13, 2024.

Griffin, John Howard. 1961. *Black Like Me.* New York: New American Library.

Guterl, Matthew Pratt. 2023. "The Curious Case of Ariana Grande: Racial Passing in the Present." *ASAP/Journal* 8, no. 2: 279—300.

Hall, Stuart. 1988. "New Ethnicities." In *Black Film/British Cinema*, edited by Kobena Mercer, 27—31. London: ICA Documents.

Halsell, Grace. 1969. *Soul Sister.* Greenwich, CT: Fawcett.

Hobbs, Allyson. 2014. *A Chosen Exile: A History of Racial Passing in American Life.* Cambridge, MA: Harvard University Press.

Jackson, Lauren Michele. 2020. "The Layered Deceptions of Jessica Krug, the Black-Studies Professor Who Hid That She Was White." *The New Yorker.* (September 12, 2020). https://www.newyorker.com/culture/cultural-comment/the-layered-deceptions-of-jessica-krug-the-black-studies-professor-who-hid-that-she-is-white. Accessed June 13, 2024.

Jeffries, Michael P. 2013. *Paint the White House Black: Barack Obama and the Meaning of Race in America.* Stanford, CA: Stanford University Press.

Keller, Morton. 2015. *Obama's Time: A History.* New York: Oxford University Press.

Krug, Jessica. 2020. "The Truth, and the Anti-Black Violence of My Lies." *Medium.* September 3, 2020. https://medium.com/@jessakrug/the-truth-and-the-anti-black-violence-of-my-lies-9a9621401f85. Accessed June 13, 2024.

Lipsitz, George. 2011. *How Racism Takes Place.* Philadelphia: Temple University Press.

Lloyd, David. 2019. *Under Representation: The Racial Regime of Aesthetics.* New York: Fordham University Press.

Lott, Eric. 2017. *Black Mirror: The Cultural Contradictions of American Racism.* Cambridge, MA: Harvard University Press.

Lott, Eric. 1995 (originally published 1993). *Love and Theft: Blackface Minstrelsy and the American Working Class.* New York: Oxford University Press.

Mailer, Norman. 1957. "The White Negro." *Dissent* (Fall 1957).

Mercer, Kobena. 1994. "Black Hair/Style Politics." In *Welcome to the Jungle: New Positions in Black Cultural Studies*, 97—128. New York: Routledge.

Michaels, Walter Benn. 1997. "Autobiography of an Ex-White Man: Why Race Is Not a Social Construction." *Transition* 73: 122—143.

Ngai, Sianne. 2005. *Ugly Feelings*. Cambridge, MA: Harvard University Press.

Oluo, Ijeoma. 2017. "The Heart of Whiteness: Ijeoma Oluo Interviews Rachel Doležal, the White Woman Who Identifies as Black." *The Stranger*. April 19, 2017. http://www.thestranger.com/features/2017/04/19/25082450/the-heart-of-whiteness-ijeoma-oluo-interviews-rachel-dolezal-the-white-woman-who-identifies-as-black. Accessed June 13, 2024.

Roach, Joseph. 1996. *Cities of the Dead: Circum-Atlantic Performance*. New York: Columbia University Press.

Roediger, David R. 2010. *How Race Survived U.S. History: From Settlement and Slavery to the Obama Phenomenon*. New York: Verso.

Sammond, Nicholas. 2015. *Birth of an Industry: Blackface Minstrelsy and the Rise of American Animation*. Durham, NC: Duke University Press.

Sedgwick, Eve Kosofsky. 1993. "Privilege of Unknowing: Diderot's 'The Nun.'" In *Tendencies*, 23—51. Durham, NC: Duke University Press.

Sieg, Katrin. 2009. *Ethnic Drag: Performing Race, Nation, Sexuality in West Germany*. Ann Arbor: University of Michigan Press.

Slotkin, Richard. 1973. *Regeneration Through Violence: The Mythology of the American Frontier, 1600—1860*. Middletown: Wesleyan University Press.

Sugrue, Thomas J. 2010. *Not Even Past: Barack Obama and the Burden of Race*. Princeton: Princeton University Press.

Sunderland, Mitchell. 2015. "In Rachel Doležal's Skin." *Vice*. December 7, 2015. https://www.vice.com/en/article/rachel-dolezal-profile-interview. Accessed June 13, 2024.

Touré. 2011. *Who's Afraid of Post-Blackness? What It Means to Be Black Now*. New York: Simon and Schuster.

Vance, J. D. 2016. *Hillbilly Elegy: A Memoir of a Family and Culture in Crisis*. New York: HarperCollins.

Wilson, Judith. 1994. "Beauty Rites: Towards an Anatomy of Culture in African-American Women's Art." *The International Review of African American Art* 11, no. 3: 11—55.

Ziyad, Hari. 2020. "The Stories and Lies of Jess Krug." *Vanity Fair*. December 17, 2020. https://www.vanityfair.com/style/2020/12/the-stories-and-lies-of-jess-krug. Accessed June 13, 2024.

Žižek, Slavoj. 1990. "Eastern Europe's Republics of Gilead." *New Left Review* 183 (September/October): 50—61.

Reading the Blackened Faces of the Ku-Klux Klan in the Reconstruction-Era United States

Elaine S. Frantz

There is a reason why it surprises us to hear that blackened faces were probably as common as forms of Klan disguise as were elaborate robes and headgear. One of the greatest successes of Ku-Klux Klan apologists was convincing many of their contemporaries, and us, that Klan violence was unique, bizarre, and novel. This supposed otherness was signified by its costume. As the canonical history of the Klan's founding in the second half of the 1860s coauthored by an original member explained, "it only required a quaint garb and some mysterious sounds to convince the uninitiated that we were spirits from another world."[1] Ku-Klux members claimed that their outlandish costume and performance was for the benefit of "superstitious freedmen." While there is scant evidence that freedpeople were frightened by the spectacular costumes rather than the deadly weapons stowed beneath them, Northerners then and historians ever since have been transfixed by the spectacle of the costume. Scholars have approached the Klan as if it were an anomaly: meaningfully distinct from the relentless white-on-black violence that preceded, surrounded and coexisted with, and followed it. We have focused unduly on a minority of Ku-Klux attackers who imported ritual and costume elements from European and Caribbean carnival traditions, masquerade balls, and fraternal orders. These attackers played weird music, developed a mysterious code language to announce their meetings in newspapers, and paraded about in a wide variety of costumes, including the expensively produced white robes with tall conical hats and masks affixed which would later become iconic. This garish performativity transmuted terrible but prosaic racist criminality into racist terrorism: it intrigued the press, which spread news of the attacks, circulating the terror beyond Klan attacks' direct victims. It also marked the wealth and resources of Klan attackers, implied extensive planning and coordination, and, essentially,

---

1   Lester and Wilson 1905, 22.

defined Klan violence as discontinuous with and distinct from the pervasive racial violence which surrounded it.[2]

To the extent that it drew upon the carnivalesque, Ku-Klux performed inversion: gendered and racial drag. While Ku-Klux were all or almost all men, they often used feminine costume elements and witnesses sometimes noted that they looked like women. The same is true with race: while Ku-Klux were all or almost all white, there are many examples of their costuming themselves as Black. I have elsewhere considered the significance of inversion as an interpretive key to Klan costumes: in representing themselves as women, Ku-Klux at once claimed, parodied, and rejected feminine qualities (Frantz [Parsons] 2005). Similarly, in evoking Blackness, Ku-Klux inhabited certain perceived strengths of Blackness, while also mocking and distancing themselves from Blackness.

As powerful as the carnivalesque is as an interpretation of Klan costumes, however, when we focus too exclusively on it, we miss most of what the Ku-Klux were signaling and doing. To begin with, we have been so transfixed by these costumes that we have seen them even when they weren't there. Only a minority of Klan attackers wore sensational costumes like the ones we imagine. A large proportion of Klan attackers wore only cheaply and easily-made costume elements or no costume at all. Such attacks were and are more easily recognizable as continuous with familiar forms of violence. Even minimal costumes could convey substantial meaning, of course. One of the most common forms of less-than-spectacular Klan costuming was blackening the face. Blackened faces were likely as common a disguise among Klan attackers as were the elaborately carnivalesque costumes which historians have associated with them. Despite the contemporary fascination with the more sensational costumes, contemporaries also knew—as later generations forgot—that many Ku-Klux simply blackened their faces. The contemporary association between violence with blackened faces and the Ku-Klux was so strong during the active period of the Klan that when four men in Pittsburgh blackened their faces in 1871 to rob a bank—a crime with no apparent political or racial motivation—a Washington, DC, newspaper entitled its article about the robbery "The Ku-Klux Klan."[3]

Ku-Klux in blackened faces foreground elements of this terrorist movement that are usually neglected and recontextualize interpretations of the Klan which focus too exclusively on carnivalesque inversion. Blackened-faced Ku-Klux—although they themselves were often or always engaged in racial drag like their more sensationally dressed peers—reveal the Klan's continuity

---

2   I have written about the significance of Klan costuming, focusing (though not exclusively) on more elaborate costumes, at greater length in "Midnight Rangers" (Frantz [Parsons] 2005).

3   *The Daily Patriot* 1871, 1.

with other violent traditions in the United States and beyond, and turn our attention to the many Klan attacks which were more spontaneous, less elaborately prepared, and required no special resources. These blackened-faced attacks had performative significance overlapping with but distinct from that of carnivalesque costumes. Focusing on Klan attackers with blackened faces underlines Klan attacks' continuity with what Kidada Williams calls "the ordinary violence of emancipation" (Williams 2012, 19). It opens up the meanings of blackened faces in the Reconstruction-era United States (1863—1877).

The Ku-Klux Klan, which emerged in Pulaski, Tennessee, sometime between the spring of 1866 and the spring of 1867, was among many anti-Black, anti-Republican terrorist groups which spread through much of the US South in the decade after the end of the Civil War. These loosely connected groups committed terroristic violence through much of the former Confederacy and parts of Missouri and Kentucky: beating, whipping, raping, driving from their homes, and otherwise abusing thousands, and killing hundreds of Black (and white) Republicans. Beginning in 1868, many of these groups adopted the name of the Pulaski-based group, calling themselves "Ku-Klux." Klan victims were only a small part of the hundreds of thousands of freedpeople and their allies terrified, injured or killed by white people acting independently or collectively in the massive struggle following emancipation.[4] Both Southern white supremacists and federal leaders, however, promoted the idea that most white-on-Black violence was Klan violence: white Southern elites hoped that the federal government might be forced to give concessions in the face of distinct and organized mass resistance to its efforts to rule the formerly insurrectionary states, and the idea of such resistance legitimized federal control in the South, and made it possible to promise that the continued oppression of Black Southerners was the kind of problem a military could solve.

Because of such pressures to present Klan violence as exceptional, attacks which were more elaborately performative received more attention than those perpetrated by uncostumed attackers or those in simple costumes such as blackened faces. The term "blackface" would not be in common use until the 1890s: instead, people referred to "blackened," "blacked," or "smutted" faces. The primary referent of "blackened face" was minstrel performance. Minstrel shows—which mainly featured white men mimicking Black men and women with faces blackened and often with wigs and grotesquely painted lips, had blanketed the mid-nineteenth-century North and South since the late

---

4   The best overview of Klan violence remains Trelease 2023 (1971). An excellent review of private, non-Klan white-on-Black violence in this period is Vandal 2000. Chapter Seven of Roth (2009) places mid-nineteenth century vigilante homicide in the broader context of other forms of inter- and intraracial homicide.

antebellum period. When Reconstruction-era Americans saw a person with a blackened face, minstrelsy would likely have been their first thought. Minstrel blackening was not meant to realistically evoke the appearance of Black human faces, of course. "Created from burnt cork mixed with grease, it was black without shading, and usually darkened to an artificial extreme" (Johnson 2012, 8). Blackened faces transformed an actor into a racist caricature and transformed a personal face into a generic signifier. Even those black actors who performed as minstrels sometimes "blacked up": Frederick Douglass noted that in adopting the racist exaggerations of white minstrelsy, they failed to represent the Black man "as he is" (Gilmore 1997, 773). Eric Lott and others have powerfully explored the complex work of minstrelsy, as actors simultaneously impersonated and dehumanized Black people (Lott 2013).

The blackened faces of Klan terrorists were usually significantly different than those of theatrical professionals. Witnesses rarely knew how Klan attackers had blackened their faces, but it is most likely that they smutted their faces with substances like dirt and soot. Yet, their faces evoked the more intensive blackening of the stage, including its claim to deindividualization. As Evelyn Annuß has put it speaking more broadly of costumed Klan violence, the terrorists themselves became "gesichtslos," or faceless.[5]

A blackened face did not only imply racial drag, however: contemporaries also associated it with other things. The first was death: newspapers described certain corpses, particularly those of people killed in sudden and violent ways, as having "blackened faces." This included those killed by poison or fire, passengers killed in steamboat explosions, soldiers killed by military explosions, and people who had been hanged.[6] In the wake of the Civil War, the association of blackened faces with quick and unnatural death would have had particular power.

The blackened face also had a strong association with nocturnal crime. American newspapers, including those in the Reconstruction-era South, regularly covered contemporary robberies or assaults by men in blackened faces.[7] Some racialized meaning attached to criminals' blackened faces: Simon Balto has recently explored the contemporary phenomenon of white people assuming racial drag in order to pin their crimes on Black people (Balto 2024). We cannot know how frequently that successfully occurred. But in many other cases, contemporaries described blackened-faced nocturnal crime without suggesting that the criminal might in fact be Black, portraying it as a pragmatic

---

5   See Annuß 2025, 169.
6   See *Fall River Daily Evening News* 1867, 1; *Franklin Democrat* 1866, 2; *Louisville Daily Courier* 1867, 1.
7   See *Chicago Tribune* 1866, 2; *Daily Dispatch* 1866, 2; *New York Daily Herald* 1866, 4.

effort to make the face less visible by moonlight or simply to obscure identity. Blackened-faced criminals were a trope in fiction as well: where a disguised criminal appeared, readers knew that a familiar face would be exposed underneath at story's end.

Newspapers reported contemporary examples of blackened-faced attackers in the North, as when a group of Ohio residents in 1866 sooted their faces to attack local "vagrants and chicken thieves," or when a group of twenty men with sooted faces in 1871 assaulted a couple they deemed to be living immorally, tarred and feathered the woman and dragged her around the yard, naked "like a stuck pig."[8] They were keenly aware as well of the blackened faces of the Irish revolutionary group, the Fenians, who were directly contemporary to the Klan.[9] While surely these "vigilante" attacks were not devoid of racial meaning, cross-racial drag seems to be secondary. In these contexts, blackened faces primarily indicated transgression itself: the intent to violate laws in order to achieve a collective goal.

Blackened-faced vigilantism connected violent men through time as well as through space. As Eric Lott's contribution to this collection argues, blackface "always carries other times in it." And, indeed, blackened faces also suggested continuity with historical acts of collective violence. As E. P. Thompson most influentially established, blackened-faced crime was a tradition stretching at least as far back as the medieval period in England.[10] Reconstruction-era Southerners were well aware of this history: Southern newspapers included romantic fiction about rural robbers and highwaymen in the early national United States or in historical England.[11] These stories did not exactly celebrate the blackened-faced robbers—the heroes were the men who discovered the criminals' identities and confronted them—but they did romanticize them as representing a freer time when government was distant and men made their choices and faced their dangers on their own.

Some historic violence in blackened face was not solely for individual gain, but was a form of collective expression of grievance against authority or of moral norms. In the early American context (and even in the Reconstruction era) attackers with blackened faces were sometimes described as "Indian" rather than "Black." Philip Deloria's *Playing Indian* decodes the multiple meanings and European precedents of dressing as Indians in the Revolutionary Era.

---

8   Newspaper article introduced into evidence during the testimony of B. F. Sawyer, see *Report of the Joint Select Committee* (hereafter referred to by KK *Report*) 1872, vol. 7, Georgia II, 898.

9   See *Daily Ohio Statesman* 1866, 2; Snay 2007.

10   See *Pittsburgh Weekly Gazette* 1871, 1; Thompson 1975, 76.

11   See *Yorkville Enquirer* 1868, 1.

Reconstruction-Era Southerners were as aware of this centuries-long tradition of blackened-faced vigilantes as they were of robbers with blackened faces. Those in the Reconstruction era repeating the iconic revolutionary story about the Boston Tea Party, for instance, referred to participants' "blackened faces."[12] The fact that blackened faces could evoke both enslaved African Americans and indigenous Americans reveals a productive slippage. If there was one thing white Americans in the 1860s and 1870s thought they knew about indigenous Americans, it was that they were close enough to gone, and it was common among white people in the Reconstruction-era South and North alike to predict that without the alleged former guidance, protection, and support of slave-holders, the "doomed race" would simply die, like the indigenous allegedly had before them, of their own deficiencies.[13] This points to a potential continuity between blackened faces and what Raz Weiner, in his essay in this volume, describes as the necropolitics of racialized drag: in blackening their faces, Ku-Klux also enacted the replacement of now-unwelcome Black Southerners.

Not only were these alternative significances of blackened faces in wide-spread national circulation—they were present in specific places important to the development of Klan terrorism. Blackened faces were present as the Klan took root and may have been the first disguise used by the men who created the Klan in Pulaski, Tennessee. One of the Klan's initiators was an editor of the *Pulaski Citizen* and in early 1867, just as the Klan was emerging locally, that paper called for a strolling minstrel band to visit town to alleviate their bore-dom, and mentioned that if one could not be hired, local men could create their own. Soon afterward, the *Citizen* published an article giving instructions on how to remove tan from one's face.[14] And early Ku-Klux own recollections, supported by an 1866 carte de visite which appears to represent the first Klan members playing musical instruments, and which refers to them as "Midnight Rangers," reveal that the men who created the Klan in Pulaski also did nighttime serenades. The carte de visite does not depict them with blackened faces, but their instruments suggest that they were performing in a style to which black-ened faces were traditional.[15]

The *Pulaski Citizen* was well aware of the connection between blackened faces and racial violence. In the summer of 1866, the *Citizen* ran a story about the recent robbery of four gentlemen by men "disguised by the blacking of their faces."[16] Between 1866 and 1871, the *Citizen* covered the Fenian uprising

---

12   Gilman 1874, 33; Etting 1876, 69; *Our Monthly* 1873, 291; Deloria 1998, 11.
13   *The Tennessean* 1867, 2. Or see *Public Ledger* 1868, 1.
14   See *Pulaski Citizen* 1867a, 3; *Pulaski Citizen* 1867b, 3.
15   Parsons 2005, 811.
16   *Pulaski Citizen* 1866, 2.

heavily and generally approvingly, though without mentioning blackened faces. In August 1868, the paper noted that Nathan Bedford Forrest, who is often thought to have been the head of the Klan but who claimed to disapprove of its excesses, had routed a group of men in blackened faces, calling themselves Ku-Klux, who were attacking Black men in Memphis.[17]

Newspapers circulating in areas with the most Klan violence also mentioned these other meanings of blackened faces. Most strikingly, in November of 1868, within one month of the first reports of Klan activity there, the newspaper in Yorkville, South Carolina, one of the biggest locations of Klan activity, gave over most of its front page to a short story about an early national robber with a blackened face.[18] Not only those who created and propagated the Klan, but presumably those who participated in and were victimized by Klan attacks, were well aware of the multiple meanings of sooted faces.

Ku-Klux also would have been aware that even before the Klan's rise, groups of men with blackened faces had been attacking freedpeople and their few white allies. In parts of Texas, the "Black Calvary" terrorized freedpeople with "blackened faces" by 1866.[19] That same year, men with blackened faces whipped a freedman teaching school in Jackson, Louisiana, and attacked a former Union soldier who was visiting relatives in Kentucky, whipping him with a cowhide.[20] In Panola, Mississippi, a white Northern Republican postmaster was driven from town by "ruffians with blackened faces" in January of 1867.[21]

When, in the spring of 1868, Klan attacks fanned through the South, it would not have seemed remarkable that many of them sooted their faces. Wearing black masks (by the Reconstruction era these were sometimes available in general stores, presumably intended for masquerades) was different than blacking the face and would have lacked some of the resonance of blackening, but black masks and blackening could also flow together in reports of attacks.[22] There are dozens of reports of Ku-Klux, and other costumed terrorist groups wearing simple black masks or black cloth hoods, across the South. C. D. Forsythe, in Paulding County, Georgia, recalled that the disguises were "a kind of black gown, and a black mask that went over the face, with places cut for the eyes, and some fantastic colors about it in places to make it look

---

17   See *Pulaski Citizen* 1868, 4.
18   See *Yorkville Enquirer* 1868, 1.
19   See *Bangor Whig and Courier* 1866, 2.
20   See *Public Ledger* 1866, 2; *Evansville Daily Journal* 1866, 8.
21   See *Memphis Daily Post* 1867, 8.
22   See testimony of Charles Smith in KK *Report* 1872, vol. 7, Georgia II, 598, where he testifies: "Some just had those faces on that you see in the stores."

frightful."[23] Victim Henry Lowther recalled that his attackers had something thin over their face, black oilcloth.[24] Elias Hill in South Carolina testified that one of his attackers had black oilcloth over his head, and something like gloves covering his hands and wrists: "I could see his face all around his eyes."[25] In 1871, a newspaper reported an attack by Kentucky Ku-Klux, wearing masks, and with faces darkened underneath them.[26]

There are dozens more instances of Ku-Klux and other terrorist bands wearing blackened faces, in Louisiana, Florida, Georgia, Mississippi, Alabama, Missouri, and North and South Carolina. A Republican political leader in New Orleans named Charles B. Young testified that in 1868 "There was another [Republican club in New Orleans], of which I was president ... known as the head club of the first ward, which was entered by about six men with blackened faces; or masks, about 10 o'clock at night, armed with double-barrel shotguns."[27] One of the most notorious early Ku-Klux murders, that of Republican leader George Ashburn in Columbus, Georgia, in March 1868, was conducted by "a party of persons in masks, and with blackened faces."[28] A man named Charles Wilson, in 1872, was taken from his house in Missouri and whipped by a "band of men with blackened faces."[29] A Mississippi victim asked to describe his attackers responded: "the fact is, I was so excited I could not take particular notice of their disguise. Their faces were blacked; and some of them had cloth hanging around the sides of their faces; they had on red pants, I believe, with a large belt around the waist, with bowie-knives and pistols."[30] A white attack victim in Florida said his attackers "had smut on their faces."[31]

Sometimes Klan blackface explicitly evoked meanings other than racial ones. The blackened face itself (and Ku-Klux costumes generally) was theoretically opaque. It had such a multitude of symbolic referents that it rarely just meant racial drag. To blacken the face was to dress like a Black man, but it was as much to dress like a white man dressed as a Black man. It was to dress like a vigilante: Ku-Klux of course liked to think of themselves as vigilantes, sometimes articulating explicitly during an attack which communal norms they were defending, sometimes reading a list of charges aloud, or even leaving a written

---

23   Testimony of CD Forsythe in KK *Report* 1872, vol. 6, Georgia I, 84.
24   See testimony of Henry Lowther in KK *Report* 1872, vol. 6, Georgia I, 360.
25   Testimony of Elias Hill in KK *Report* 1872, vol. 5, South Carolina III, 1408.
26   See *Chicago Tribune* 1871, 2.
27   "Testimony Taken in the Sub Committee of Elections" 1870, 484.
28   Meade 1868, 6.
29   Lawrence 1872, 693.
30   Testimony of Cornelius McBride in KK *Report* 1872, vol. 11, Mississippi I, 327.
31   Testimony of R. W. Cone in KK *Report* 1872, vol. 13, Florida I, 69.

account of the reason for their visit.[32] Connecting themselves to vigilantes tied Ku-Klux to time-tested, and transatlantic traditions in a way that perhaps they believed lent legitimacy to their violence. It was to dress as a thief: in addition to their personal violence, Ku-Klux regularly stole things. They often stole things of value such as money, guns, clothing, presumably for pragmatic reasons. But the fact that they also stole small things, like a slate pencil, from the people they attacked, might suggest a deliberate performance of or nod to blackened-faced burglary.

To blacken one's face was also to dress as a dead man: Ku-Klux frequently called themselves ghosts. They referred to themselves as dead Confederates back from the grave, or claimed to be specific deceased people.[33] The first Ku-Klux group, in Pulaski, Tennessee, leaned heavily into a "ghostly" identity, and apparently claimed to be "spirit[s] from another world ... killed at Chickamauga."[34] One group of racial terrorists in Missouri was alternately known as "Ku-Klux" and "Dead Men."[35] When a group of Ku-Klux, some of whom were wearing masks and others of whom "had just blacked up the biggest part of the face," confronted Mitchell Reed in Georgia, "They said they were Ku-Klux and came out of the ground."[36] Another Black victim in that state, Charles Smith, attacked by a group of men who were "just blacked and marked up," had been warned by his former master that the Ku-Klux might come for him. The white man told him that "they are men that rise from the dead."[37] Prominent Democrat James Holt Clanton, called to give an overview of the Klan in Alabama, was asked for instances of Klan violence. He recalled that one boy had decided to scare Black people by dressing up in a mask in a graveyard. Rep. Job Stevenson asked: "The idea was that kuklux came out of graveyards?"[38] and Clanton responded only that the boy was foolish.

When Ku-Klux and other anti-Black terrorists adopted these blackened faces, part of what they were doing was racial masquerade, usually performing as Black men, occasionally as "Indians." Sometimes they "tangled their hair"[39] along with blackening their faces. Sometimes they "black[ed] their faces and dress[ed] up like negro troops."[40] Sometimes they added a stereotyped

---

32 See Waldrep 2002.
33 See testimony of Mary Anne Norvill in KK Report 1872, vol. 2., North Carolina I, 473, and testimony of Simpson Bobo in KK Report 1872, vol. 4, South Carolina II, 802—803.
34 Lester and Wilson 1905, 73.
35 The News 1871, 2.
36 Testimony of Mitchel Reid in KK Report 1872, vol. 7, Georgia II, 647.
37 Testimony of Charles Smith in KK Report 1872, vol. 7, Georgia II, 598—599.
38 The News 1871, 2.
39 Testimony of Mary Brown in KK Report 1872, vol. 6, Georgia I, 376.
40 Charles City Intelligencer 1866, 1.

racialized performance, such as making war-whoops or performing elements of minstrel shows, by cracking jokes or performing music, or by forcing their victims to assume minstrelesque behaviors.[41]

At least some, and arguably all Ku-Klux who blackened their faces, then, were in racial drag. Some of these, but not others, intended or hoped to be mistaken for Black. The Democratic Party during the Klan period embraced a Big Lie: many claimed that most or all Ku-Klux violence was a "humbug" and a "bug-a-boo" or even denied that real Ku-Klux existed. This denialism spread from rural white Southerners to the halls of Congress. There was so much evidence of Klan violence, however, that some attacks had to be explained away rather than denied. Blackening their faces made it possible for Klan apologists to claim that certain terrorist acts had been committed by Black men disguised as Ku-Klux. This claim was pervasive in the Democratic press: even the *New York Herald* claimed that "Three-fourths or more of the crimes committed in [the South] have been wrongly attributed to the Ku-Klux. Many in fact have been committed by the negroes and their radical carpet bag allies who pretend to have such a horror of the Ku-Klux."[42]

It is hard to say whether white American Klan deniers truly believed that Klan violence was committed by Black people, or whether they made this claim for strategic reasons or because they found it entertaining to do so. This was a period of popular fascination with disguise: people tended to be credulous about the power of "ingenious disguises," and newspaper accounts casually suggested that blackened faces could cause white people to pass for Black, even in daylight.[43] Klan attacks generally happened at night, and witnesses often saw attackers at a distance, or while under great duress, so visibility would have been low. Some people did testify that costumes successfully obscured the race of attackers. When a man named Nelson Harris was taken from a jail in Union, Alabama, tortured, and killed, his (presumably white) jailers later said: "These persons [who abducted him] came in with their faces blacked, or were black men."[44] John A. Minnis, the district attorney for the Northern District of Alabama, claimed of a group of attackers in Limestone, Alabama: "They were in disguise, and nobody could identify them either as colored or anything else."[45] Like these two witnesses, claims to the racial ambiguity of attackers were often made not by the victims themselves, but by white people called upon to explain

---

41   For more discussion of minstrelesque performance during attacks, see Frantz [Parsons] 2015, 101—107.

42   *New York Daily Herald* 1871, 6.

43   *The Fairfield Herald* 1872, 1.

44   Testimony of William Miller in *KK Report* 1872, vol. 8, Alabama I, 3.

45   Testimony of John A. Minnis in *KK Report* 1872, vol. 8, Alabama I, 539.

the attacks, presumably sympathetic to the Klan's goals. These speakers had a transparent ideological motivation to keep open the possibility that these blackened-faced attackers were, in fact, Black.

Claims to the racial ambiguity of attackers made by victims are harder to explain away: but they are rare and almost entirely made by the minority of victims who were white. Drury Goings, a white radical who was brutally attacked by the Klan in Union, South Carolina, said that "they were so perfectly disguised that I could not tell if they were black or white men."[46] But Goings was confused not by blackening or even black masks but by (not black) disguises which covered the entire head: "it seemed a kind of paste-board in a square, and with holes in it at the top of them, and a kind of horse's ears."[47] Florida E. Cone, a white victim of an attack in Florida, noted that while she knew and immediately identified her attackers, the blackening of one of the men's faces was "very dark, almost as dark as a colored person any way. You could hardly tell if it was smut or the natural color; that is, a person who did not know him."[48]

John O. Perry, a white man in Georgia to whose home two Black men fled when the Klan was pursuing them, likely understood that the men approaching were white before he saw them because the men hiding in his home had alerted him that the Ku-Klux was on their heels, but his wording suggests how, on a dark night, illuminated only by the light of a match, blackening or a black mask or veil could confuse race: "I saw enough to know that they looked like negroes ... Their faces either had something black on them or something black over their faces .... they were blacked or had something over them."[49]

The aftermath of one particularly horrific Klan attack shows the internal mechanics of how blackened faces could produce the illusion of racial ambiguity even when it failed to fool witnesses. Robin Westbrook, a Black man living in Jefferson, Alabama, was "a kind of a man that would not take any foolishness from a white man."[50] Ku-Klux surrounded his home: three entered and beat, shot and killed him as his wife, Betsy, and stepson, Tiller Reese, watched in horror. Betsy and Tiller later testified that despite the fact that one of these three was wearing a knit cap pulled over his face, and another had his face smutted, they were confident not only of the racial identities but of the specific identities of those who were inside the house and most central to the violence. They were all white neighbors, and Tiller and Betsy named them, explaining the specific

---

46   Testimony of Drury Goings in *KK Report* 1872, vol. 4, South Carolina II, 1074.
47   Testimony of Drury Goings in *KK Report* 1872, vol. 4, South Carolina II, 1072.
48   Testimony of Florida E. Cone in *KK Report* 1872, vol. 13, Florida I, 74.
49   Testimony of John O. Perry in *KK Report* 1872, vol. 6, Georgia I, 538.
50   Testimony of Tiller Reese in *KK Report* 1872, vol. 9, Alabama II, 1249.

grievances each had with Robin.[51] As a Black neighbor explained, "[Betsy] said she could not see their faces, but she was right there with them, and knew them all her life pretty well, and knew the shape, and how the men were made."[52] Nevertheless white witnesses repeatedly claimed that Betsy Westbrook had been unsure of the racial identity of the attackers, or had claimed the attackers were Black. Dr. Seth D. Smith informed the committee that a "Squire Smith" had told him that Betsy Westbrook had sworn that the perpetrators were Black men.[53] When the Sheriff of the county, Jacob Michael, Jr., was first asked about the Westbrook murder, he quickly remarked, "they didn't know whether [the attackers] were black or white." [54]

This story illustrates the most significant function of blackened faces within Klan attacks, and suggests that the disguises were for the larger public—newspaper readers and political leaders—as much or more than for the eyes of victims or witnesses. Klan attackers in racial drag were sometimes attempting to pass themselves off as Black men. But blackened faces, to be effective, did not require verisimilitude: Black witnesses, and even white Republicans, had so little credibility in the eyes of whites in power, and so little control over local discourse, that even the most transparent disguise was sufficient to discredit their testimony, retroactively projecting onto them a confusion about the race their attackers that they had not experienced.

When Ku-Klux bands donned racial drag, they knew that their allies in the Democratic press would take advantage of this ambiguity. If part of the work of blackface Klan attacks was activating a necropolitics of replacement, it is ironic that Ku-Klux often used blackface to suggest that they, themselves didn't exist. Kentucky Klan attackers wearing blackface under their masks were attempting, the newspaper covering the attack speculated, "to create the report that they were negroes, as it has been the fashion of the Democratic press of Kentucky to accuse negroes of engaging in such work."[55] This dynamic shaped a powerful pro-Klan national counterdiscourse which provided plausible deniability to Republican narratives of Klan outrages.[56] Southern papers also stirred the waters by referring to any groups of Black men committing or threatening acts of violence, legally sanctioned or not, as "Negro Ku-Klux."[57] Pro-Klan newspa-

---

51   See testimony of Betsy Westbrook in *KK Report* 1872, vol. 9, Alabama II, 1243—1244, and testimony of Tiller Reese in *KK Report* 1872, vol. 9, Alabama II, 1248.
52   Testimony of George Jones in *KK Report* 1872, vol. 9, Alabama II, 1392.
53   Testimony of Seth Smith in *KK Report* 1872, vol. 9, Alabama II, 1253.
54   Testimony of Jacob Micheal, Jr. in *KK Report* 1872, vol. 9, Alabama II, 1373.
55   *Chicago Tribune* 1871, 2.
56   See *The Daily Journal* 1868, 3.
57   *Nashville Union and American* 1871.

pers like the *Yorkville Enquirer* and the *Union Times* frequently claimed that Black men staged Ku-Klux outrages by attacking one another in order to justify federal military intervention.[58]

The stacked multiple meanings of blackened faces made them a powerful symbol: a Ku-Klux in blackened face was engaging in racial drag. But also: evoking of grotesque death, criminality, communal vigilantism, and traditions of lawlessness that spanned time and place. Not far beneath it all lurked a necropolitics of replacement. The Ku-Klux's blackened face was a particularly multivalenced form of racial drag, far from simply carnivalesque. This multiplicity of meaning was a crucial aspect of the effectiveness of this particular iteration of white terror.

Contemporary media and historians alike often struggle to hold open the analytical complexity of violent attacks. Our primary obligation, when confronted with violence, is to prevent it (at the moment) or condemn it (in retrospect). For that, we want clarity. So we strip the scene of violence of its detail and complexity as we focus on that crucial task. Despite their seeming "mysterious" nature, elaborately costumed Klan, which "came from nowhere," emerging in 1867, and disappeared, a few years later, as quickly as they had appeared, are a problem in a box, and one that one can imagine solving. Their blackened-faced fellow terrorists are harder to pin down, more obviously continuous with and intricately connected to a broader culture of violence. This less-spectacular Klan neither arrived nor left, so has remained in the shadow of more spectacular forms of violence.

References

Annuß, Evelyn. 2025. *Dirty Dragging: Performative Transpositionen.* Wien/ Bielefeld: mdwPress (English version forthcoming 2026).

Balto, Simon. 2024. "Racial Framing: Blackface Criminals in America." *Journal of American History* 111, no. 2: 290—308.

Bangor Whig and Courier. 1866. "Reconstruction in Texas." November 24.

Charles City [IA] Intelligencer. 1866. "The Rebel Army Doing Its Work." April 19.

Chicago Tribune. 1866. "A Night Surprise." April 1.

Chicago Tribune. 1871. "Ku-Klux in Kentucky." January 28.

Daily Dispatch [Wilmington]. 1866. "New York Correspondence." January 2.

Daily Ohio Statesman [Columbus]. 1866. "Summary Justice." July 16.

Deloria, Philip. 1998. *Playing Indian.* New Haven: Yale University Press.

---

58   See *Yorkville Enquirer* 1872, 2.

Etting, Frank Marx. 1876. *An Historical Account of the Old State House of Pennsylvania Now Known as the Hall of Independence.* Boston: James R. Osgood and Co.

Evansville Daily Journal. 1866. "An Outrage on a Union Soldier." September 7.

Fall River [MA] Daily Evening News. 1867. "The Coal-Pit Explosion in England." January 2.

Franklin [IN] Democrat. 1866. "Summary of the Week." December 6.

Frantz [Parsons], Elaine. 2005. "Midnight Rangers: The Costume and Performance of the Reconstruction-Era Ku Klux Klan." *Journal of American History* 92, no. 3: 811—836.

Frantz [Parsons], Elaine. 2015. *Ku-Klux: The Birth of the Klan during Reconstruction.* Chapel Hill: University of North Carolina Press.

Gilman, Caroline Howard. 1874. *Recollections of the Private Centennial Celebration of the Overthrow of the Tea.* Cambridge, MA: Press of John Wilson and Son.

Gilmore, Paul. 1997. "The Genewine Artekil: William Wells Brown, Blackface Minstrelsy, and Abolitionism." *American Literature* 69, no. 4: 773.

Johnson, Stephen, ed. 2012. *Burnt Cork: Traditions and Legacies of Blackface Minstrelsy.* Amherst: University of Massachusetts Press.

Lawrence, Eugene. 1872. "Mr. Charles Schurz and His Victims." *Harper's Weekly* 16, no. 819: 693—694.

Lester, J. C. and D. L. Wilson. 1905. *The Ku Klux Klan: Its Origin, Growth and Disbandment.* New York: The Neale Publishing Company.

Lott, Eric. 2013 (originally published 1993). *Love and Theft: Blackface Minstrelsy and the American Working Class.* New York: Oxford University Press.

Louisville [KY] Daily Courier. 1867. "Further Particulars of the Explosion of the David White." February 15.

Meade, George Gordon. 1868. *Major General Meade's Report on the Ashburn Murder.* Atlanta: Judge Advocate's Office, Headquarters Department of the South.

Memphis Daily Post. 1867. "Outrages." January 23.

Nashville Union and American. 1871. "A Serious Affray with Negro Ku-Klux at Hopefield." May 30.

New York Daily Herald. 1866. "Outlaws in Kentucky." November 11.

New York Daily Herald. 1871. "Frauds, Social Disorganization, and Political Troubles in the South." November 15.

Our Monthly. 1873. "Revolutionary Tea: A Centennial Tribute." Vol. 8 (October).

Pittsburgh Weekly Gazette. 1871. "Telegraph Office Robbery." May 20.

Public Ledger [Memphis]. 1866. "An Ebony Ruby in Trouble: A Colored Teacher Rudely Handled." July 20.

Public Ledger [Memphis]. 1868. "The African at Home." March 5.

Pulaski Citizen. 1866. "A Daring Robbery." July 6.

Pulaski Citizen. 1867a. "Amusement Wanted." January 11.

Pulaski Citizen. 1867b. "Removing Tan." May 3.

Pulaski Citizen. 1868. "General Forrest after the Kuklux." August 21.

Report of the Joint Select Committee to Inquire into the Condition of Affairs in the Late Insurrectionary States [KK Report]. 1872. Volumes 1—13. Washington: Government Printing Office.

Roth, Randall. 2009. *American Homicide*. Cambridge, MA: Belknap Press.

Snay, Mitchell. 2007. *Fenians, Freedmen, and Southern Whites: Race and Nationality in the Era of Reconstruction*. Baton Rouge: Louisiana State University.

"Testimony Taken in the Sub Committee of Elections in Louisiana." 1870. In *United States Congressional Serial Set*. Serial no. 1435. 41st Congress, 2d session, House of Representatives, misc. doc. no. 154, 484. Washington, DC: Government Printing Office.

The Daily Journal [Wilmington NC]. 1868. "The Ball Opens." February 1.

The Daily Patriot. 1871. "The Ku Klux Klan." March 20.

The Fairfield Herald [Winnsboro, SC]. 1872. "A Campaign Story." November 27.

The News [Lynchburg]. 1871. "Reign of Terror in Missouri." October 16.

The Tennessean. 1867. "Emancipation and Degeneration." November 3.

Thompson, E. P. 1975. *Whigs and Hunters*. New York: Pantheon Books.

Trelease, Allen W. 2023 (originally published 1971). *White Terror: The Ku Klux Klan Conspiracy and Southern Reconstruction*. With a Foreword by Karen Cox. Baton Rouge: Louisiana State University Press.

Vandal, Giles. 2000. *Rethinking Southern Violence: Homicides in Post-Civil War Louisiana*. Columbus, OH: Ohio State University Press.

Waldrep, Chris. 2002. *The Many Faces of Judge Lynch*. New York: Palgrave MacMillan.

Williams, Kidada. 2012. *They Left Great Marks on Me: African-American Testimonies of Racial Violence from Emancipation to World War One*. New York: New York University Press.

Yorkville [SC] Enquirer. 1868. "A Black Mare with a White Star." November 12.

Yorkville [SC] Enquirer. 1872. "Scraps and Facts." August 8.

Gender Bending in the Southern Babylon: Black "Female Impersonators" in 1940s to 1960s New Orleans

Aurélie Godet

While Judith Butler's and Marjorie Garber's works have been invaluable for challenging the supposedly natural relationships between the sex binary, gender, and sexuality, their theoretical insights have sometimes been criticized for their apparent disconnection from specific sociohistorical contexts in which "gender trouble" (Butler 1990) and "category crises" (Garber 1993) may emerge.[1] This chapter investigates one such context: that of mid-twentieth-century New Orleans, a city often described as a "mecca" for sexual dissidents or a "Southern Babylon," due to its supposedly "lax moral code, its situation as a port and its association with customary port vices, its openness to nonconformists, its regional and national reputation as a sin city—a reputation both deplored and carefully nurtured—and its exoticism" (Mitchell 1995, 141).[2] Using a combination of photographic, textual, and oral evidence, I investigate the ways in which Black "female impersonators," i.e., artists who practiced the male-female reversal as part of a usually professional comic act (Newton 1972, 3),[3] challenged

*   Research for this article was completed in the fall of 2023 thanks to a Dianne Woest fellowship at the Historic New Orleans Collection. I am grateful to the director and to the reference associates of the Williams Research Center for their warm welcome and assistance.

1   For criticism or supplementation of Butler's and Garber's ahistorical approach, see Ferris 1993; Stryker 2006; Sears 2015; Hartman 2019.

2   Similarly, George Chauncey described Harlem in the 1920s as a "homosexual mecca" (Chauncey 1994, 244).

3   In 1910s New Orleans, the term also referred to a popular Mardi Gras performance in which men masqueraded as women in the streets. See the captions to the John T. Mendes Photograph Collection (n.d.) at the Historic New Orleans Collection. Today, the term is no longer popular among drag performers. US television personality RuPaul, for instance, is known to have said, "I do not impersonate females! How many women do you know who wear seven-inch heels, four-foot wigs, and skintight dresses?" (quoted in Corso 2009)

the gender, sexual, and racial norms of Cold War America through performance, built community in spaces that may have appeared "queer-resistant," and ultimately transcended contextual constraints to become celebrated figures on the local (and national) stage. In so doing, I attempt to resist the imposition of contemporary gender and sexual identities onto past cross-dressing practices by shifting attention away from a metaphoric use of drag or a recognizable gender-bending *figure* to multiple gender-bending *practices* in one specific locale.

Limits of Gay-Centered or Regionalist Approaches to Black Drag Performance in New Orleans

While clearly lacking nuance,[4] the association between female impersonation and homosexuality is deep-rooted. English poet Edward Carpenter, credited with the earliest use of the term "cross-dressing" in the *Oxford English Dictionary*, stated in 1911: "Cross-dressing must be taken as a general indication of, and a cognate phenomenon to, homosexuality" ("Cross-dressing" n. d.). In 1971, an article in Lee Brewster's *Drag Queens* magazine characterized the drag queen as a "homosexual transvestite" who is hyperfeminine, flamboyant, and militant (Brewster 1971, 11—12).

In New Orleans, drag certainly played a key role in the emergence of a gay community, as Howard Philips Smith recently summarized: "This inversion dominated the early gay balls in New Orleans, where almost every costume was either camp or ultrafeminine drag. These balls united gay men, who became swept up in the Carnival season, and became a source of fierce competition and pride" (Philips Smith 2017, 323). The label "gay," however, does not do justice to the complexity of impersonations of femininity in New Orleans. One needs to beware especially of conflating gender expression and sexual orientation when discussing these ball or nightclub performances.

Similarly, one needs to beware of regional essentialization that, for instance, connects the appeal of drag in New Orleans with an ongoing fascination with the mythical Southern figures of "the lady" and "the belle" that came to embody the area's conservative sexual identity after the Civil War.[5] Indeed, while the recurrence of Southern belle imagery in queer culture is

---

4   Contemporary sociological studies have determined that most men who cross-dress are actually heterosexual (see Dynes 2016, 1312).

5   "Although drag is not an exclusively southern development, it does resonate within the region. It can be seen as a response to the excessively performative nature of southern femininity.... Drag modalities repurpose white southern femininity, model-

corroborated by archival evidence from the 1950s to the 1970s (see Figs. 1 and 2), this explanation overlooks the history of Black drag shows in New Orleans, for whom Southern white femininity was, if not exactly ignored,[6] at least just one inspiration among many.

Figure 1. Jimmy Callaway, a white New Orleans female impersonator working at Club My-O-My, performing in "Southern belle" garb on April 12, 1951 ("Mr. Pat Waters" 1951).

---

ing new ways of being southern that can sometimes break free from a tired old recycling of the myths of the lady and the belle" (McPherson 2003, 194).

6   Black female impersonators did occasionally model their skits on the "southern belle" trope, thus engaging in the sort of whiteface parodic performativity that "ethnic drag" has been shown to include (see Sieg 2002).

Figure 2. The biggest LGBT+ festival in New Orleans today, Southern Decadence, started as a simple costume party on Labor Day weekend 1972 for which the following invitation—designed by Robert Laurent and featuring a libertine Southern belle—was issued ("Southern Decadence Party Invitations" n.d.).

The converse notions that the South was essentially inhospitable to queer identities or that Black communities there have been largely and consistently homophobic must also be shed (for a refutation of this thesis see hooks 1989, 120—126; Constantine-Simms 2000, 211—225). In other words, before the question of what drag meant to mid-twentieth-century Black performers of New Orleans can be addressed, one must first mine the archival record for snippets of information about nineteenth- and early twentieth-century Black queer lives.

Excavating Black Queerness from the New Orleans Archival Record

Little is known about the queer Black men who inhabited antebellum New Orleans. While it is assumed locally that the keeping, by many white men, of free women of color as mistresses found a parallel, albeit smaller, in some white men's keeping of free Black youths, there is (so far as I know) no material evidence for it. Abolitionist literature produced in the early nineteenth century, however, was quite prolix about the ways that "oppression under slavery c[ould] queer gender identities and marital and family relations, including driving enslaved people to acts of cross-dressing in order to escape white surveillance and the South itself" (Bibler 2013, 192).[7] Some works, such as Frederick Douglass's novella *The Heroic Slave* (1852), even mobilized explicitly homoerotic forms of sentimentality to attract white men to the abolitionist cause.

In the late nineteenth century, discourses of race, gender, and sexuality increasingly deployed models of codified identity categories that defined individuals as discrete and immutable types, giving rise to the split between "heterosexual" and "homosexual" at the same time as Southern authorities instituted stricter methods for segregating "white" from "black." While certain literary works such as *The Adventures of Huckleberry Finn* (1885) and *Pudd'nhead Wilson* (1894) by Mark Twain challenged accepted boundaries by linking scenes of racial and gender disguise with male homoeroticism, the romanticized attachments between former slaves and their white masters in the works of Thomas Nelson Page and Joel Chandler Harris were clearly more about reinforcing social and racial divides (Gebhard 1997, 132—56).

In the early twentieth century, most interracial same-sex relations occurred in a context of prostitution. In their study of turn-of-the-century New Orleans, Katy Coyle and Nadiene Van Dyke have argued that many of the African American and Black Creole prostitutes who sold sex to the city's white elite engaged in lesbian sexual practices both professionally, for their clients' voyeuristic pleasure, and privately, for their own pleasure (Coyle and Van Dyke 1997, 54—72).

New Orleans's famed vice district, Storyville (1897—1917), also included a male brothel run by a burly madam named Big Nellie, in which white customers often solicited Black young men. There, performers with names such as Lady Richard, Mammy George, and La Sylvester, who sang, danced, and dressed in imitation of women, constituted a significant part of the entertainment (Rose 1974, 15). As Black newspapers suggest, such acts soon gained a national audience. *The Freeman*, for instance, followed the career of adopted New Orleanian Augustus Stevens,[8] who danced the cake walk in various Black traveling shows (Fig. 3). And, as shown by Eric Lott, nineteenth-century minstrel shows notoriously included homosexual imagery (Lott 2013, 27, 55—6, 90, 126, 168—171).

Religious authorities were powerless against it, as suggested by a lawsuit filed by a Black church (the Union Chapel Methodist Episcopal Church) against

---

7   See especially Williams Wells Brown's novel *Clotel; or, the President's Daughter* (1853) and William Craft's *Running a Thousand Miles for Freedom* (1860).

8   A later article about Augustus Stevens commented admiringly on his ability to counterfeit a woman's appearance (see Fig. 3): "As a female impersonator in actions, talk, singing, dressing and performing, up the present date of them all, our dear friend, Augustus Stevens, is the leader. He is so perfect in his make-up that persons talk to him, men get stuck on him before they find out the real facts" (*The Freeman* 1903).

the City of New Orleans in the late nineteenth century (Long 2005, 128—139). Ultimately, it was the U.S. Navy that closed Storyville in 1917, claiming that its proximity from the naval training station was a "bad influence" on recruits.

AUGUSTUS STEVENS, FEMALE IMPERSONATOR.

Figure 3. Photographs of Augustus Stevens in *The Freeman* (1901). Stevens started his career in a Chicago medicine show that established him "as one of the best female impersonators in the country," before joining A. G. Allen's New Orleans Minstrels and performing under the name Papinta.

Following the discontinuation of the Storyville experiment, many Black male prostitutes found new employment opportunities in music and night clubs. Many of these clubs were located on Rampart Street, a site immortalized in Ida Cox's song *Blues for Rampart Street* (1923) and in the comedy song *Saturday Night Fish Fry* (1947), in which Cox claimed the street for Black New Orleanians: "Rampart Street in New Orleans town, / Known to everyone for miles around. / Colored music and real jazz bands, / That's the best spot in all the land" (quoted in Simmons 2015, 70). Meanwhile, New Orleans was also the site of drag balls similar to those organized in New York and Chicago during the 1920s and 1930s.[9] Though the connection between New Orleans Black impersonation of femininity with this national phenomenon was not always acknowledged in the print culture of the period, it is hard to ignore today.

---

9   In Harlem, the Masquerade and Civic Ball—also known as "Faggots Ball" or "Fairies Ball"—was actually established as early as 1869 by the Hamilton Lodge of the Grand United Order of Odd Fellows, an African American association independent of other US fraternal orders that did not accept Black men. Musicians and literary figures like Langston Hughes and Bessie Smith were often in attendance in the 1920s to 1930s (see Garber 1989, 318—331; Wilson 2011, 33—34).

During World War II, queer Black soldiers were able to maintain a vibrant subculture. A crucial testimony in this regard is that of George Eagerson, a. k. a. "Countess Vivian" (1912—2012). When he was interviewed by E. Patrick Johnson in 2005, just a week before Mardi Gras, the former nurse at Charity Hospital lived alone in a "shotgun" house (i. e., a house with a hallway at the center, down which you can see the back door) just one block from where St. Ann intersects Bourbon Street, marking the divide between its "straight" and "gay" ends. Before evoking his experience in the U. S. Army, Eagerson told Johnson about Black gay life in the 1920s and 1930s, emphasizing its almost complete separateness from New Orleans white gay life:

> [G.E:] [A]t that time I did not know or realize that they had white sissies … 'cause everything was segregated. And over here, the only time you would come over here [in the French Quarter] would be if you was *working.*
> [E. P.J:] *And so there were lots of black gay bars?*
> Oh yeah, I hope to tell you, there was a whole lot of them. … Just like they have gay bars, white queer bars today and black gay bars, there were black gay bars then. And, of course, the only difference was the black stayed in their place, the whites stayed in their place. (Johnson 2008, 483)

He mentioned the existence of Black drag queens, "more than a couple of them," including one Julia Pimpay whom I have not been able to track down. He added that they "used to dress, put on dresses and dance and hustle at night" and that they lived in precarious conditions: "They wouldn't have nothing in the room but the bed and the one chair" (ibid.). Later, when Johnson asked him if he met other gay men in the army, he answered that there were in fact "God knows how many of them" and that they would always recognize one another: "They had their hats, those little caps that we used to wear, fixed all kinds of ways on their head and everything else, child. And you could tell that they were, of course, like me" (ibid.). This correlates with the findings of Allan Berubé who, in *Coming Out Under Fire,* has revealed that "soldiers shows" put on by both Black and white soldiers during World War II (independently, since the armed forces were still segregated) were fertile ground for the exploration of new gender or sexual identities (Berubé 2020).[10] Wartime media reviews of these

---

10   While some of them were essentially "pony ballet" numbers, in which groups of masculine-looking GIs dressed in tutus and performed ballet routines, and others were of the minstrel show kind, yet others featured skilled singers and dancers. The first all-Black soldier show, *Jumping with Jodie,* was produced by the soldiers of the 3966th

numbers helped to counter potentially negative reaction by reframing the discussion on these drag performers as ordinary male soldiers doing their duty to entertain their peers and promote good morale among the troops. Thanks to this inadvertent patronage, the shows "opened up a social space in which gay men expanded their own secret culture" (Berubé 2020, 72). There were limits to this official tolerance, however. Proposals to detain homosexuals in camps were secretly discussed by Navy officials at least twice during the conflict. The second time was in July 1944, when the commandant of the 8ᵗʰ Naval District in New Orleans, A. C. Bennett, sent a confidential letter to Secretary of the Navy Frank Knox in which he depicted the discharge of gay servicemen as a threat to civilian society and recommended that "homosexuals and/or perverts ... be segregated ... for the duration of the war ... for the good of the military service but also [as] an obligation which the Navy owes to society generally" (quoted in Berubé 2020, 215). Knox ultimately rejected the proposal, but the language in which the letter was couched clearly foreshadowed the antiqueer climate of Cold War New Orleans.

During the so-called Lavender scare of the 1950s, undercover cops entrapped gay patrons in Crescent City bars, queer bashing became a popular pastime of drunken fraternity members,[11] and visible signs of effeminacy (dress, makeup, even gestures) could get men arrested. Paradoxically, however, the queer world also "enjoyed an openness and exuberance that seemed to defy the national postwar atmosphere of suppression" (Philips Smith 2017, xiv).

When queer Black soldiers returned to preintegration New Orleans, some of them were able to find work as musicians and waiters in the newly established white gay bars of the French Quarter, so long as they entered clubs via back doors and took their breaks in back rooms and off side streets (Eric Seiferth, quoted in Walker 2020). Yvonne "Miss Dixie" Fasnacht, the owner of Dixie's Bar of Music (established in 1939 as a straight bar on St. Charles Avenue, before relocating to Bourbon Street where it became a hub of queer life, with a side door "For Male Bachelors Only"), famously employed gay Black bartenders, all wearing traditional waiter outfits (Philips Smith 2017, 307).

There were also music and night clubs that featured queer performers. Compared with Detroit (1937) or Baltimore (1938), no police commissioner's edict or law banning female impersonators from appearing in night spots

---

Quartermaster Truck Company in Germany, and included a nightclub number set in Harlem featuring female impersonators (see Jura 2021).

11   In 1958 a Mexican tour guide named Fernando Rios was lured from a Bourbon Street gay bar and then ambushed and beaten to death. His three confessed attackers, undergraduates from nearby Tulane University, were found not guilty by a jury because Rios had allegedly made an "indecent advance" (see Delery-Edwards 2017).

across the city to cut down on "sex crimes" was ever voted (Gallon 2018, 391), and female impersonators were therefore able to make a living in New Orleans beyond the 1940s, whereas they disappeared from clubs in most cities after World War II. Though legally segregated, the Dew Drop Inn, the Caledonia Inn, Club Desire, and Club Tiajuana[12] featured such extraordinary talent that white music enthusiasts occasionally infiltrated them, at risk of arrest, which is why the New Orleans Police Department occasionally conducted raids to uphold segregation laws.[13] And though they mostly catered to a heterosexual audience, they became sites of queer desire and gender-nonconforming expression in Black life, thus functioning as "interzones," the concept that Kevin Mumford has used to refer to sex districts in turn-of-the-century Chicago and New York City (Mumford 1997).

Resurrecting the Lives of Black Female Impersonators: Archival Challenges

According to E. Patrick Johnson, "Neglect on the part of historians of the South, black sexual dissidents' complicity of silence around issues of sexuality, and Southerners' habitual taciturnity on things of a 'private nature,' all have colluded

---

12   Started as a barbershop run by entrepreneur Frank Pania at 2836 LaSalle Street, in Central City, a predominantly Black neighborhood, the Dew Drop Inn then blossomed into a restaurant and hotel featuring the "swankiest" night club in New Orleans from 1939 until 1972. After the club closed, it operated as an inn but then eventually stood empty after Hurricane Katrina. In 2010, it was designated a historic landmark, and the club reopened in March 2024 as a historic hotel and venue (see McNulty 2024; "Dew Drop Inn" n. d.). Located on St. Philip Street, just outside of the French Quarter in the Tremé area, the Caledonia Inn was owned and operated by the female impersonator from whom it took its name. According to New Orleans residents, this Caledonia was the inspiration for the all-Black musical comedy film short "Caledonia," produced in 1945, which featured Louis Jordan. The lyrics to the blues classic "Caledonia" ("Caledonia, Caledonia, what makes your big head so hard?") take on a whole new meaning when one realizes that the song was about a drag personality (see Bartlett 2004, 72; "Caldonia Inn" n. d.). The history of Club Desire, established at 2604 Desire Street, was recently told by historian Nick Weldon (2022; see also "Club Desire" n. d.). As for Club Tiajuana, it was a cheaper establishment located at 1209 Saratoga Street, near Earhart Boulevard (see "Club Tiajuana" n. d.).

13   Pania was one of these club owners who defied rigid Jim Crow racial boundaries by occasionally allowing white spectators into his club. A series of police raids pushed him to challenge the constitutionality of the segregation laws of the city in the mid-1960s, and he won, successfully securing an injunction against the police in 1967 ("Pania v. City of New Orleans" 1967).

to keep the stories of Southern black gay men's lives 'hidden in plain sight'" (Johnson 2008, 5). Without necessarily agreeing with Johnson's essentializing perspective on the South (or on sexual orientation), I have found the process of gathering information on the Black female impersonators who worked at the Dew Drop, Caledonia, Club Desire, and Club Tiajuana quite painstaking indeed.

Magazines featuring female impersonators, including *Letters from Female Impersonators*, published by Nutrix Co. from 1961 to 1963, were of no big help, for instance, as their New Orleans contributors or interviewees were exclusively white (*Letters from Female Impersonators* 1962). The discovery of Thomasine Marion Bartlett's dissertation, titled "Vintage Drag, Female Impersonators Performing Resistance in Cold War New Orleans," initially lifted my spirits (Bartlett 2004). However, while it includes short sections on the Dew Drop Inn and the Caledonia Inn, it mostly sheds light on the history of three white clubs: the Powder Puff, the Wonder Club (on the levee of Lake Pontchartrain), and its successor Club My-O-My.[14] The rich collection of oral testimonies gathered by the author in the early 2000s does not include any Black performer, as they regretfully acknowledge (Bartlett 2004, 39).

Fortunately, the Black press of the mid-twentieth century (at least, until the mid-50s[15]) covered female impersonators more so than white newspapers, thus providing a wealth of information about Black New Orleans performers—though necessarily incomplete as it did not encompass the private space of

---

14   The city's first club featuring female impersonators, the Powder Puff, opened on Decatur Street in the French Quarter around the mid-1930s and closed in 1937 for ordinance violations. Opened by the same owners in 1938, the Wonder Club was situated in a lightly policed border-space in Jefferson Parish, just outside of New Orleans, and flourished until it was destroyed by a hurricane in 1947. The same year, Club My-O-My opened and competed with the Wonder Club for "the best impersonators." After a fire destroyed its first location, it reopened in the space vacated by the now-defunct Wonder Club. It remained in operation on the lakeshore until it was destroyed by fire in 1972 (see Bartlett 2004, 63—72).

15   In 1954, the year the Supreme Court handed down its decision on school integration, *Ebony* (est. 1945) stopped publishing articles about homosexuality (replacing them with sections titled "Family," "Marriage," "Children," "Military," and "Work") and the Black newspapers of Detroit, New York, and Chicago ended their coverage of drag shows. Martin Luther King was one of many civil rights figures who believed that attaining full citizenship for African Americans was dependent on the creation of a heteronormative Black culture (see Russell 2008, 114, 116, and 121). *Jet* (est. 1951), which was geared more toward a working-class readership and was less concerned with "respectability," did continue to cover drag balls, however (see Conerly 2001, 386 and 389).

the home as a site of Black queer sexuality.[16] The typical article on 1950s female impersonator shows in publications like *Ebony, Jet*, the *Pittsburgh Courier*, the *Baltimore Afro-American*, and *The Louisiana Weekly* passed no negative judgments, and often included detailed descriptions of the performers' outfits. Intentionally or not, this attentive coverage called into question the respectable heterosexual identity constantly extolled in the Black press as a long-standing institution of racial uplift.

Over the course of my research, I also benefited from the wonderful Ralston Crawford Collection of Jazz Photography acquired by Tulane University in 1961, as well as from the interviews conducted by Jason Berry, Jonathan Foose, and Jeff Hannusch in the early 1980s (Berry, Foose, and Jones 1986, 54—64, 88—91; Hannusch 2001, 135—38) and by anthropologist Nick Spitzer in 2016 (Spitzer 2016). Together, these resources convinced me that important questions about how Black female impersonators understood their relationships to local Black communities, how they experienced and resisted racial oppression, and how they dealt with pressures to adhere to gender and sexual norms were perhaps not as unanswerable as I initially thought. Before dealing with these questions in more detail, however, I propose to flesh out three of these performers' biographies so as to identify possible commonalities.[17]

Three Profiles in Courage

Irving Hale, a. k. a. Patsy Vidalia (1921—1982)

Irving Hale was born in Vacherie, Louisiana, midway between New Orleans and Baton Rouge—a sugarcane-centered agricultural community from where

---

16   We know that queer Black men congregated in clandestine clubs such as Fourth World, which met in private homes. Sadly, no record of these festive events has survived (see Fieseler 2023). For an examination of the range of sexualities that existed behind closed doors in 1920s Harlem, see Robertson et al. 2012.

17   The reason why I settled on Patsy Vidalia, Little Richard, and Bobby Marchan as emblems of the Black female impersonator scene of the 1940s—1960s period had to do as much with source availability as with their significance to New Orleans performance culture. Other Black "female impersonators" such as Elton Paris (1922—2007) and Sir Lady Java (b. 1943) were ultimately left out because, though born in the city, they became famous elsewhere: in San Francisco for Elton Paris, in Los Angeles for Sir Lady Java. Another New Orleans native, Stormé DeLarverie (1920—2014), born from a wealthy white father and a Black mother, was omitted both because they were a male (not female) impersonator and because their career as a performer quickly took them to California (DeLarverie n. d.).

Antoine "Fats" Domino's family also hailed. After his father died, he moved to New Orleans with his mother and became fascinated by the local female impersonator scene. In 1947 he started working at the Dew Drop Inn at the request of Frank Pania who had seen him perform at Club Desire. There, he became the club's resident emcee—a gig that included a room at the club—and hosted an annual Halloween Ball as Patsy Vidalia (after the mild-flavored Vidalia onion that was also slang for sex workers), Valdez, or Valdelar (the name he chose when he recorded for the Mercury label in 1953). He also worked as part-time bartender and singer in a drag troupe called the Valdalia Sisters.

Interviewed in 1981 by Jason Berry, the self-proclaimed "Toast of New Orleans" remembered introducing the Dew Drop Inn variety shows with a sonorous "Ladies and Gentlemen, it's showtime at the Dew Drop!" (quoted in Berry, Foose and Jones 1986, 62). Patsy's theme song was a raunchy shake dance titled "Hip Shakin' Mama" (first recorded by Chubby Newsom). Comic acts, shake dancers, and novelty skits wove in and out of numbers played by the home band: "Everybody came and did a number, singing and dancing" (ibid.). The schedule of entertainment would continue until hours that ranged from 2:00 to 4:00 in the morning. According to musician Charles Neville (1938—2018):

> Patsy served the same function as a majordomo would serve at a supper club. He was that, plus he was a big part of the entertainment. He also worked as a waitress. I've seen him behind the bar. I've seen him really dressed up at the door bringing people to the tables, and he could do that with dignity, man; then at showtime he would become the MC. There was no caste difference. (quoted in Berry, Foose, and Jones 1986, 58)[18]

More recently, local musician Deacon John Moore (b. 1941) referred to the Halloween Ball hosted by Patsy as the place to be:

> That was like the big event of the year you know—the most talked about show of the year: Patsy's annual gay ball. People from all walks of life. And everybody would be piling in there, because every year Patsy would try to outdo herself from the previous year and everybody couldn't wait to see what she[19] was gonna wear ... (quoted in Spitzer 2016).

---

18   Note the emphasis on "dignity" (a remnant of the Civil Rights movement ethics of respectability) and on the absence of hierarchy among club workers.

19   Though most sources use the pronoun "he" when referring to Hale, according to musician Harold Battiste, who in 1995 was the director of jazz studies at the Univer-

In 1953, Patsy Vidalia was featured in a rhythm-and-blues package show that toured the North and Deep South, including cities like Mobile, Alabama, for example, where she had a reportedly "smashing" two-week engagement. Indeed, the Dew Drop Inn doubled as a booking agency, sending bands to perform at other venues across the region. Her performances were a strong influence on Little Richard, for whom the Dew Drop Inn became a second home in his eight years as a touring musician.

Irving Hale stopped performing regularly at the Dew Drop in the mid-1960s but became the first Black female impersonator to break the color line in the 1970s, when he took over as host at Club My-O-My (Bishop 2025). His last public appearance was in 1980 when he participated in Jazz Fest's late-night "Dew Drop Revisited" concerts alongside other club alumni like Walter "Wolfman" Washington (1943—2022) and Charles Neville (1938—2018). He died at home in New Orleans in 1982.

Richard Penniman, a. k. a. Princess Lavonne, a. k. a. Little Richard (1932—2020)

Kicked out of his home in Macon, Georgia, at the age of fourteen, Richard Penniman flourished onstage as "Princess Lavonne," a minstrel-show drag queen, and by eighteen he was a fixture of the variety shows and revues that toured the South, learning the tricks of his trade from female impersonators who danced and sang alongside him (Hamilton 1998). He was based at New Orleans's Club Tiajuana for several months in 1952.

When he turned to rhythm and blues in 1953 under the assumed name Little Richard, he got rid of the drag queen's dresses but, as noted by Marybeth Hamilton, he retained the sequins, makeup, pompadour, strut, and volubility. "This is Little Richard, King of the Blues," he reminded his audience in Black nightclubs, adding with a cunning smile, "and the Queen, too!" (quoted in Hamilton 1998, 162; Cortés 2023)

In 1955 his producer Robert Blackwell sent him to New Orleans to record new music at Cosimo Matassa's J&M Studios. There, Richard relaxed at the Dew Drop Inn nightclub, and the experience famously inspired him to write a risqué blues song titled "Tutti Frutti." A sanitized version of this hit became one of the first records to bring the underground queer Black culture of the South to the

---

sity of New Orleans, "She was always a woman—she lived as a woman. ... She would make fun of herself and what she was" (quoted in Bartlett 2004, 68).

mainstream. In 1970, Little Richard released his tribute song "The Dew Drop Inn," insisting that this was where "you meet all your fine friends."

Little Richard's case illustrates the documented connections between jazz/blues and queerness (Lhamon 2002, 86—97 and Carby 1994). We know of at least a dozen New Orleans jazz/rhythm & blues musicians who were gay or trans (openly or not), including Tony Jackson (1882—1921), who played piano in several brothels and wrote *Pretty Baby*, singer Larry Darnell (1928—1983), and James Booker (1939—1983), a frequent Dew Drop Inn act whom Doctor John supposedly called "the best black, queer, one-eyed junkie piano genius New Orleans has ever produced."[20] Others, like Louis Armstrong, had close ties with female impersonators without being gay (*Pittsburgh Courier* 1945a; *Pittsburgh Courier* 1948).

Oscar James Gibson, a. k. a. Roberta (1930—1999)

Born in Ohio, Oscar James Gibson arrived in New Orleans in 1953 with a female impersonator revue. He was soon hired as a singer and an emcee at Club Tiajuana and the Dew Drop Inn. On weekends (Friday, Saturday, and Sunday), he performed as Bobby Marchan at the Dew Drop Inn, and on weekdays he performed as Roberta (sometimes spelled Loberta, as in the 1953 song "Tipitina" by pianist Professor Longhair) in the Powder Box Revue at the Dew Drop, and later at Tiajuana, while wearing cocktail dresses sewed by hand.

As explained by John Wirt in a recent biographical sketch, Gibson's musical career began in 1953 with a single for Aladdin Records in Los Angeles. In his second single, "Chickee Wah-Wah" (1957), he played the role of a wide-eyed young man who attracts an aggressive woman. He subsequently sang for several Huey Smith and the Clowns recordings, including the call-and-response romp "Don't You Just Know It."

In 1959, Gibson found inspiration for his first solo hit during a nightclub engagement with his female impersonator troupe in Omaha, Nebraska. He sent a copy of "There's Something on Your Mind," a tale of passionate love and murder, to Bobby Robinson, one of the earliest Black producers and record company owners in the United States. The song was an instant hit. "I got booked to do a solo tour for a thousand dollars a night," Gibson told interviewer Ben Sandmel on the Allison Miner Music Heritage Stage during the 1998 New Orleans Jazz and Heritage Festival. In the 1980s and 1990s, Gibson hosted as

---

20   While used in a variety of publications, the quote has never been adequately referenced.

Bobby Marchan for popular talent shows and performed regularly at Jazz Fest. During the final decade of his life, he transitioned to rap music impresario, contributing to the success of the Cash Money Records label. He died in 1999 at the age of sixty-nine (Wirt 2023).

What these three profiles suggest is that Black female impersonators could live as men or as women, that they could desire same-sex partners or not (Little Richard was openly bisexual for part of his career), that they were some of the most gifted artists of the period, in a city that counted many, and that they took cues from one another's performances to improve their standing in the "showbiz circuit." In other words, Black female impersonation was not just a "pleasurescape" but a significant part of Black performance labor from the 1940s to the 1960s. Finally, the careers of Irving Hale, Richard Penniman, and Oscar Gibson indicate that gender-nonconforming individuals were fully accepted in the musicians' community. Does this mean that their acts were perhaps not as subversive as people today think they were?

Reading the Performance

The following selection of pictures taken by photographer Ralston Crawford at the Dew Drop Inn in 1952 and 1954 testifies to the diverse, complex portrayal of femininity on stage in a Black night club. Figure 4 (showcasing Patsy Vidalia and other dancers, with Bobby Marchan acting as the emcee) suggests that Black female impersonators of the 1940s to 1960s "conditioned their body and looks to emulate femininity … as opposed to make mockery of it," in line with E. Patrick Johnson's definition of female impersonation (Johnson 2008, 351). Figure 5, however, provides evidence for how rooted Black female impersonation as a profession was in vaudeville theater. They show Black comedian Lollypop Jones performing the asexual "mammy" minstrel show stereotype, thus playing to stereotypes about older Black women. Figure 6, finally, shows that female impersonators often shared the stage with female entertainers, including shake dancers, acrobats, fire eaters, and sword swallowers.

Figure 4. Dew Drop Inn entertainment featuring Patsy Vidalia in 1954 (Box 6 #109, Ralston Crawford Jazz Photography).

Was there a common denominator to these performances? Not necessarily. They offered Black performers a wider range of cultural characters and archetypes than had been the case on the nineteenth-century stage (probably wider than today, in fact). According to drummer Earl Palmer (1924—2008), "I don't ever remember being on a show where there wasn't some gays, you know on Vaudeville shows. Because entertainment was much more broader than it is now" (quoted in Spitzer 2016). While parodic performances of the mammy or Southern belle kind amounted to "playing for laughs," performances in which Irving Hale, Richard Penniman, or Oscar Gibson "passed" as women were more subtle.

Figure 5. Comedian Lollypop Jones performing at the Dew Drop Inn in 1952 (Box 7 #118, Ralston Crawford Jazz Photography).

In a recent article, music scholar Tom Attah has argued that Little Richard consciously adopted the trappings of the "sissy" as a deliberate ploy to defuse and deflect accusations of sexual interest in the young white women attending his shows after 1955 (Attah 2023, 14). Speaking in 1997, Little Richard indeed confirmed that

> it wasn't just a gay thing. To be black and work for white girls, I had to look that way. If I didn't wear make-up and look feminine, I couldn't work the white clubs, they wouldn't let me be with the white girls. The more effeminate I looked, they didn't mind me being with the white women. They'd say, "Oh Richard, there ain't nothin' to him" (quoted in ibid.).

Figure 6. Shake dancer on the stage of Club Tiajuana in 1951 (Box 8 #141, Ralston Crawford Jazz Photography).

In the context of a Black club and a predominantly Black audience (Fig. 7), the choice of a female persona probably had a different meaning and must have elicited a different response.

Figure 7. Patrons at Tiajuana Club, including James "Sugar Boy" Crawford (well-known author of "Jock-A-Mo") on the right, 1953 (Box 8 #139, Ralston Crawford Jazz Photography).

To cisgender, straight Black men in the audience, watching a female impersonator on stage may have been a way to toy with heteronormativity without endangering it. In the performance of their own femininity, Patsy, Princess Lavonne, and Roberta embodied bawdy, up-front, actively flirtatious women, but Hale, Penniman, and Gibson deactivated the act's threatening potential by claiming "mere" performance. Looked at in this light, the female impersonators were not threatening to hegemonic masculinity, and a man could respond to the "girl" on his lap without being assigned to the effeminacy or homosexuality that such behavior would have suggested if indulged in a different venue.

For all that they threatened traditional sexual patterns, "pansy acts" paradoxically "confirmed the masculinity of non-freakish black men" by casting queer men as curiosities (Hamilton 1998, 171). At the same time, if femininity could be performed, and was acknowledged as performance, it was logical to infer that masculinity was also performed. This logic inverted the insider joke, creating an uneasy insecurity about the foundations of assertive masculinity, while also establishing a "secret" alliance between the female impersonator and the Black heterosexual male audience. Both knew that unassailable masculinity was a cultural fiction.

Figure 8. A dancer on the lap of a friend at Tiajuana Club, 1951 (Box 8 #144, Ralston Crawford Jazz Photography).

To Black female spectators (the least empowered in the masculinist, segregationist system of the "New South"), the female impersonators' flamboyant performance of femininity may have had great appeal too. Their active sexuality and personal agency challenged the notion of women as passive and dependent. Patsy Vidalia was the voice of authority at the Dew Drop Inn—the enforcer of owner Frank Pania's policies. She always used her masculine body in her act to remind audience members of her power. Musician Harold Battiste (1931—2015) recalled that she would "tease and flirt with the audience before reminding them 'not to mess with her' because of her actual manhood" (quoted in Bartlett 2004, 11). At the Caledonia Inn, Caledonia, the female impersonator was the owner. Although Caledonia lived as a woman, her bodily use of masculinity gave them the active credentials to engage in business and successfully run a bar. As models for a potentially different way of performing femininity, while remaining attractive to men, the freedom from gender restraints enacted by the female impersonators offered an alternative to traditional, respectable but dependent, femininity.

Gay men in the audience must have been moved by the sexual freedom of Patsy Vidalia, Little Richard, and Roberta. Indeed, though there appears to have been a general agreement on their part to "suspend disbelief" and to accept the notion of the performance as a purely theatrical event, outside the domain of ordinary life, drag acts also created an expectation of coherence between the performer's social/performance front and their "true" inner self (Goffman, 1990, 56). As such, the performance pointed not just to a utopia but to an achievable goal.

In other words, while the New Orleans female impersonators were never on a soapbox lobbying for political overthrow, their performance effectively challenged the gender, sexual, and indeed racial binary. Not only was their flamboyant perfectionism neither male nor female; it also did a lot to attract white spectators to Black New Orleans clubs. In fact, they performed the impossible: gender-bending Black men, staging themselves as the lowest segment of the social order (Black women), receiving applause from both racially mixed audiences and respect for a job well done, in "a dress-rehearsal for a new social order" (Bartlett 2004, 155).

Perception of Black Female Impersonators across the Color, Gender, and Sexual Lines

As successful as they were on stage, female impersonators lived in precarious conditions once they stepped outside of the clubs in which they performed. Indeed, because cross-dressing in the streets was illegal in New Orleans, artists who did not leave their persona at the door risked arrest.[21] During the 1950s, local harassment ordinances to "drive out the deviates" expanded, mandating the firing of "immoral workers" and the eviction of queer tenants. Being arrested for any of these offenses often led to unwanted public attention, as names, addresses, and charges were frequently published in well-read crime sections of major newspapers such as the *Advocate* or *The Times-Picayune*. This kind of exposure typically resulted in job loss and social exclusion from community networks (Fieseler 2023).

---

21   "It is unlawful to appear masked or disguised in the street or any public place" (*Code of the City of New Orleans* 1956, 580). This is the main ordinance that was used to persecute female impersonators, though queer individuals could also be arrested for "obstruction of free passage," legalese for blocking a sidewalk. This ordinance is still on the books, but modified to allow for some exceptions such as "promiscuous masking" during the periods of Mardi Gras and Spring Fiesta and "participating in … exhibitions of minstrel troupes, circuses or other dramatic or amusement shows" (*Code of the City of New Orleans* 1995, Article VI, Division 1, Section 54—313 "Masks or disguises in public"). It is rarely enforced.

If white queer men could experience harassment, exposure, and violence, despite their economic privilege or social status, queer Black men were in fact isolated threefold: by the straight white community, the queer white community,[22] and the straight community. On this last point, however, there is a modicum of disagreement between scholars. Laura Grantmyre and Daneel Buring, in their study of Pittsburgh and Memphis Black female impersonators from the early to mid-twentieth century, have highlighted a live-and-let-live ethos that allowed female impersonators to "perform in nightclubs, participate in parades, socialize in beauty parlors, sing in church choirs, and gather in neighborhood bars" (Grantmyre 2011, 987; Buring 1997). Laurence Senelick has similarly argued that, while white American drag artists before the 1970s closeted their sexuality when off-stage, Black performers "lived as unabashed 'sissies' and 'fags' offstage" (Selenick 2000, 338). But Brett Beemyn, writing about "drag queens who performed before an overwhelmingly heterosexual audience" in Washington, DC's Black entertainment district, has noted that "while they may have received a certain level of acceptance ... it was only as long as they remained a form of exotic entertainment" (Breemyn 1997, 194).

Where does New Orleans fit in the acceptance-to-hostility continuum? According to musician and poet Eluard Burt (1937—2007), "All the musicians really loved Patsy and they respected what he was" and queerness in New Orleans "was just automatically acceptable in the black community. ... And there was never—what later we get a gay-bashing thing, that never happened in the black communities. Because in the entertainment world you never know who is who, or who is what" (quoted in Spitzer 2016). Outside of the musicians' community, however, things were more complex, as Figure 9 attests. Even when "they lived their life and they didn't bother anybody" (Grantmyre 2011), Black female impersonators elicited a variety of responses in the Crescent City, from hostility to tolerance to full acceptance.

Many Black New Orleanians remember being warned against the "unhealthy" environment of the Dew Drop Inn and South Rampart Street by their parents or other figures of authority. "[The Gilbert Academy school principal] warned us in a voice drenched in acid: 'Stay away from South Rampart Street, or you'll end up there. A hint to the wise is sufficient,'" writer Tom Dent reminisced in the late 1970s (quoted in Rogers 1995, 6). Millie McClellan Charles lived only a few blocks from the Dew Drop Inn, but she was forbidden to go to there, as well as to the Tick Tock Tavern on South Rampart Street (Simmons

---

22 Until the 1970s, gay bars in and near the French Quarter sought to keep Black patrons out (or keep their numbers minimal). According to Howard Philips Smith, only three establishments—Gigi's, the Safari House, and Café Lafitte in Exile—genuinely welcomed Black men (see Philips Smith 2017, 246).

2015, 75). Clearly, "respectable" working-class parents did not want Black girls mingling with cross-dressers or scantily clad shake dancers. They feared Black nightlife on Rampart and its overt manifestations of sexual and bodily freedom. Worshippers at the soon-to-be-politically influential New Zion Baptist Church, which was located around the corner of the Dew Drop Inn, were similarly hostile to "gender rebels."

Figure 9. Sign on Burgundy Street advertising rooms for all "colored" people except female impersonators, 1950s (Box 9 #169, Ralston Crawford Jazz Photography).

On the other hand, the fact that Black female impersonators were often seen in the New Orleans cityscape on festive occasions—much like in Memphis, where Peaches, the city's foremost African American female impersonator, marched through Black neighborhoods on Saturdays as a "majorette-in-drag" and participated in the Black community's citywide Cotton Carnival Jubilee Parade (Buring 1997, 107—8)—points to a certain level of acceptance in New Orleans's Black community.[23]

So do the many testimonies of straight women befriending female impersonators in the Crescent City. One of them, when interviewed by LaKisha Simmons in 2007, said that she "often went to clubs where she enjoyed music, danced, and delighted in the excitement of Black queer performers, whom she considered her friends" (quoted in Simmons 2015, 73).

---

23   Local lore has it that in 1948, the carnival parade organized by the Zulu Social Aid and Pleasure Club incorporated a Black female impersonator named "Corinne." Details about "Corinne the Queen" can be found in *Gumbo Ya-Ya*, a collection of folk tales and gossip on Louisiana published in 1945 under the auspices of the Louisiana Writers' Project (see Saxon 2008, 26).

Figure 10. Four men in drag in the French Quarter, ca. 1951—1954 (Milton E. Melton, gift of Stephen Scalia, The Historic New Orleans Collection, 2012.0172.27).

Overall, therefore, it seems that New Orleans Black female impersonators of the 1940s to 1960s were what Patricia Hill Collins termed "outsiders within" (Collins 1986, S14—S32; see also Dunning 2009). By virtue of their racial identity, they occupied the same geospatial and social locations as other Black men, but they remained outside the full recognition accorded them in everyday life as a result of their challenge to gender and sexual norms. This is consistent with the findings of Kim Gallon, who in her study of the way Black queer performances in Washington, DC, were received by Black institutions such as Howard University, Black churches, and Prince Hall Masonic Temples, concluded that gender-nonconforming performances and homosexual expression were actually sustained by them, albeit with varying degrees of complexity and resistance (Gallon 2018). While queer individuals were not always embraced in Black families and communities, they were at least sufficiently protected to safely navigate the streets of their neighborhoods (hooks 1989).

Conclusion

Investigating the gender-bending practices of African American female impersonators in mid-twentieth-century New Orleans makes it possible to reflect on the long history of Black drag performance in the "Big Easy," from Augustus Stevens to Patsy Vidalia to, I would add, contemporary bounce superstar Big Freedia.[24] Long thought to be derivative of white carnival practices, or oppositional to it, Black gender bending had in fact been part of the city's cultural landscape since at least the nineteenth century, and developed almost independently from white gender-nonconforming practices.

A second takeaway of this study is that, while George Lipsitz's statement that "In New Orleans, [masquerade and imposture] are necessary tools for self-defense and survival in the one-sided war that white supremacy wages against African people in America" certainly rings true (Lipsitz 2011, 281), labeling cross-dressing as a "weapon of the weak" (Scott 1985) does not quite convey the complexity of the performance. For 1940s—1960s drag artists, the female persona was both an opportunity to challenge the expected racial, sexual, and gender norms of post-World War II America and a way to carve out a niche for the Southern (or national) blues circuit. Audience response was at least as equivocal: while spectators may have read the performance as a challenge to the heteronormative system, others may have seen it as "innocent fun" directed at "sissies" and women.

One more lesson from this historical analysis is that, outside of the music and night club environment, female impersonators did not meet an unqualified response either: embraced by the musical world, they were also treated as "freaks" by straight white fraternity members or as a threat to the Civil Rights movement's ethics of racial, gender, and sexual respectability by local church members.[25] As suggested by Laura Grantmyre in 2011, it seems that we cannot fully grasp the core of this history—with its ever-shifting yet consistently porous racial, sexual, and gender boundaries—if we rely solely on teleological or binary narratives of segregation versus integration, invisibility versus visibility, or margin versus mainstream. The reality, as I have hopefully shown, is more complicated.

One avenue for further research concerns the potential influence of Black female impersonators on local understandings of femininity. To what degree did local women borrow stylistically from female impersonators?

---

24   On gender-bending practices in New Orleans bounce music, see Schoux Casey and
     Eberhardt 2018. On bounce as a queer "black safe space," see Chastagner 2024.
25   "The politics of respectability offered no place for sissies," as historian Jerry Watkins
     crudely puts it (Watkins 2017, 126).

And to what degree did female impersonators' performances of femininity influence local heterosexual male desires? One story offers the beginnings of an answer here: the fact that soul singer Irma Thomas patterned her stage shows after Patsy Vidalia's performances. "He gave me tips on how to wear make-up, what clothes to wear, how to move on stage and how to get off and on the bandstand," she recalled in 1999 (quoted in Hannusch 2001, 136). Thomas learned the choreography and the song *Hip Shakin' Mama* from Vidalia, sensuously provoking desire in her audiences with an act that was her impersonation of a female impersonator. There are probably other, similar instances of cross-fertilization in New Orleans history, and exploring them would help gauge the centrality of drag to the performance of gender in New Orleans over the *longue durée*.

References

Primary Sources

The Code of the City of New Orleans, Louisiana. 1956. New Orleans: Hauser Print Co.

Code of the City of New Orleans, Louisiana. 1995. https://library.municode.com/la/new_orleans/codes/.

DeLarverie, Stormé. N.d. "Stormé DeLarverie Papers." Schomburg Center for Research in Black Culture, Manuscripts, Archives, and Rare Books Division, The New York Public Library.

The Freeman, An Illustrated Color Newspaper. 1901. "Augustus Stevens, Female Impersonator." Digital Transgender Archive. www.digitaltransgenderarchive.net/files/kw52j838h. Accessed May 7, 2024.

The Freeman, An Illustrated Color Newspaper. 1903. "Stage." Edited by "Woodbine." Digital Transgender Archive. https://www.digitaltransgenderarchive.net/files/6682x430x. Accessed May 7, 2024.

"John T. Mendes Photograph Collection." N.d. The Historic New Orleans Collection, Louisiana Digital Library. https://louisianadigitallibrary.org/islandora/object/hnoc-p15140coll1%3Acollection. Accessed May 7, 2024.

Letters from Female Impersonators. 1962. Volume Number Ten. Digital Transgender Archive. www.digitaltransgenderarchive.net/downloads/pn89d6592. Accessed May 7, 2024.

"Mr. Pat Waters Very Smart Club My-O-My Proudly Presents The World's Most Beautiful Boys in Women's Attire." 1951. Flyer from April 12. Queer Music Heritage. www.queermusicheritage.com/fem-myomya.html. Accessed May 7, 2024.

"Pania v. City of New Orleans." 1967. https://www.leagle.com/decision/1967913 262fsupp6511787. Accessed May 7, 2024.

Pittsburgh Courier. 1945a. "Louis Armstrong, Native New Orleans Boy, Gets Homecoming Welcome Sunday." October 21.

Pittsburgh Courier. 1945b. "Display Ad 1—No Title." October 21.

Pittsburgh Courier. 1948. "Clicks in Mardi Gras Town: Armstrong Hot as Good Gumbo in N.O." May 1.

Ralston Crawford Collection of Jazz Photography, William Ransom Hogan Jazz Archive, Howard-Tilton Memorial Library, Tulane University.

"Southern Decadence Party Invitations." N.d. Flyers from several dates. LGBT+ Archives Project of Louisiana. https://lgbtarchiveslouisiana.org/southern-decadence-party-invitations/. Accessed May 7, 2024.

Secondary Sources

Attah, Tom. 2023. "The Boy Can't Help It: Little Richard's Disruption and Reconstruction of Black Male Screen Performativity." In *Pop Stars on Film: Popular Culture in a Global Market,* edited by Kirsty Fairclough and Jason Wood, 11—29. New York: Bloomsbury.

Bartlett, Thomasine. 2004. "Vintage Drag: Female Impersonators Performing Resistance in Cold War New Orleans." PhD dissertation, Tulane University.

Berry, Jason, Jonathan Foose, and Tad Jones. 1986. *Up from the Cradle of Jazz: New Orleans Music since World War II.* Athens: Georgia University Press.

Berubé, Allan. 2020. *Coming Out Under Fire: The History of Queer Men and Women in World War II.* Twentieth anniversary edition. Chapel Hill: University of North Carolina Press.

Bibler, Michael P. 2009. *Cotton's Queer Relations: Same-Sex Intimacy and the Literature of the Southern Plantation, 1936—1968.* Charlottesville: University of Virginia Press.

Bibler, Michael P. 2013. "Queering the Region." In *The Cambridge Companion to the Literature of the American South,* edited by Sharon Monteith, 188—203. Cambridge: Cambridge University Press.

Beemyn, Brett. 1997. "A Queer Capital: Race, Class, Gender, and the Changing Social Landscape of Washington's Gay Communities, 1940—1955." In *Creating a Place for Ourselves: Lesbian, Queer, and Bisexual Community Histories,* edited by Brett Beemyn, 183—210. New York: Routledge.

Bishop, Quinn. "My-O-My: The Forgotten History of How New Orleans' Black Drag Queens Helped Shape Rock 'N' Roll." *Gambit* 46, no. 25: 13—17.

Brewster, Lee G., Kay Gybbons, and Laura McAllister, eds. 1971. "Drag Queen vs. Transvestite." *Drag Queens: A Magazine About the Transvestite* 1, no. 1: 11—12.

Buring, Daneel. 1997. *Lesbian and Queer Memphis: Building Communities behind the Magnolia Curtain.* New York: Garland Publishing.

Butler, Judith. 1990. *Gender Trouble: Feminism and the Subversion of Identity.* New York: Routledge.

"Caldonia Inn." N. d. A *Closer Walk NOLA.* https://acloserwalknola.com/places/caldonia-inn/. Accessed September 7, 2024.

Carby, Hazel. 1994. "'It Jus Be's Dat Way Sometime': The Sexual Politics of Women's Blues." In *Unequal Sisters: A Multi-cultural Reader in American History,* 2nd edition, edited by Vicki L. Ruiz and Ellen Carol DuBois, 238—249. New York: Routledge.

Chastagner, Claude. 2024. "The Queer Spaces of Black Dance Music." *Popular Culture Studies Journal* 12, no. 1: 12—41.

Chauncey, George. 1994. *Gay New York: Gender, Urban Culture, and the Making of the Gay Male World, 1890—1940.* New York: Basic Books.

"Club Desire." N. d. A *Closer Walk NOLA.* https://acloserwalknola.com/places/club-desire/. Accessed September 7, 2024.

"Club Tiajuana." N. d. A *Closer Walk NOLA.* https://acloserwalknola.com/places/club-tiajuana/. Accessed September 7, 2024.

Conerly, Gregory. 2001. "Swishing and Swaggering: Homosexuality in Black Magazines during the 1950s." In *The Greatest Taboo: Homosexuality in Black Communities,* edited by Delroy Constantine-Simms, 384—395. Los Angeles: Alyson Books.

Constantine-Simms, Delroy, ed. 2001. *The Greatest Taboo: Homosexuality in Black Communities.* Los Angeles: Alyson Books.

Corso, Susan. 2009. "Drag Queen Theology." *Huffington Post.* April 15, 2009. https://www.huffpost.com/entry/drag-queen-theology_b_175120. Accessed September 7, 2024.

Cortés, Lisa, director. 2023. *Little Richard: I Am Everything.* New York: Magnolia Pictures.

Coyle, Kate and Nadiene Van Dyke. 1997. "Sex, Smashing, and Storyville in Turn-of-the-Century New Orleans. Reexamining the Continuum of Lesbian Sexuality." In *Carryin' on in the Lesbian and Queer South,* edited by John Howard, 54—72. New York: New York University Press.

"Cross-dressing." N. d. *Oxford English Dictionary.* https://www.oed.com/dictionary/cross-dressing_n. Accessed September 7, 2024.

Delery-Edwards, Clayton. 2017. *Out for Queer Blood: The Murder of Fernando Rios and the Failure of New Orleans Justice.* Jefferson, NC: Exposit Books.

"Dew Drop Inn." N. d. A *Closer Walk NOLA.* https://acloserwalknola.com/places/dew-drop-inn/. Accessed September 7, 2024.

Dunning, Stefanie. 2009. *Queer in Black and White: Interraciality, Same Sex Desire, and Contemporary African American Culture*. Bloomington: Indiana University Press.

Dynes, Wayne R. 2016 (originally published 1990). "Transvestism (Cross-dressing)." In *Encyclopedia of Homosexuality*, vol. 2, edited by Wayne R. Dynes, 1312—1313. New York: Routledge.

Ferris, Lesley, ed. 1993. *Crossing the Stage: Controversies on Cross-Dressing*. London: Routledge.

Fieseler, Robert W. 2021. "LGBTQ+ Rights Movement in Louisiana." *64 Parishes*. April 9, 2021, last updated March 24, 2023. https://64parishes.org/entry/lgbtq-rights-movement-in-louisiana. Accessed September 7, 2024.

Gallon, Kim. 2018. "'No Tears for Alden': Black Female Impersonators as 'Outsiders Within' in the 'Baltimore Afro-American.'" *Journal of the History of Sexuality* 27, no. 3, 367—394.

Garber, Eric. 1989. "A Spectacle in Color: The Lesbian and Queer Subculture of Jazz Age Harlem." In *Hidden from History: Reclaiming the Gay and Lesbian Past*, edited by Martin Duberman, Martha Vicinus, and George Chauncey, 318—331. New York: Meridian Books.

Garber, Marjorie. 1993. *Vested Interests: Cross-Dressing and Cultural Anxiety*. New York: Routledge.

Gebhard, Caroline. 1997. "Reconstructing Southern Manhood: Race, Sentimentality, and Camp in the Plantation Myth." In *Haunted Bodies: Gender and Southern Texts*, edited by Anne Goodwyn Jones and Susan V. Donaldson, 132—156. Charlottesville: University Press of Virginia.

Godet, Aurélie. 2025. "Betwixt Fear and Despair: Joy in French Colonial Louisiana, 1682—1769." Unpublished manuscript.

Godet, Aurélie. 2021. "Racial Passing at New Orleans Mardi Gras from Reconstruction to World War II: Flight of Fancy or Masked Resistance?" In *Erasure and Recollection: The Memory of Racial Passing Within and Beyond the United States*, edited by Aurélie Guillain and Hélène Charlery, 57—104. Brussels: Peter Lang.

Goffman, Erving. 1990 (originally published 1956). *The Presentation of Self in Everyday Life*. London: Penguin.

Grantmyre, Laura. 2011. "'They Lived Their Life and They Didn't Bother Anybody': African American Female Impersonators and Pittsburgh's Hill District, 1920—1960." *American Quarterly* 63, no. 4: 983—1011.

Hamilton, Marybeth. 1998. "Sexual Politics and African-American Music; or, Placing Little Richard in History." *History Workshop Journal* 46, no. 1: 161—176.

Hannusch, Jeff. 2001. *The Soul of New Orleans: A Legacy of Rhythm and Blues*. Ville Platte: Swallow.

Hartman, Saidiya. 2019. *Wayward Lives, Beautiful Experiments: Intimate Histories of Social Upheaval*. New York: W.W. Norton.

Hill Collins, Patricia. 1986. "Learning from the Outsider Within: The Sociological Significance of Black Feminist Thought." *Social Problems* 33, no. 6: 14—32.

hooks, bell. 1989. "Homophobia in Black Communities." In *Talking Back: Thinking Feminist, Thinking Black*, 120—126. Boston: South End Press.

Johnson, E. Patrick. 2008. *Sweet Tea: Black Queer Men of the South*. Chapel Hill: University of North Carolina Press.

Jura, Aaron. 2021. "GI as Dolls: Uncovering the Hidden Histories of Drag Entertainment During Wartime." *The National WWII Museum New Orleans*. June 15, 2021. https://www.nationalww2museum.org/war/articles/drag-entertainment-world-war-ii. Accessed September 7, 2024.

Lhamon, Jr., W.T. 2002. *Deliberate Speed: The Origins of a Cultural Style in the American 1950s*. Cambridge: Harvard University Press.

Lipsitz, George. 2011. "New Orleans in the World and the World in New Orleans." *Black Music Research Journal* 31, no. 2: 261—290.

Long, Alecia. 2005. *The Great Southern Babylon: Sex, Race, and Respectability in New Orleans, 1865—1920*. Baton Rouge: Louisiana State University Press.

Lott, Eric. 2013 (originally published 1993). *Love and Theft: Blackface Minstrelsy and the American Working Class*. New York: Oxford University Press.

McNulty, Ian. 2024. "Dew Drop Inn, a Nearly-Lost New Orleans Treasure, Is Back." *Nola.com*. March 1, 2024. https://www.nola.com/entertainment_life/eat-drink/dew-drop-inn-reopens-as-historic-hotel-venue-in-new-orleans/article_2a08cec8-d732-11ee-b06d-0f58fb23cdseehtml. Accessed September 7, 2024.

McPherson, Tara. 2003. *Reconstructing Dixie: Race, Gender and Nostalgia in the Imagined South*. Durham, NC: Duke University Press.

Mitchell, Reid. 1995. *All on a Mardi Gras Day: Episodes in the History of New Orleans Carnival*. Cambridge, MA: Harvard University Press.

Mumford, Kevin. 1997. *Interzones: Black/White Sex Districts in Chicago and New York in the Early Twentieth Century*. New York: Columbia University Press.

Newton, Esther. 1972. *Mother Camp: Female Impersonators in America*. Chicago: Chicago University Press.

Philips Smith, Howard. 2017. *Unveiling the Muse: The Lost History of Gay Carnival in New Orleans*. Jackson, MS: University of Mississippi Press.

Robertson, Stephen, Shane White, Stephen Garton, and Graham White. 2012. "Disorderly Houses: Residences, Privacy, and the Surveillance of Sexuality in 1920s Harlem." *Journal of the History of Sexuality* 21, no. 3: 443—466.

Rogers, Kim Lacy. 1995. *Righteous Lives: Narratives of the New Orleans Civil Rights Movement*. New York: New York University Press.

Rose, Al. 1974. *Storyville, New Orleans: Being an Authentic, Illustrated Account of the Notorious Red-Light District*. Tuscaloosa: University of Alabama Press.

Russell, Thaddeus. 2008. "The Color of Discipline: Civil Rights and Black Sexuality." *American Quarterly* 60, no. 1: 101—128.

Saxon, Lyle. 2008 (originally published 1945). *Gumbo Ya-Ya*. Boston: Houghton Mifflin.

Schoux Casey, Christina and Maeve Eberhardt. 2018. "'She Don't Need No Help': Deconsolidating Gender, Sex and Sexuality in New Orleans Bounce Music." *Gender and Language* 12, no. 3: 318—345.

Scott, James C. 1985. *Weapons of the Weak: Everyday Forms of Peasant Resistance*. New Haven: Yale University Press.

Sears, Clare. 2015. *Arresting Dress: Cross-Dressing, Law, and Fascination in Nineteenth-Century San Francisco*. Durham, NC: Duke University Press.

Senelick, Laurence. 2000. *The Changing Room: Sex, Drag and Theatre*. London: Routledge.

Sieg, Katrin. 2002. *Ethnic Drag: Performing Race, Nation, Sexuality in West Germany*. Ann Arbor: University of Michigan Press.

Simmons, LaKisha. 2015. *Crescent City Girls: The Lives of Young Black Women in Segregated New Orleans*. Chapel Hill: University of North Carolina Press.

Spitzer, Nick. 2016. "The Dew Drop Inn." *American Routes Shortcuts*, podcast. December 2, 2016.

Stryker, Susan. 2006. "(De)Subjugated Knowledges: An Introduction to Transgender Studies." In *The Transgender Studies Reader*, edited by Susan Stryker and Stephen Whittle, 1—17. New York: Routledge.

Walker, Dave. 2020. "Take a Tour of Bourbon Street's Music Scene of the 1950s." *The Historic New Orleans Collection*. June 5, 2020. https://hnoc.org/publishing/first-draft/take-tour-bourbon-streets-music-scene-1950s. Accessed September 7, 2024.

Watkins, Jerry. 2017. "Keep on Carryin' On: Recent Research on the LGBTQ History of the American South." *History Compass* 15, no. 11: 124—128.

Weldon, Nick. 2022. "The Downtown Club with Uptown Ideas." *The Historic New Orleans Collection*. September 2, 2022. https://hnoc.org/publishing/first-draft/the-downtown-club-with-uptown-ideas. Accessed May 7, 2024.

Wilson, James F. 2011. *Bulldaggers, Pansies, and Chocolate Babies: Performance, Race, and Sexuality in the Harlem Renaissance*. Ann Arbor: University of Michigan Press.

Wirt, John. 2023. "The Irrepressible Bobby Marchan." *64 Parishes*. February 28, 2023, last updated June 1, 2023. https://64parishes.org/the-irrepressible-bobby-marchan. Accessed September 7, 2024.

FACING CONTEMPORARY
COMMODIFICATION

Digital Blackface and Memetic Ambiguity

Katrin Köppert

Memes as Happy Objects of White Supremacy

Some memes, "[b]y fate, or like magic" (Jackson 2019, 88), manage to extend their lifespan against the ephemerality of the internet, writes Lauren Michele Jackson in her 2019 book *White Negroes*, which followed her legendary article in *Teen Vogue* two years earlier. In this article, she had introduced the terminology of digital blackface to a large audience and described it as an embodiment practice of Blackness that, in reference to the minstrelsy tradition in the USA, depicts the racist sentiments of society online (Jackson 2017). Alongside games, TikTok videos, emojis, etc., memes are a genre of digital blackface. They circulate primarily in the form of so-called reaction images as embodiments of Blackness: these memes, which draw on the visual archive of Black facial expressions and gestures to illustrate and communicate a feeling, are the form of performative appropriation of Blackness or Black as performance transferred to the internet globally. According to Jackson, the popularity of such reaction images is often linked to their short-lived nature: as quickly as some memes with titles such as "Crying Jordan," "Damn, Daniel," "Sweet Brown" appear, they are gone, "just like that" (ibid., 87). However, some never fade away because they are "too attuned to our baser sensibilities" (ibid., 88).

This is the case with the "You Get a Car" meme[1] at the center here, which has resisted the online logic of transience since 2004 and returns at regular intervals. This meme, which medializes Oprah Winfrey's outburst of joy in her 2004 television show and exaggerates Black female affect as grotesque, does not fade because it touches on racism as a basic sentiment. However, unlike Jackson, I would like to claim that it is not so much the baser sensibilities that this meme appeals to. Rather, I am interested in examining it as an example of a dynamic that—especially in the context of the US—*produces* the meme

---

*   Parts of this article were published in German under the title "Meme(tische) Gespenster" (Köppert 2025a).

1   See "Oprah's 'You Get a Car,'" n. d.

in analogy to the historically generated, racist idea of Blackness as something inferior in order to create a feeling of superiority, of *white*[2] supremacy. It is precisely in this constitutive dynamic that the feeling of happiness associated with memes can be located. This was only revived in 2024, when Oprah Winfrey amused an entire room at the 29th Critics Choice Awards with just a small reference to the "You Get a Car" meme.

"Oprah Winfrey pays homage to THAT iconic 'you get a car' meme as she takes the stage in slinky dress that showcases slim figure after weight loss drug use," headlined the *Daily Mail* the day after Winfrey's appearance at the 29th Critics Choice Awards on January 15, 2024 (Daily Mail 2024). Winfrey, in her introduction speech for Best Actor, wished she could tell the audience "You get a trophy, you get a trophy, and you get a trophy." This smiling allusion to the most parodied moment in television history,[3] according to the *Daily Mail*, when Winfrey gave everyone in the audience a new car by shouting "You get a car" in her 2004 show, immediately sparked amusement and laughter among those present at the awards ceremony. The laughter probably proves the virality of the "You Get a Car" meme, which was created twenty years ago, and the sustainable effectiveness of this meme in a digital culture that is fast-moving and tends to forget. The transgenerational longevity of the so-called Oprah meme (Köppert 2022, 227) refers to a certain extent to the hypermemetic culture in which (political, public) discourses are shaped by memes in the long term—and no longer limited to the USA (von Gehlen 2020, 50). Memes, for that matter, prove to be happy objects and are symptomatic of the affective discourse that determines them normatively. This means that with the circulation of the meme as a cultural object, archives and discourses that tend to amass unhappiness are associated with pleasure and thus take on the form of happiness. Sara Ahmed refers specifically to heterosexual marriage as an archive of (economic, legal, etc.) unhappiness for women, which however—circulating as a happy object—stands for (phantasmatic) happiness (2010, 31). Memes serve as a promise of happiness too, which is important for heteronormative and—as will be seen—*white* discourses. And indeed, the literature on memes is permeated by questions of humor (Moebius 2018, Dargiewicz 2022, Nowotny and Reidy 2022), wit (von Gehlen 2020), the frivolous (Galip 2021), the exaggerated masquerade (King 2021). Even when their polarizing and destructive power takes

---

2   I use italics to emphasize the social construction of the category of whiteness. However, based on the social constructivist approach, I choose to capitalize Blackness to account for lived or embodied experiences, particularly in the context of antiracist resistance movements (see Eggers et al. 2005).

3   See "Oprah Winfrey Pays Homage," 2024.

center stage in the context of right-wing instrumentalizations, memetic irony is an essential point of reference.

The joyful excitement in the audience of the 29th Critics Choice Awards makes it clear how sticky—in Ahmed's terms—happiness is and how intensely the feeling of entertainment is attached to a meme though it has long since been discussed publicly and critically in the context of digital blackface (see Daily Mail 2021). So the question is: What idea of the world, what political discourse is formed when, despite the brutal history of blackface reproduced in the meme, the desire for happiness is articulated in the laughter of the audience? Which chapter of history wants to be kept affectively open here, and why? What role do memes play in their mediality and to what extent are they a medium for delaying an affective closure. And to what extent can this delay be understood as exemplary of how race is also produced through its connection with technology (Chun 2009)? So how can memes be understood as technologies in which race is performed, and performed differently? To approach these questions, I will first discuss digital blackface as the subject of a digital image culture of "affect as racialization" (Blickstein 2019). The second part will then deal with memes as ghosts and, in this context, as machines of Blackness or as Black technical objects according to Ramon Amaro (2022), but also of Black techno-conjuring according to Ezekiel Dixon-Román (2021). Particularly with regard to Black techno-conjuring, I would like to discuss the tension between memetic haunting and its potential for undoing racist violence and redress (Dixon-Román 2021, 5). Even though it will be issued very late in this article and is still quite cursory here, though more elaborated elsewhere (Köppert 2025a, 2025c), I would like to deal with practices of resignifying colonial and racist histories of blackface and ethnic drag and highlight the question of how digital blackface can be decolonized in the second part of this text.

Digital Blackface—Navigating Crises

The primarily *white* audience, which reacted with amusement in 2024 in memory of the "You Get a Car" meme that has been distributed and modified on a massive scale since 2004, kept an affective space open in which blackface is not a trigger for criticism or indignation. On the contrary: digital blackface can be understood as part of a boom in the affective navigation of various crises in which whiteness emotionally finds itself, contrary to all facts of still being privileged. By updating a meme that is exemplary for digital blackface, control can be established over everyday life, which increasingly threatens to slip away in the face of political conflicts, climate change and social injustice. Within such a *white* emotional culture the invoked meme is then less of a "province of meaning" that can be used to leave the dominant everyday world in a carnivalesque manner (Moebius 2018, 6). Rather, it seems to me that the grotesquely exaggerated emotional outburst in the meme becomes a medium for instantiating a controlled and controllable everyday life at the moment of its revival during the award ceremony. If everyday life is perceived as a circus, then the meme once again has the function of providing stability. Blackface provides *white* stability and is actualized—especially since the Black Lives Matter protests and the toppling of colonial-racist monuments in the US context and beyond—for the purpose of self-affirmation and *white* happiness in the field of digital culture. Central to such an assertion are 1) the medial racialization of affect, to be discussed here as memetic distortion (defacement) and animation of the face; and 2) the appropriability of affect, which in the context of the media history of amateur photography refers to the colonial-racist logic of fungibility (Hartman 1997).

Memetic Defacement

The deranged face captured in the "You Get a Car" meme and the grotesquely overdrawn laugh that exposes Winfrey's teeth can be understood as visualizations of blackface on a motivic level. Alongside the blackening of skin, the toothy smile is one of the most important topoi of racist Othering, which became part of US-American mass culture in the form of minstrel shows in the nineteenth century and spread internationally in the course of transmedial translation into photography and film in the twentieth century. On the level of meme-specific characteristics, the montage of the image's motif with text, but also the loop in the GIF version,[4] function like an additional animation of the face. From a historical perspective, the meme reproduces the racialization of affect or the affective charge of racism via animation (Blickstein 2019).

In his racist pamphlet *Notes on the State of Virginia* (1785), Thomas Jefferson described the Black face as an immovable veil that was incapable of any emotion (quoted in Yao 2021, 18). Frustration with this opacity of the face informed the dehumanizing discourse of Black subjects' inherent insensitivity. As a result of this frustration, the overemphasis on liveliness or affectability generated by blackface in the minstrel shows showed the supposedly Black subject as affected, not to prove their humanity, but to visibly emphasize that Black affect was different, abject and less valuable (Ngai 2015, 95, see also Chen 2012 and

---

4   See the GIF at https://i.kym-cdn.com/entries/icons/original/000/012/809/oprah-free-car.gif, accessed May 15, 2024.

Köppert 2022, 231).[5] The grotesque exaggeration of affect as a characteristic of blackface—for example, the oversized, laughing mouth and gesticulating hands—is obviously repeated in Winfrey's meme.

The animation, which is either created by short agitating text messages that are mounted over the image or played as a GIF, is, beyond the distorted face, a technological condition of the racialization of affect as animatedness (see Ngai 2015). This means two things:

1) In a meme, the image is animated on the basis of the text, insofar as the image becomes a story, which in most cases of "You Get a Car" memes known to me has an innervating character. Winfrey appears either as an apocalyptic oracle (You Get the Flu!) or an inciting hate preacher (You Go to Hell!) and is thus associated with the image of the over-emotionally racialized subject who is in turmoil (Ngai 2015, 91).

2) The GIF in turn animates by means of editing and looping. The Black female body is magically set in motion by the invisible cut, but is trapped in this movement due to the loop. Following Sianne Ngai's (ibid., 100) remarks on early animated film and its racialization, it could be said that the GIF version of the Winfrey meme functions in the ambiguity of showing an uncontrollable body that is at the same time immobile. With the GIF, emotional vivacity and mechanistic containment coincide once again. Similar to what Rey Chow (1993) states for early film, it seems to me that the ambiguity does not coincidentally conflate with the moment in which digital image culture begins to take shape in the twenty-first century. However, I believe that, contrary to what Chow claims for the film, memes do not only use the Black body to *show* that in the digital age the human being is an automaton in which social injustice and mechanization processes take on a life of their own in an uncontrolled manner. Rather, the memes/GIFs are integrative technologies of a digital culture that *carry out* the automation of the Black body and at the same time capture the transgressive potential of the emancipation of Blackness.

It is not only the loop that holds the ecstatic movement captive; many of the texts also function according to the principle of calling up Blackness as threatening and controlling it at the same time: many variations of the "You Get a Car" meme catch up with the threatening invocation of the "You" through the more metaphysically universalizing "Everyone." The meme thus accomplishes within its elements what had functioned—as Evelyn Annuß (2014, 68) has

---

5   In this context, it is interesting to note that the abolitionists had previously also worked with dramatizations of animation—with the aim of recoding dehumanization. As Sianne Ngai points out, the fact that Black people were animated like dolls for the purpose of achieving this is just another form of objectification (see Ngai 2005, 99).

argued—partitioned on stage and backstage in 1920s film, particularly in *The Jazz Singer* (1927). The stage as a site of blackfacing, the disfiguring of expression through the comic-like exaggeration of mouth, eyes, and hands, was crucial to integrating into the dominant *white* culture of the US, which had been symbolized in the film by the backstage space occupied exclusively by *white* people. In relation to the meme, it seems to me that with the allusion to "Everyone," the backstage as a metaphor of the invisible but universalized *white* dominant culture enters the visible field of the stage. Whiteness no longer operates out of its unmarkedness, but explicitly communicates itself within the meme as the principle of everyone, which keeps the supposedly threatening potential of the appeal associated with the Black female body ("you") under control. If *white* normativity in film was derived from the hidden everydayness of the backstage, so that it could remain invisible behind the black mask during the carnivalesque stage spectacle, in the context of digital cultures it is pushed visibly into the picture as "Everyone." The "You Get a Car" meme therefore seems to me to be a technology for regaining a supposedly lost control, which, in contrast to the historical blackface in the film, is not based on invisible ventriloquism, but must take place on an open stage—on the digital stage of the meme.

Memetic Fungibility

Previously unmentioned, but also relevant for the "You Get a Car" meme, is the logic of transferability. The "You Get a Car" meme is exemplary for the way in which Black people's facial expressions and gestures are depicted, which—collaged with text or animated in the case of GIFs—are used by *white* people for reaction images, for example on X (formerly Twitter), to express a feeling or make a joke.[6] This imitation or transmission of emotional expression generated in the use and distribution of images as an emotional reaction or commentary corresponds to the "absolute fungibility" (Palmer 2017, 38, see also Palmer 2020) of Black people's affective articulations. The appropriability and consumability of Black people's affective expression—created under the auspices of elaborate constructions—for the communication of their own feelings marks the structural position that Blackness has historically occupied for subjectivation within *white* supremacy and repeatedly fills in the context of digital image cultures. The practice of transferring visibly affected Blackness to the communicative actions of *white* people on social media platforms can be understood as the

---

6   See Katrin Köppert and Simon Strick's research project "Digital Blackface: Racialized Affect Patterns of the Digital," funded by the Volkswagen Foundation.

ability of *whiteness* to possess Black affect and to not being called into question in its own articulation of feeling.

Tanya Sheehan (2014) has demonstrated this appropriation in the US history of private amateur and snapshot photography. After the toothy smile was attributed to the Black body shortly after the abolition of slavery in order to discipline it (photographically), it was later adopted by the *white* middle class in self-portraits. In order to free themselves from the social restrictions of sentimental inwardness, the toothy smile was used in the private photography of the *white* bourgeoisie at the beginning of the twentieth century, using racially charged watermelon slices held in front of the face or body as a "prosthetic grin" (ibid., 149). In the following, I would like to argue that the "You Get a Car" meme mirrors this history of amateur photography in digital space, yet transforms it. With the adoption of the affective transgression of Black people produced as a stereotype, a vitalization of the users takes place, which, however, coincides with the moment when the power of *whiteness* is increasingly affirmed again (Alt-Right, Trump, etc.). So even if it can be assumed that the constructed stereotype of Black expression is appropriated in the sense of a desire for the associated intensity of feelings with the reaction image, this does not mean that the hegemonic feeling of *white* interiority is called into question. As Tanya Sheehan writes, following Saidiya V. Hartman (1997):

> such appropriation did much more than imagine blackness as an "abject and degraded condition"; it fulfilled a "desire to don, occupy, or possess blackness or the black body as a sentimental resource and/ or locus of excess enjoyment" without compromising the audience's "serious" performances of whiteness and respectability elsewhere. (2014, 146)

In light of this history of amateur photography, the Black body turns into an emotional resource for the production and balancing of one's own feelings.

Digital blackface in the form of reaction images also seems to tie in with the history of minstrel shows, which after the abolition of slavery in the US took on the function of defining *white* feeling—with the effect of pointing out to Black people "their place" in society. Winfrey's meme seems to be an example of a present in which Black people are once again being referred to their place, albeit in a different media-specific setting, and thus excluded from the affective register of *white* supremacy, perhaps especially in the case of a Black woman like Oprah Winfrey, who has generated a great deal of economic and cultural capital.

The reference to minstrel shows makes it possible to point out the difference to the media history of snapshot photography: Whereas the appropriation of the toothy smile was popularized in the medium of snapshot photography and celebrated in the context of family rituals in front of the camera, with the memetic use and distribution of the exaggerated feeling of happiness we are witnessing the publicizing of a once private media use. On the one hand, this testifies to the diffusion of privacy and the public sphere that has gone hand in hand with digitalization and, on the other, to the transformation of everyday life into a stage, into a show—in which, however, it is not the state of exception but affective normality that is to be established.

The meme, which I discussed in this first part as an example of digital blackface in the context of affect theory, is an example of a digital image culture in which affects are racialized in the form of animation and transmission and distributed as media for the production of *white* supremacy. I would now like to focus on it as an object that is not only racially charged, but also represents a technology of race. On the one hand, I am interested in the extent to which the meme can be understood as a specter that haunts the internet and digital culture as a reminder of the colonial history of dehumanization. On the other hand, I am interested in looking at this haunting in its antiracist potentials of undoing and reparation.

Memetic Specters

The introduction to the *Critical Meme Reader* I (2021) states that memes combine two types of domination: that of social subjugation at the level of signification and that of machine domination at the level of asignification (Arkenbout and Scherz 2021, 10).[7] While on the one hand they act on the basis of ideology and interpellation, on the other they act by means of deterritorialized codes or signs outside of a reference to human subjectivity. Insofar as the nonrepresentative logic takes precedence within information and computer technology, memes can also be understood as media that are less powerful due to their content than their machinic dimension. Due to this asignifying dimension, they are referred to in the introduction as "mutating energy" (ibid., 11), as "bastard" (ibid., 8), "informational obesity" (ibid., 11), or "perverse delight" (ibid.).

I want to argue that these classifications mark memes as technologies of race, that is, as technologies organized around the presupposition of racist categorizations, as Ramon Amaro (2022, 13) explicates using the example of machine learning. The meme is thus operative at the level of a machinic

---

7   This paragraph is based in part on my text "Meme(tische) Gespenster," published in German (Köppert 2025a).

dimension whose attributions as "perverse," "obese," and "mutated" repeat the racist history in which technology was constituted on the basis of Blackness as an abstraction of signification. Memes are thus haunted by a history that links Blackness to asignification or objecthood and to the associated pleasure in the spectacle of the other and the monstrous. This spectacularization of Blackness as an object or apparatus in the context of minstrelsy, which is decisive for the history of technology, has been demonstrated by Louis Chude-Sokei (2016), among others, using the example of Joice Heth. In *The Sound of Culture: Diaspora and Black Technopoetics*, he describes how in 1835 P. T. Barnum, an American showman and "pioneer" of the "modern circus," presented Heth, a Black enslaved woman, alongside the most famous machine of the time—the Mechanical Turk chess machine—for the purpose of spectacle and curiosity in Boston (2016, 21—26). In this demonstration, Heth is shown as an apparatus, whereas the machine of the Mechanical Turk is insinuated as human-like. The uncanny valley of similarity between human and machine is traversed by means of an image of Black femininity (ibid., 23), which stands for the dissimilarity or mutation of an understanding of computers that can be apostrophized with signification (see also Köppert 2025b). The dissimilarity that is required in rela-tion to similarity in order to accept technology instead of humans is generated by the fact that Black femininity is performed as machinic in the sense of a wooden surface or affective opacity. This opacity is important for the asignify-ing contagion or machinic subjugation of the human being. What is left out is the association of Black femininity with the system of machinic signification or the idea of a computer capable of inner depth.

With reference to the meme as mutating energy in the sense of asignifica-tion, the digital present is haunted by this history of minstrelsy and the meme is the specter of this performative dehumanization. As such, it does not operate on the level of what can be seen in the meme, but what can be affectively perceived with the meme without having to be aware of it (Dixon-Román 2021). Following Ezekiel Dixon-Román, it could be said that I am interested in the "haunting logics of colonialism in the epistemology of [meme]-technology" and the question of the extent to which blackface, also with regard to memes, "represents the link between centuries and the primary manifestation of a racialized version of what counts as the uncanny" (Chude-Sokei 2016, 15)—"that unsettling sense of familiarity and difference as when we encounter dolls, masks, anthropomor-phized machines, and ... blacks in a time when their humanity continued to be in question" (ibid., 15).

The question is to what extent the uncanniness that accompanies the meme as a ghost of colonial-racist pasts is also the condition of the possi-bility of addressing reparation and thus reorientation (Dixon-Román 2021, 5). The unsettling feeling of affectively registering something familiar—blackface minstrelsy—with the "You Get a Car" meme recursively unfolds Blackness as a asignifying apparatus and affecting spectacle. According to Ezekiel Dixon-Román, however, this temporality of recursion that is central to haunting is not characterized by a self-identical repetition (ibid., 4). Instead, due to recursion, it is enriched with contingencies and indecisions. In this sense, haunting conditions the possibility for the transformative power of the creative indecision of Blackness (ibid., 5). This is an operation of Black techno-conjuring. Dixon-Román describes this Black technoconjuring of indecision that cannot be calculated by machine systems. He uses the example of deepfakes made with Generative Adversarial Networks, which have blurred dots or mismatched accessories that he interprets as diffractive wave patterns in Karen Barad's sense, that is, patterns of overlap that "make a difference because they produce differences" (ibid.). He sees the double face of haunting in these patterns: the exhumation of colonized bodies "in the violent wake of the algorithm" (ibid.) and the potential to change the logic of the systems.

The magic of haunting, as described by Dixon-Román using the example of algorithms, cannot be easily translated to memes, even though algorithms play a role in their dissemination. Nonetheless, with recourse to the "You Get a Car" meme, I would like to suggest that it too has an inherent magic that operates not only as a revenant of colonial-racist pasts, but also as a way of opening up the possibility of reparation or undoing violence. With regard to the aforementioned GIF version, it is striking to what extent the loop produces the animation described above while at the same time restricting the radius of movement. On the other hand, however, a movement is created that not only insinuates a dance movement in the up and down or back and forth triggered by looping, but also creates a certain blurriness, a slight dizziness. I understand this dizziness in the sense of the specter's two-facedness and as a force of the uncanny, which, according to Samira Kawash, can be described as decolonial because it can neither be directed teleologically towards certain goals of liberation, nor can it be traced in social reality (Kawash 1999, 239). Rather, this force takes place in the technological asignification of Black conjuring. I understand the decolonial power of this Black conjuring, which I would like to propose as an uncanny deception of blurring movements, as exemplary of the ambiguity of the ghostly nature of memes. It articulates itself as an unsettling sense.

The materiality of the sensuality of this deception could also be linked to Armond R. Towns's concept of Black radicalism, derived from the zombie. In *On Black Media Philosophy*, Towns initially refers to Jussi Parikka's concept of zombie media, which, in the form of residues, electronic waste, and toxic chemicals, lead an afterlife and transform our world (Towns 2022, 151). Towns questions this media history or archaeology, which is always portrayed as raceless, by referring to the Black history of the zombie, which is not only a product of popular *white* imagination, but also of Black emancipation history in Haiti (ibid., 152). The idea of dying in the struggle for liberation, yet not being able to leave the plantations, but having to continue living as the undead according to the wishes of the *white* people, organized Black radicalism in Haiti, just as Black radicalism structured the fear of *white* people.

According to Towns, it is not the zombie as a metaphor that shapes fear, but rather the zombie as a material embodiment of the Black struggle. In contrast to Parikka's concept of the zombie, the materiality of this radicalism does not refer to the apocalyptic end of the world (Parikka 2012), but rather the affirmation of ambiguity. In Black radicalism, materiality is closely related to unpredictability. Or to put it another way: ambiguity is Black worldmaking (Towns 2022, 153). The GIF can also be understood in terms of world creation, in which materiality means ambiguity rather than objectivity. The dance created by editing and looping keeps the swaying of the meme as a zombie open in the sense of what Tavia Nyong'o understands as the delay of becoming an object in his examination of the public reenactment of Michael Jackson's zombie walk during the Occupy protests in London (Nyong'o 2012, 144).

In this delay—I would call it memetic ambiguity—Black worldmaking occurs, again following Towns. So even though the "You Get a Car" meme perpetuates the cycle of accumulation through the dehumanization-related dispossession of Black femininity, the swaying, dizzying zombie dance of the animated meme also enacts an incalculable form of Black worldmaking. This is an expression of Black radicalism, a right to reparations, as Towns explains in reference to Fred Moten and Stefano Harney (2013), which is located in the discovery of an alternative epistemology of meme technologies (Towns 2022, 155).

References

Ahmed, Sara. 2010. "Creating Disturbance: Feminism, Happiness and Affective Differences." In *Working with Affect in Feminist Readings*, edited by Marianne Liljestrom and Susanna Paasonen, 31—44. New York: Taylor & Francis.

Amaro, Ramon. 2022. *The Black Technical Object: On Machine Learning and the Aspiration of Black Being*. London: Sternberg Press.

Annuß, Evelyn. 2014. "Blackface and Critique: From T. D. Rice to Frederick Douglass." *Forum Modernes Theater* 29, no. 1—2: 64—72.

Arkenbout, Chloë and Laurence Scherz. 2022. "Introduction." In *Critical Meme Reader II: Memetic Tacticality*, edited by Chloë Arkenbout and Laurence Scherz, 10—18. Amsterdam: Institute of Network Cultures.

Blickstein, Tamara. "Affects of Racialization." In *Affective Societies: Key Concepts*, edited by Jan Slaby and Christian von Scheve, 152—164. New York: Routledge.

Dargiewicz, Anna. 2022. "Was gibt es hier zu lachen? Zu Internet-Memes als Quelle des Humors am Beispiel von Corona-Memes." In *Mit Humor ist nicht immer zu spaßen: An der Grenze von Spaß und Ernst*, edited by Mariusz Jakosz und Iwona Wowro, 169—188. Göttingen: V&R unipress.

Dixon-Román, Ezekiel and Ramon Amaro. 2021. "Haunting, Blackness, and Algorithmic Thought." *e-flux Journal* 123 (December 2021). https://www.e-flux.com/journal/123/437244/haunting-blackness-and-algorithmic-thought/. Accessed May 15, 2024.

Chen, Mel Y. 2012. *Animacies: Biopolitics, Racial Mattering, and Queer Affect*. Durham, NC: Duke University Press.

Chow, Rey. 1993. "Postmodern Automatons." In *Writing Diaspora: Tactics of Intervention in Contemporary Cultural Studies*, 55—72. Bloomington: Indiana University Press.

Chude-Sokei, Louis. 2016. *The Sound of Culture: Diaspora and Black Technopoetics*. Middletown: Wesleyan University Press.

Chun, Wendy. 2012. "Race and/as Technology." In *Race after the Internet*, edited by Lisa Nakamura and Peter Chow-White, 38—60. New York: Routledge.

Eggers, Maureen Maisha et al. 2005. "Konzeptuelle Überlegungen." In *Mythen, Masken und Subjekte: Kritische Weißseinsforschung in Deutschland*, edited by Maureen Maisha Eggers, Grada Kilomba, Peggy Piesche, and Susan Arndt, 11—13. Münster: Unrast Verlag.

Galip. Idil. 2021. "The 'Grotesque' In Instragram Memes." In *Critical Meme Reader I: Global Mutations of the Viral Image*, edited by Chloë Arkenbout, Jack Wilson, and Daniel de Zeeuw, 27—39. Amsterdam: Institute of Network Cultures.

Gehlen, Dirk von. 2020. *Meme: Muster digitaler Kommunikation*. Berlin: Verlag Klaus Wagenbach.

Harney, Stefano and Fred Moten. 2013. *The Undercommons: Fugitive Planning & Black Study*. Brooklyn: Autonomedia.

Hartman, Saidiya V. 1997. *Scenes of Subjection: Terror, Self-Making, and Slavery in Nineteenth Century America*. Oxford: Oxford University Press.

Jackson, Lauren Michele. 2019. *White Negroes: When Cornrows Were En Vogue ... and Other Thoughts on Cultural Appropriation*. Boston: Beacon Press.

Kawash, Samira. 1999. "Terrorists and Vampires: Fanon's Spectral Violence of Decolonization." In *Frantz Fanon: Critical Perspectives*, edited by Anthony C. Alessandrini, 239—240. London: Routledge.

King, Andy. 2021. "Weapons of Mass Distraction: Far-Right Culture-Jamming Tactics in Memetic Warfare." In *Critical Meme Reader I: Global Mutations of the Viral Image*, edited by Chloë Arkenbout, Jack Wilson, and Daniel de Zeeuw, 217—235. Amsterdam: Institute of Network Cultures.

Köppert, Katrin. 2022. "Oprah Memes: Dis-articulations of Affect." In *Critical Meme Reader* II: *Memetic Tacticality*, edited by Chloë Arkenbout and Laurence Scherz, 226—236. Amsterdam: Institute of Network Cultures.

Köppert, Katrin. 2025a. "Meme(tische) Gespenster." TFMJ *Journal for Theatre, Film and Media Studies* 3—4, Twilight Zones: 245—257.

Köppert, Katrin. 2025b. In print. "Zur Technopoetik von Holz: Flüchtige Ontologien digitaler Differenz." In *Matters of Difference: Filmische, mediale und diskursive Differenzverflechtungen*, edited by Natalie Lettenewitsch, Sabine Nessel, and Tullio Richter-Hansen. Berlin: Neofelis.

Köppert, Katrin. 2025c. "'Knowing Memes Means Knowing the Internet as Irrevocably Black as Fuck': Memetische Enteignung und/als Emanzipation." *Zeitschrift für Medienwissenschaft* 33, no. 2, Aneignungen revisited: Memes: 45—54.

Moebius, Simon. 2018. "Humor und Stereotype in Memes: Ein theoretischer und methodischer Zugang zu einer komplizierten Verbindung." *kommunikation @ gesellschaft* 19: 1—23. https://nbn-resolving.org/urn:nbn:de:0168-ssoar-56036-3. Accessed May 15, 2024.

Mori, Masahiro. 2012. "The Uncanny Valley." IEEE *Spectrum*. June 12, 2012. https://spectrum.ieee.org/the-uncanny-valley. Accessed May 15, 2024.

Ngai Sianne. 2005. *Ugly Feelings*. Stanford: Harvard University Press.

Nowotny, Joanna and Julian Reidy. 2022. *Memes: Formen und Folgen eines Internetphänomens*. Bielefeld: transcript.

Palmer, Tyrone S. 2020. "Otherwise than Blackness: Feeling, World, Sublimation." *Qui Parle: Critical Humanities and Social Sciences* 29, no. 2: 247—283.

Palmer, Tyrone S. 2017. "'What Feels More Than Feeling?' Theorizing the Unthinkability of Black Affect." *Critical Ethnic Studies* 3, no. 2: 31—56.

Sheehan, Tanya. 2014. "Looking Pleasant, Feeling White: The Social Politics of the Photographic Smile." In *Feeling Photography*, edited by Elspeth Brown and Thy Phu, 127—157. Durham, NC: Duke University Press.

Steyerl, Hito. 2011. "In Free Fall: A Thought Experiment on Vertical Perspective." *e-flux Journal* 24 (April 2011). www.e-flux.com/journal/24/67860/in-free-fall-a-thought-experiment-on-vertical-perspective/. Accessed May 15, 2024.

Yao, Xine. 2021. *Disaffected: The Cultural Politics of Unfeeling in Nineteenth-Century America*. Durham, NC: Duke University Press.

Websites and Online Sources

"Don't Post Oprah Memes if You Are Not Black." *Daily Mail*. March 12, 2021. www.dailymail.co.uk/femail/article-9355601/White-non-black-people-told-NOT-share-Oprah-memes-digital-blackface.html. Accessed February 8, 2024.

Jackson, Laureen Michele. "We Need to Talk About Digital Blackface in Reaction GIFs." *Teen Vogue*. August 2, 2017. www.teenvogue.com/story/digital-blackface-reaction-gifs. Accessed February 8, 2024.

"Oprah's 'You Get a Car.'" N. d. *Know Your Meme*. https://knowyourmeme.com/memes/oprahs-you-get-a-car. Accessed September 10, 2024.

"Oprah Winfrey Pays Homage to THAT iconic 'You Get a Car' Meme as She Takes the Stage in Slinky Dress that Showcases Slim Figure after Weight Loss Drug Use." *Daily Mail*. January 15, 2024. www.dailymail.co.uk/tvshowbiz/article-12963521/Oprah-Winfrey-pays-homage-iconic-meme.html. Accessed February 8, 2024. Also: www.tiktok.com/@dailymail/video/7324229574391450926. Accessed September 10, 2024.

On Arab Masquerades and Necropolitics: Invisibilization and Hypervisibilization in Israeli Popular Culture

Raz Weiner

Performance scholar Katrin Sieg coined the term ethnic drag in her book on racial, ethnic, and gender mimicry in Germany, where she extends the category of drag to include cross-ethnic performances. For Sieg, ethnic drag stands for a practice that

> excludes the material bodies of cultural Others and appropriates or ventriloquises their voices. The displacement, which reiterates the symbolic of colonial histories and attendant subject formations, instructs spectators how not to see the power and property relations that underwrite constructions of nationality even after race was elided from official discourse. It offers a critical vantage point from which the internal logic of nationality, race, and gender can be understood, as well as marking the locus of its most acute internal instability. (Sieg 2009, 86)

Not unlike the early 1990s discourse of gender performativity (Butler 1990), Sieg identifies the operations of drag as an interruption of regimes of perception and as a marker of their instability. However, several difficulties emerge from her concept of ethnic drag. Firstly, although taking care not to "postulate gender, sexuality, and race as analogues" (Sieg 2009, 22), the very grouping of her different case studies reflects an understanding of drag as reliant on performances of crossing between binary categories. Sieg also ignores the genealogies of practice and etymology of the term, which she refers to as "classic drag" (Sieg 2009, 28); this is imbricated with particular traditions of queer performance and, when attended to form within the idiosyncratic logic of its practitioners, is not necessarily synonymous with crossing, bending, or even with mimicry. Secondly, Sieg's careful and convincing attempts to create an epistemology through which to comprehend a wide range of heterogeneous representational performance practices hinges on the study of nation, national subject formation, and "the intricate ways in which race ... and sexuality" are predicated on [the nation] and vice versa" (Sieg 2009, 23). While this conceptual orientation may be adequate for the German or even broader Western European context, with its particular traditions of nationalism, colonialism, fascism, and performance, it falls short in the context of Israel-Palestine, where the cultural tropes I explore are located. In fact, the prevalent assumption of the sameness of national formations problematizes Sieg's alignment of heterogeneous materials such as Lessing's *Nathan the Wise* (*Nathan der Weise* 1779) to those studied by historian Eric Lott on the nineteenth and twentieth-century American minstrel show, for example (1995), even if in both cases white people masked as non- or other-than white people. While Sieg's archive is rooted in and resulting from a European national project generating its constitutive Others in the form of (racial, ethnic, religious, sexual, etc.) minorities, Lott's subject material is constituted by settler-colonial power relations. As such, the mimicry and impersonation of Blacks in the US cannot be isolated from the function of exogenous groups (whether as enslaved or as immigrant laborers) who are meant to replace indigenous labor (Mamdani 2015). The absence of this perspective from the well-established study field of American blackface and minstrelsy—an influential scholarship hinging on the American discourse of race, which informs the study of tropes of racial mimicry worldwide—represents an acute gap in research.

This gap becomes clear with regard to other geopolitical contexts. In his study of the history of blackface in Hebrew-speaking Israeli theater, cultural anthropologist Eitan Bar-Yosef cites performance scholar Catherine Cole, who notes that what made the US-American minstrel show so racist "was that blackness and African American culture became the unequivocal signifier for ignorance, disorder and the grotesque" (Cole in Bar-Yosef 2013, 128). However, Bar-Yosef contends, "outside the United States, blackface could attain different meanings, divorced from the ideological weight associated with the specific race hierarchies germane to a particular culture" (ibid.). This is an important qualification in relation to studies such as Cole's on blackface in postcolonial Ghana (Cole 2001), Nadia Davids and Chinua Thelwell's on blackface in South Africa (Davids 2013; Thelwell 2013), Tracy Davis on minstrels in Britain (Davis 2013), or Halifu Osumare on mimicry of Blacks in Japanese Hip-Hop (Osumare 2001). However, the relevance of the US-American minstrel show as a product of settler culture, when compared to racial mimicry of Blacks in the 1950s and 1990s Habima, i.e., Israeli national theater productions of the racially charged musical *Cry the Beloved Country*, is entirely missing from Bar-Yosef's analysis.[1] Such research is oriented to a perspective of hegemonic experiences of empire and nation, risking the enhancement of settler-colonial processes rather than advancing their exposure and critique.

In turning to Sara Ahmed's phenomenological approach (Ahmed 2006), I instead pose the question of whose identity and agency were relegated to the background and made "invisible" with regard to contemporary Israeli popular culture. This analysis points to the understanding of performances of racist mimicry of Arabs within this context in order to pose a more general claim: that there is a continuum between ethnic mimicry and necropolitics (Mbembe 2003). I compare two audiovisual examples, each with distinct aesthetics, that together emblematize a near-dichotomy of strategies of defacement by means of representation. I read them as the two ends of the same technology of visuality. While one presents a general caricature of an Arab singer, the other capitalizes on the hyperrealistic impersonation of Palestinians. In both of them, the face of the Palestinian Other is out of focus for the Israeli and international viewer, impossible to discern and therefore dehumanized. These seemingly benign forms of popular culture are consumed, celebrated, normalized and identified with uncritically, not by a fundamentalist minority of messianic settlers, but by the mainstream of Israeli society and a significant share of global viewership. Contrary to the prevalent appeal to exceptionality in the Israeli case, I contend that a degree of the necropolitical is endemic to any case of ethnic drag practice embedded in colonial relations. Shefita and Fauda are but a suffocating reminder that the stakes of ethnic mimicry, appropriation, and the theatrical (ab)use of an/other's face are not the insult or the political incorrectness but the facilitation of real destruction of real bodies, homes, and lives.

Shefita, Fauda, and The Necropolitical Hypercontemporary

Shefita is a peculiar though resilient phenomenon in Israeli popular culture, often regarded as a multicultural innovation. A persona created by the Jewish-Israeli performer Rotem Shefi, Shefita specializes in covering English songs with a unique twist: using a fake grotesque Arabic accent. The television series *Fauda* (in Arabic فوضى; "chaos" or "disorder") fictionalizes the activity of a specialized

---

1   Habima (Hebrew: The Stage) is Israel's national theatre. Founded in 1918 in Moscow as an avant-garde Hebrew-speaking theatre group, their immigration to Palestine in 1931 (officially endorsed as a national theater in 1958) was a well-publicized symbolic milestone of Zionist settlement and naturalization of the settlement project by means of erecting national institutions (see Tartakovsky 2013).

security force unit of "Mista'arvim" whose members disguise themselves as Palestinians and infiltrate Palestinian society to collect intelligence and execute "sensitive" operations. Created by Israeli-Jewish makers, both Shefita and *Fauda* rely on the representation of an Arab Other, articulating its meanings and symbolic economies. The emergence of two such distinct cases of popular representation of "Arabness," in the case of Shefita and of Palestinians in that of *Fauda*, is intriguing when considered against the backdrop of Jewish-Israeli public discourse. In the last two and a half decades, public opinion in Israel has sweepingly gravitated towards nationalistic, separatist, and xenophobic sentiments. Since the Second Intifada in 2000, Palestinian citizens of Israel have gradually been marked as external to the state's body-politic de facto, a trend visible in openly ethnocentric legislation and culminating in the parliamentary discourse leading up to the 2022 elections and their aftermath (Arablouei 2024; Alterman 2022). The legitimacy accorded by the Israeli mainstream to, and its compliance with, the state-sanctioned violence and military oppression of Palestinians in the West Bank and especially Gaza have reached unprecedented heights. Within this political and social climate, the appearance and popularity of the two performance tropes is at least conspicuous. It encourages us to rethink popularity as an indicator of social trends and a decipherer of cultural currents as biopolitical. What does the impersonation of an "Arab" or of "Palestinians" signify within contemporary Israeli culture? I propose that— in a manner which exposes inherent contradiction with nationalism—the more violence is directed towards Palestinians, the more visibly they cohere as political subjects. The related but essentially different examples of Shefita and *Fauda* outline two strategies of disavowal emanating from this (apparent) paradox. While *Fauda's* ethnic drag capitalizes on extreme mimetic adjacency and is more impervious to criticism (claiming to "give a face to the other side"), Shefita's Othering masquerade dialectically opens itself to decolonizing trajectories.

Although significantly routed within the local contexts of their formation, both Shefita and *Fauda* have proliferated and are being viewed globally through online streaming platforms. Shefita was titled "the Arab diva who broke the internet" after viewings of her music-video exceeded a million views on YouTube in August 2015 (*Orly & Guy Morning Show*). *Fauda* is the first Israeli television production not only to be bought by the global streaming giant Netflix for distribution but also production, rebranded as a Netflix Original in November 2016 (Shechnik 2016). This made the show's second season an international coproduction rather than a singly Israeli cultural product. Both Shefita and *Fauda* are also reported to have been watched with fascination in the Arab world (Noriel 2017), traditionally regarded in Israel as hostile or oblivious to Israeli content. The exceptional attention directed towards these two performances of ethnic drag and their commercial success highlights their relevance for the study of contemporary cultural representations and the public they assemble globally. Furthermore, they bring to the fore the role of new viewing cultures in commodifying and circulating local discourses of performance and their demurral of the local-global binary. As such, they expose how networks of racist violence and occupation exceed the local and—again, the national—through commodification, which in turn normalizes and whitewashes violence. We should think of them and theorize them as produced and perpetuated by global networks of power, dovetailing, or as it appears in this case, foreshadowing, disaster capitalism, arms trade (Klein 2008), and even genocide.

Shefita's FreeFrom Arab

Rotem Shefi is a trained singer-songwriter who has attempted to break into the Tel Aviv music scene for several years. While this did not happen to Shefi, it did happen to her made-up persona, Shefita, whose cover version of Radiohead's 1990s hit song *Karma Police* went viral on YouTube in 2013 (Shalev 2003). Shefi features in the video dressed in an oriental garment and riding an old horse cart in the streets of Jaffa's gentrified flea market. Two distinctly Arab markers of the cover version are the use of instruments typical of Arabic classical music and Shefi's accent. The latter functions as the main signifier of Arab Otherness, as did the burnt cork marked Blackness in the US minstrel. This element is the most revealing of Shefi's practice as pejorative mimicry, exercised from an uncritical, privileged position and one that exceeds the innocent bad taste of mimicking another's speech. In the reality of segregation, surveillance, and population control in Israel, accents play a crucial role in official and unofficial systems of racial profiling and discrimination. Numerous documentaries and news reports in Israeli media have exposed how speaking Hebrew with a discernible Arabic accent results in fewer opportunities to attain a job, rent a flat, or enter a nightclub, even when "Arabness" is not signified through physical appearance, religious affiliation, or place of residence (Barbiro and Koperman 2010; Dahan and Rivlin 2015; Tzion 2021). The focus on the voice as the locus of racist mimicry is an elusive and often overlooked formal element in different traditions of ethnic drag. Lott remarks that "every time you hear an expansive white man drop into his version of Black English, you are in the presence of blackface's unconscious return" (Lott 1993, 5). Indeed, visual devices like blacking-up (or adorning prostatic long noses; Sieg 2009) are more readily policed and banned by liberal regimes of political correctness than the use of voice and accent. The anxiety around the tone of voice tends to take center stage in situations where the tone of the skin is inadequate to signify racial difference.

As Sieg shows in her work, such was the case in the performance tradition of Jewface in nineteenth to mid-twentieth-century Germany, capitalizing on what was known as the "Jewish voice" (Sieg 2009, 35).

But Shefi does not intend to parody or ridicule. She insists in her early interviews that her performance of Shefita is motivated by love and respect for Arabic culture. She offers the example of hearing the sound of the call for prayer coming from the mosque of the Arab village neighboring her native town as an example of personal relation and identification (Shalev 2013). The isolation of the accent component as a leading aesthetic device of mimicry is further enhanced by Shefita's refrain from actually speaking Arabic. This is perhaps more than anything due to Shefi's complete lack of knowledge of the Arabic language. Since *Karma Police*, Shefi has released at least five more music videos in which she covers English songs of Nirvana, Alanis Morrissett, and Aerosmith as Shefita. Although none of them has gained the outstanding online popularity of the first Karma Police video in 2013, Shefi has not continued to perform her own music. Her first interview as Rotem Shefi and not Shefita since 2013 was in 2023 (Mako 2023), and another in 2024, where in light of the October 7 attack, she renounced her Shefita. During this decade, she has only been interviewed as Shefita, insisting on speaking her Arabic-accented English.

As a cultural fiction, Shefita offers an abstract, updated quotation of Arabness with no source; a simulacrum. More than anything, Shefi's "Arab diva" lacks any marker of Palestinian identity or agency. In her early shows, Shefi made it a point to inform her audiences that Shefita was "born in a rich village between Dubai and Iran and accidentally arrived in Israel with which she fell in love immediately" (Brener 2015). As such, this fiction aligns the public she creates with the West-facing prosperity of the Gulf States, in which indigenous Palestinians are implicitly deducted from the sum group of "Arabs." In this way, Shefi provides Israeli audiences with a kosher oriental fantasy of a generalized Arab whose language and jokes they understand. This is a character that, by coming from the outside, orientates them as locals, indeed natives. In the world of this fantastic ethnic drag, the Palestinians whose mosque prayer calls have inspired Shefi and on whose lands of destroyed villages Shefi's native town was erected have never existed, nor has their language. Due to this characteristic of the Shefita act, I call this mode of ethnic drag "FreeFrom," following the logic of unhealthy food produce engineered to contain no sugar, gluten, caffeine, or fat, thus allowing consumers to eat it without risking their health. Shefita fictionalizes and trades an Arabness devoid of "Palestinianness" as signifying political claims and rights, and it is in this quality that her popularity inheres.

In fabulating Shefita's biography, Shefi foreshadowed the political reality which materialized with the signing of the Abraham Accords in 2020, consolidating diplomatic relations and mainly trade (Maoz 2020) between Israel, the

UAE, and Bahrain. Unlike the peace treaties between Israel, Egypt, and Jordan and the Oslo Accords with the PLO, the Abraham Accords ignore Palestinian claims completely. In this, the long-standing position of unrecognition and non-normalization of Israel at the expense of the Palestinians by the Arab states was broken. What served to recover Trump's and Netanyahu's waning support due to their failed coping with the COVID-19 crises (ibid.) now allowed Israelis to fly from Tel Aviv to Dubai and back without ever noticing the West Bank underneath—bypassing it as if it never existed. It's a fantasy of a Middle East free from Palestinians.

Considering Shefita solely as a cultural phenomenon within a nation risks mistaking it for cultural appropriation. This interpretation would assume some underlying societal-ideological and legislative systems that account for these minorities, defining and protecting them and their culture or failing to do so—a situation where the hegemonic group is reproduced by a dialectic relation to them. As cited earlier, in theorizing practices of impersonation of Native Americans in postwar Germany as a reaction to the Nazi genocide (by means of embodying a surrogate victim of genocide according to Sieg), Sieg finds that this ethnic drag "instructs spectators how not to see the power and property relations that underwrite constructions of nationality even after race was elided from official discourse" (Sieg 2009, 86). Here, however, the national—that is the Israeli-Jewish public gathering to face Shefita as their Arab Other—makes possible the unseeing of Palestinian Arabs and the reality of occupation. If they embrace her as an Arab, it is only as fiction, as a cartoon, and endorsing her seemingly expresses inclusivity, tolerance, openness, and mostly good humor. Though appropriation may alter an object, it inevitably preserves its existence and often enhances it. Whatever established signifiers of Arabness are at Shefi's disposal, which are very few, the context within which she operates necessarily frames her signification as erasure and elimination rather than appropriation, at least as far as Arabness pertains to Palestinians in Israel-Palestine. When we ask who Shefia is "free from," the violence of this act becomes far more apparent.

In a workshop I conducted with a mixed working group of Jewish and Palestinian youth in Jaffa in January 2017, I screened several of Shefita's music videos and asked the participants to comment. Most Palestinian participants had not seen Shefita before, and the first one to respond said, "I don't under-stand the words she is singing; is she from India?" When I explained that this performance was meant to signify an Arabic accent, most Palestinian partic-ipants burst out laughing. As many of the Jewish participants already knew Shefita before, their reactions oscillated between embarrassment and disbelief at the Palestinians' failure to decode Shefita's "Arabness," and they launched an avid defense of the talent and playful inventiveness of the singer. As part of the ongoing activity of an established political youth partnership (Sadaka-Reut NGO, https://reutsadaka.org/en/), the setting for the workshop was part of the organization's pedagogy of decolonizing education. Both Jewish and Palestinian youth group members, who, at the time of the workshop, had already worked together for several months, were familiar with each other and with a critical political discourse. Yet, the Jewish members of the group were unable to recognize the repercussions of the symbolic elimination of Palestinians generated by Shefita's act, and the Palestinian members struggled to articulate their resistance to it (indeed, how can one prosecute Shefita for appropriating Arab culture when a moment before one decoded her as Indian?). The Jewish participants highlighted Shefita's talent and comedic qualities by refuting any suggestion that the imitation might be problematic. A mere few took a critical stand towards it, deeming it racist or offensive. Only at this part of the discussion, where the gap between the two groups was exposed as phenomenological—what does one *see* or *not see*—did the Palestinian participants express their anger at both the performer and their fellow groupmates for endorsing her. It is not so much what Shefita *does* as much as what she *means* in the context of Israeli contemporary politics—or rather, what she does phenomenologically.

In 2019, Shefita participated in the reality TV song contest Hakokhav Haba (in Hebrew "rising star"), which nominates the Israeli representative for the 2019 Eurovision (mako.co.il). This show exposed her to millions of viewers and turned the discourse around her act and its questionable ethics into a heated debate in printed and social media. On the one hand, the acceptance and normalization of her act on such a magnified scale and the opportunity to voice objections to it, on the other, facilitate the "presencing" of power relations even when their articulation in discourse is still incoherent and vague. One such example was the initiative of Fakhri Sa'id, a Palestinian student of the Tel Aviv University College in Jaffa, to cancel her show on campus, leading to a televised debate between Shefi and Sa'id (Cohen and Loksh 2019). Through talking back to Shefita, Sa'id was able to perform a resistance to the broader mechanisms of oppression, greater and graver than the specific situation. In this, the made-up drag of ethic-crossing momentarily served to suspend the straightening devices of disavowal. The decoy that Rotem Shefi created and named Shefita was used inversely in this case as a concrete target for political dissent. It allowed denied power relations to become somewhat exposed.

Shefita's case frames drag as marking practices that produce phenomenological interference, an intervention that suspends or resists naturalized, normalized regimes of perception. As a practice of drag, Shefita's ethnic fiction challenges orientations: the ways concrete bodies and their significations are found in space (Ahmed 2006). The implication of masquerading as an Arab—even in the FreeFrom style exercised by Shefi—in a space devoted to the disavowal of Palestinian Arabs cannot but draw attention to how Arabness is constructed, to begin with, and, by that, reintroduce the disavowed Palestinian into view. This dynamic is further complicated in the following example of ethnic drag, where, in a completely opposite fashion to Shefita's, the mimicry of Palestinians claims the utmost detailed accuracy and authenticity.

Fauda's Superarab

The tactics of ethnic impersonation deployed in the action television fiction *Fauda* (2015) expose an opposite route of appropriation and erasure. The series portrays the activity of Mista'arvim—a specialized undercover military unit that undertakes sensitive operations within the Palestinian civilian areas of the West Bank. What "undercover" means in this context is that Jewish-Israeli soldiers are trained to mimic Palestinians to perfection, mastering typical styles of dress, walking, body language and dialect. In other words, the units of Mista'arvim use racial cross-dressing for military purposes. What the makers of *Fauda*, Lior Raz and Avi Issacharov, have done, in turn, is to use their military experience of Mista'arvim ethnic drag for entertainment purposes. As *Fauda* is now being broadcast in numerous countries, Raz and Issacharov can be said to have launched the entertainment equivalent of the Israeli security industry, which exports worldwide the technology and knowledge developed for the occupation, surveillance, and population control of Palestinians.[2] The abundance of Israeli manufactured weapons featuring in the series indeed suggest reciprocity which is more than a mere formal likeness of these two industries.

Fauda's allusion to performance traditions of racial mimicry is apparent already in its marketers' choice of visual language, presenting the main characters in a double picture, comparing them as they are dressed up as Palestinians and when they are dressed as "themselves," that is, as "Israeli," as "normal." Most likely unintended and uninformed, these images quote rather faithfully the aesthetic logic of nineteenth-century poster advertisements from US minstrel shows. Even the subtleties of typography are recruited to express the delicacy of mimicry when diacritic signs are replaced almost unnoticeably between the Arabic and the Hebrew logos. All of these are joined to the recurring theme to which considerable *Fauda* screen time is dedicated: the act of dressing up, applying makeup, dying hair and beards, perfecting accents, and mastering

---

2   The popular US series *Homeland* (2011) preceded *Fauda* (2015) but is itself an adaptation of the Israeli series *Hatoofim* (2010).

mannerisms. Through these means, the Israeli protagonists flawlessly transform into Palestinians. The spectacle and challenge of passing authentically,
pertinent to many mimetic practices, is a vital component in *Fauda's* dramatic
structure and its aesthetic appeal.

The stakes of ethnic mimicry are demonstrated in the first minute of the
first episode. The short scene opens with an aerial shot of the inside of a large
mosque, where people are seen praying. In the next shot, loud banging on
the mosque's doors is heard, joined by nervous cries for help, as an ill-look-
ing person is rushed into the main praying hall by two men and supposedly
a woman in a long black dress and hijab. They are asking the people in the
mosque to bring him water while the man is clutching his chest, suggesting he
might be having a heart attack. As the people who were praying gather around
them to help, the ill person quickly turns to one of them, pulling out a gun
while the group who brought him in follows suit, thus revealing themselves to
both the viewers and the Palestinian characters in the mosque as Mista'arvim.
They abduct one of the people in the mosque while threatening the others
with guns to keep them from interfering. When a person standing behind the
Mista'arvim pulls out a gun, he is quickly shot dead by the woman figure waiting
by the mosque's entrance. The next shot follows a car that had waited for the
Mista'arvim unit outside the mosque, into which they all climb and quickly drive
off. The woman removes her headscarf inside the vehicle, revealing herself as
a Mista'arev man. The narrative of the rest of the episode follows them, and we
never get to see the people who were left behind in the mosque. In this snap
performance of infiltration and abduction, ethnic impersonation and gender
cross-dressing unite. This synecdochic establishment scene confirms a state
of being in which, for Palestinians, no one and nowhere is safe, while for Israeli
Mista'arvim, nowhere and nothing is out of reach.

While conspicuously absent from Shefita's fantasy, the hyperbolic presence
of Palestinians in that of *Fauda* serves as a crucial point of comparison. The
series' commitment to authentic representation dictates that all characters are
depicted by actors of their respective national/ethnic group. Palestinians play
Palestinian characters and Jewish-Israelis Jewish-Israeli ones, respectively.
Furthermore, the makers have stated in an interview that special Palestinian
advisers were employed on the set to supervise the meticulously accurate
depiction of Palestinians in all scenes alongside military and secret service
experts (Noriel 2017). A non-Israeli friend who follows the show shared with me
that he often finds it difficult to distinguish the Israelis from the Palestinians
as, in many situations, the only clear distinction is indicated through the use of
either Hebrew or Arabic. This may bear on the very intelligibility of the show's
narrative, as much of the tension that sustains the plot emanates from the ability to disguise and infiltrate. Within *Fauda*, the Palestinian characters inevitably

serve as dupes whose failure to recognize the true Israeli identity of the soldiers serves as the ultimate indication of the mastery of the Mista'arvim's mimicry. The gender scholar Amy Robinson describes the act of passing as a "triangular theatre of identity," where "a member of the in-group witnesses the failure of a person outside the group to register the identity of another in-group member" (Robinson 1994, 716). Appropriating the model which originally describes the ways queers and people of color negotiate white and/or heteronormative environments, for the most part in *Fauda*, both the viewers and the Mista'arvim are set up as members of the same group and the Palestinians as the duped Other.³ This relationship is turned around at one point when a young widowed Palestinian woman dresses as an Israeli to blow herself up in a Tel Aviv night club, avenging the death of her husband by the Mista'arvim. Rather than signaling a potential reciprocity of passing, this scene seems to alert the danger of the reversal of mimicry as a weapon when Palestinians use it against Israelis. The roles of infiltrator and duped might have reversed, but the spectator remains the detector.⁴

The symbolic and aesthetic implications of *Fauda*'s performance of crossing are severe. Unlike Shefita, the appropriation of culture, dress, speech, and body language, all framed through the performance of authenticity and accuracy, are turned necropolitical (Mbembe 2003). Due to structural segregation and discrimination, the clear majority of Jewish Israelis are Arabic illiterate. At the same time, most Palestinians have at least some knowledge of Hebrew, and many have a complete mastery of it. In this reality, the Arabic lingual sphere remains to some degree shielded from hegemonic penetration and appropriation, preserving a Palestinian discursive zone to which most Israelis would find it difficult to enter. Priding themselves on bringing Palestinian Arabic to Israeli television primetime (Noriel 2017), *Fauda*'s makers fabulate and dramatize the piercing of this somewhat protected sphere, subtitling and making accessible to non-Arab viewers what until now was out of an immediate reach and gaze. This fictional dynamic of undermining Palestinian closed private spheres is extended in *Fauda* to physical spaces such as mosques, homes, bedrooms, and showers, where the camera invades and exposes. *Fauda*'s cinematic syntax pays special attention to the bodies of Palestinian women, where plot and filmography occasionally collide in providing opportunities to peek under hijabs and bourkas. The role of the detector assigned to the viewer through

---

3   Sieg also borrows Robison's "triangular theatre of identity" in her study of antisemitic Jewish impersonation on the German stage (see Sieg 2009, 19).

4   The second season, which aired in 2018, features more mimicry of Palestinians as Israelis. This might be related to Netflix's greater involvement in the script and production.

witnessing Palestinians being duped is thus extended to constitute them as the Mista'arvim themselves. It fictionalizes them as the infiltrators whose privileged gaze is permitted into life's most intimate and closed-off areas. The real-life precarity of Palestinian bodies routinely under occupation in the West Bank, where the first two seasons are set, provides all the opportunities and contextual legitimacy for this fantasy of absolute control.

To articulate the specific defacing mechanization of *Fauda* as ethnic drag, I turn to a 1993 critique of the feminist performance scholar Peggy Phelan on the implications of gender drag for women. Phelan argues that:

> within the economy of patriarchal desire, which frames ... male cross-dressing, the figure of the woman is appropriated as a sign to validate male authority. His authority is determined by how fully he can "wear" her; in wearing her, however, he renders her actual presence unnecessary. ([1993] 2005, 99)

Significantly, Phelan provided this observation in the context of the debate surrounding Jennie Livingston's film *Paris is Burning* on Harlem drag balls of the 1980s (Livingston 1990). Since then, not only the binary approach that discusses the symbolism of drag in terms of "man-dressed-as-woman" was challenged by queer theory and more forcefully by queer performers and their practice, the very use of the term and the development of queer performance since rendered it partial and insufficient. However, when adapted to the context of the kind of ethnic drag that is circulated, even celebrated, in *Fauda* and later in the posted images of IDF soldiers, Phelan's position is rather useful.

The form of symbolic displacement and erasure of the Palestinian agency that takes place in *Fauda* is doubled. First, in paraphrasing Phelan's insight, the mimicry of Palestinians is constructed so convincingly that it constitutes the Mista'arev as a potential surrogate. Its aesthetics imply that the "adorning" of Palestinians constitutes an exciting element of contemporary Israeliness. Similarly, Philip Deloria places the assimilative practice of "playing Indian" to white Americans (Deloria 1998, 7). Secondly, within *Fauda*'s fiction, the Mista'arvim characters are very good at talking like them, walking like them, falling in love with other Palestinians like them, even resisting Zionist colonialism like them, to the extent that "real" Palestinians are deemed somewhat redundant. The excess of drag takes this logic further precisely because it is a performance, a costume. The Mista'arev represents a fantasy in which an Israeli is not only everything a Palestinian can ever be but more. Firstly, because he is protected and guided by the powerful apparatus of the Israeli intelligence and security forces. This is realized in *Fauda* through the recurring drone images of Palestinian cities and the role of the commander who is streaming intelligence and tipping off the soldiers in action through an unseen earphone, endowing them with a clear strategic advantage over the less technologically advanced Hamas warriors. Secondly, while Palestinian agency is static and predetermined, the Mista'arev is both Israeli and Palestinian, alternately and never together. It consumes and contains everything. If Shefita fashions a palatable Arabness, free-from Palestinian reference, *Fauda*'s Mista'arev not only can substitute the Palestinian Arab; he represents an improved model: a "Superarab."

*

Fauda's third season, which aired in 2020, became the only representation of Gaza and Gazans on Israeli TV screens outside the regular circulation of bombing footage on the news. Its fourth (2022; On Netflix 2023) focused on Hezbollah in Lebanon and, like the third season, followed a plotline of kidnapping of Israelis. My case studies and conclusions predate the unfathomable destruction of Gaza and the genocide of its people at the hands of the Israeli army since 2023 (see Mordechai 2024). However, in an interview with an American newspaper in March 2024, *Fauda*'s makers announced that its fifth season, which is currently in the making, will deal with the Hamas attack of October 7, 2023, and its aftermath. Lior Raz explained:

> We try to give faces to the other side and feel compassion for the other side ... Now I assume it's going to be very hard to do that ... I don't think it will be possible to show Hamas as humans, but we have to bring a good story ... (Cohen 2024)

Fauda's camera desecration of intimate Palestinian spaces is echoed in a social media trend which proliferated during 2024, after Israel's invasion of Gaza: IDF soldiers photograph themselves presenting and often modeling women's undergarments in houses they have destroyed. Outing these private, regularly hidden-away items asserts a similar testimony of complete and utter control over Palestinian lives and fate. Its often homoerotic stance and its deliberate act of humiliation notwithstanding, the dragging in these images participates in the reductive dissection of Palestinian people to materiality, to a garment and a makeup, to mannerism and a gait to be mimicked, to props on a set. The displaced dresses and lingerie items on the bodies of IDF soldiers become the negative space of its displaced or murdered owners.

References

Ahmed, Sara. 2006. "Orientations: Toward a Queer Phenomenology." *GLQ: A Journal of Lesbian and Gay Studies* 12, no. 4: 543–574. doi. org/10.1215/10642684-2006-002.

Alterman, Jon. 2022. "Israel's Rightward Shift." *Center for Strategic & International Studies.* November 29, 2022. www.csis.org/analysis/israels-rightward-shift. Accessed September 10, 2024.

Arablouei, Ramtin. 2024. "The Rise of the Right Wing in Israel." NPR. March 7, 2024. www.npr.org/2024/03/07/1198908601/throughline-the-rise-of-the-right-wing-in-israel. Accessed September 10, 2024.

Barbiro, Rafi and Maya Koperman. 2010. "'Aravia? Lo relevanti' kshegizanut venadlan nifgashim" (Arab? not relevent': when racism and real estate meet). *Ynet.* December 29, 2010. www.ynet.co.il/articles/0,7340,L-4003547,00. html. Accessed September 10, 2024.

Bar-Yosef, Eitan. 2013. "Zionism, Apartheid, Blackface: 'Cry the Beloved Country' on the Israeli Stage." *Representations* 123, no. 1: 117–153. doi.org/10.1525/rep.2013.123.1.117.

Brener, Mai. 2015. "Miri Paskal Meachoraichh: Hikonu Lehitahev BeShefita (Wtachout Miri Paskal: Get Ready to Fall in Love with Shefita)." *Achhbar Ha'ir.* www.mouse.co.il/music/articles/1.3261266. Accessed August 23, 2024.

Butler, Judith. 1990. *Gender Trouble: Feminism and the Subversion of Identity.* New York: Routledge.

Cohen, Haley. 2024. "Next Season of 'Fauda' Will Take on Oct. 7 Attacks, Show Creators Say." *Jewish Insider.* March 12, 2024. https://jewishinsider. com/2024/03/fauda-oct-7-season-5-lior-raz-avi-issacharoff/. Accessed September 10, 2024.

Cohen, Nir and Alexandra Loksh. 2019. "Shefita al HaHofa'a SheButla: 'Lo Loeget LeAravim ve LeMizrahim Ela LeAnaship Tku'im'" (Shefita on the show's cancelation: "I do not mock Arabs or Mizrahis, only boring people"). *Ynet.* February 25, 2019. www.ynet.co.il/articles/0,7340,L-5469607,00.html. Accessed September 10, 2024.

Cole, Catherine M. 2001. *Ghana's Concert Party Theatre.* Bloomington: Indiana University Press.

Dahan, Naor and Haim Rivlin. 2015. "Gizanut BeAlbar: Lo Maskirim leAravim (Racism in Albar: No Renting to Arabs)." *Hadashot (News)* N12. www.mako. co.il/news-israel/local-q2_2015/Article-e88dabc95e62e41004.htm. Accessed September 10, 2024.

Davids, Nadia. 2013. "'It Is Us': An Exploration of 'Race' and Place in the Cape Town Minstrel Carnival." *TDR The Drama Review* 57, no. 2: 86–101. doi. org/10.1162/DRAM_a_00262.

Davis, Tracy C. 2013. "'I Long for My Home in Kentuck': Christy's Minstrels in Mid-19th-Century Britain." *TDR The Drama Review* 57, no. 2: 38—65. doi. org/10.1162/DRAM_a_00262.

Klein, Naomi. 2008. *The Shock Doctrine: The Rise of Disaster Capitalism.* First edition. London: Penguin.

Lott, Eric. 1995 (originally published 1993). *Love and Theft: Blackface Minstrelsy and the American Working Class.* New York: Oxford University Press.

Mamdani, Mahmood. 2015. "Settler Colonialism: Then and Now." *Critical Inquiry* 41, no. 3: 596—614. doi.org/10.1086/680088.

Mbembe, Achille. 2003. "Necropolitics." Translated by Libby Meintjes. *Public Culture* 15, no. 1: 11—40.

Mordechai, Lee. 2024. "Bearing Witness to the Israel-Gaza War." https://witnessing-the-gaza-war.com/.

Noriel, Yehuda. 2017. "Oto Hakfar (The Same Village)." *Ynet.* July 14, 2017. www. yediot.co.il/articles/0,7340,L-4987631,00.html. Accessed September 10, 2024.

Osumare, Halifu. 2001. "Beat Streets in the Global Hood: Connective Marginalities of the Hip Hop Globe." *Journal of American & Comparative Cultures* 24, no. 1—2: 171—181.

Phelan, Peggy. 2005. *Unmarked: The Politics of Performance.* New York: Routledge.

Robinson, Amy. 1993. "To Pass//In Drag: Strategies of Entering into the Visible." PhD dissertation, University of Pennsylvania.

Shalev, Ben. 2013. "Lama Rotem Shefi Mesalselet et Radiohead (Why is Rotem Shefi Singing Radiohead)." *Ha'aretz.* May 10, 2013. www.haaretz.co.il/gallery/music/.premium-1.2015009. Accessed September 10, 2024.

Shechnik, Raz. 2016. "Netflix rachsha et Fauda (Netflix bought Fauda)." *Ynet.* August 11, 2016. www.ynet.co.il/articles/0,7340,L-4875932,00.html. Accessed September 10, 2024.

Sieg, Katrin. 2009. *Ethnic Drag: Performing Race, Nation, Sexuality in West Germany.* Ann Arbor: University of Michigan Press.

Tartakovsky, Yelena. 2013. *Habima HaMoreshet Harusit (Habima The Russian Heritage).* Safar.

Thelwell, Chinua. 2013. "'The Young Men Must Blacken Their Faces': The Blackface Minstrel Show in Preindustrial South Africa." *TDR The Drama Review* 57, no. 2: 66—85. doi.org/10.1162/DRAM_a_00261.

Tzion, Hila. 2021. "'Hayiti maskira lach et hadira aval hashchenim yahargu oti" (I would have rented you the flat but the neighbors will kill me). *Ynet.* August 6, 2021. https://www.ynet.co.il/economy/article/syfgrzfyy. Accessed September 10, 2024.

STAGING (POST)COLONIAL
RELATIONS

Borrowed Plumes, Jesuit Drag, and Costumes as Uncontrollable Residuals

Karin Harrasser

In this article, I discuss a possible deep history of the practice of "dressing up as Indian," a deep history of adorning oneself with borrowed plumes. Who does it do, when and where and for what purpose? I argue that this history of appropriation should start in the early modern period, long before the modern, romanticized nineteenth-century image of "the North American Plains Indian" accompanied real fierce resistance to genocide all over the Americas. The first part of the chapter will engage with what could be called a drag appearance of an aristocrat as allegory of Lady America. It was staged and performed as part of European diplomatic encounters in the late sixteenth century. I will unfold the circumstances and intentions of this appropriation of the Indigenous "Other" in European cultural techniques of court diplomacy. A second part will look into what I tentatively call "Jesuit drag." I will comment on the accommodation strategy of Jesuit missionaries, especially their appropriation of indigenous concepts and figures for the sake of conversion in South America in the seventeenth and eighteenth centuries. The later subsections will also discuss cases of counterappropriation of Jesuit performance culture by indigenous people. I shall conclude with reflections on contemporary versions of the excess of mimesis that Édouard Glissant characterized as central for a "Baroque abroad in the world" (Glissant 1997, 77).

Borrowed Plumes: Duke Frederick Dresses Up as Lady America

In a carnival procession and as part of a "ring race," a tournament in medieval style, the protestant duke Frederick I of Württemberg presented himself in 1599—about one hundred years after the first contact with Abya Yala[1]—to guests

---

1   I use the term Abya Yala as is suggested by decolonial authors such as Silvia Rivera Cusicanqui. The term aims to correct the misnomer America for the double continent and is used by the Kuna of Panamá (see Cusicanqui 2020).

from the German countries as a powerful and sexually attractive, naked and tattooed, Lady America. The event is fairly well documented: we have drawings of the planned scenes that are archived in the graphic collection of the Stiftung Weimarer Klassik and a detailed description of the event by the schoolmaster M. Jacob Frischlin from 1602. Frischlin recorded what he saw (at least he gives us the impression of having been an eyewitness) in rhyme. Frischlin's description largely coincides with the drawings, giving us quite a vivid picture of the actual event.

Part of a diplomatic encounter of the German Protestant nobility, the ring race opened with scenes depicting adventurous encounters with Abya Yala. This theme was followed by other costumed performances of characters including the Assyrian King Ninus, the Persian King Cyrus, Alexander the Great, and Julius Caesar, as well as marches of Swabian peasants, Capuchin monks, etc. Frischlin opens onomatopoeically, echoing drum and pipe sounds, thereby dramatizing Frederick's entry as America:

> Vide pomp / pim / pom / vide / pomp / pim / pom / Hertzog Friderich komt / pom / pim / pom / Hertzog Friderich / Friderich kompt / er kommet / er kompt / America kompt / sie kompt / sie kommet / America kompt / die Könige kompt / sie kompt / sie kompt / das pimperle pom / das pimperle pom / pom / pom / Vide pomp / Vide pomp / das pomperle pom / pomp pimp pomp / etc. (Frischlin quoted after Bujok 2004, 14)[2]

Figure 1. Scene with Christopher Columbus and Amerigo Vespucci at the Stuttgart Court, Carnival 1599 (Stiftung Weimarer Klassik, from Elke Bujok, *Neue Welten in europäischen Sammlungen; Africana und Americana in Kunstkammern bis 1670*, Berlin, Reimer 2004, Abb. 1/1).

---

2   The arrival of Frederick as America is framed rhythmically, with evoked drumming sounds (pom, pomp, pomperle). The designations "Frederick" and "America" are used synonymously.

The characters leading the procession are noblemen in costumes of the explorers, Christopher Columbus and Amerigo Vespucci.

Frischlin reports and comments:

Derowegen wir ...	Therefore we ...
Christophorum Columbum & Vespucium	Christophorum Columbum & Vespucium
Americum	Americum
... beruffen lassen	... allow to ask
Mit dem Begeren	With desire
... daß sie uns ...	... that we may ...
als erfahrne Pelotten zu unser Schwester	as experienced travelers join our sister
begleyten wölten	which she approved without any com-
welches sie ohn einig Beschweren bewilligt.	plaints.
Den Indianern ähnlich schier	Resembling the Indians
Trugen gar seltzam Kappen auff	They wore strange caps
Gelb und blaw Taffet underm Hauff.	Yellow and blue taft under feathers.
Der erst Columbus sich nennet	The first called himself Columbus
Auß America sonst erkennet	Beyond America he was known as
Juncker Philip von Lamersheym	Juncker Philip of Lamersheym
Führt mit sich und in gleichem Schein	He carries with him and in the same
Dann Carle Egen war der andr	semblance
Americam welchr thet durchwandrn	Carle Egen, the other
Weil er drey Jahr drinn gwesen ist.	Who had travelled in America
(Frischlin quoted in Bujok 2004, 15)	He was inside for three years.
	(Trans. KH.)

Figure 2. Frederick I performing Lady America, Carnival 1599 (Stiftung Weimarer Klassik, from Elke Bujok, *Neue Welten in europäis n Sammlungen: Africana und Americana in Kunstkammern bis 1670*, Berlin, Reimer 2004, Abb. 1/6).

Frischlin's comment is interesting insofar as he informs the readers that Columbus and Vespucci—the Europeans with their borrowed plumes—looked exotic enough to "pass" as "Indians." Also, we know from his descriptions which real person portrayed which character. In the case of Carl Egen, who performed as Amerigo Vespucci, we learn that he had been to Abya Yala in real life and was probably chosen for this role because of this fact.

The next scene or image in the parade was a mythical water tree, from which it was said that water flowed all by itself. Theodor de Bry's *Arrival of Columbus in the New World* (1594/96) served as the basis of this image. As Elke Bujok (2004) has demonstrated, images from de Bry's publication provided the templates for much of the performance in general.

This is followed by the entrance of America, ergo Frederick I:

Die Künigin war also bkleydt	This is how the queen was dressed
Wie ich ungefehrlich dich bescheidt	I will inform You honestly
Auff ihrem Häupt hatt sie ein Cron	On her head she had a crown
Auß Federn gmacht	Made from feathers
wie ich verstohn	as I understand
Von Papengäy	From Papagai
blaw, grün und rot	Blue, green and red
Gleich wie ein schöner Krantz auffstoht:	High standing like a wreath
Die Schämen oder Masca war	Her mask resembled a beautiful woman
Eim schönen Weibsbildt ähnlich gar	
Darnach der Leib und gantze Wath	Her whole body
Wie eins nackenden Menschen stath	Appeared as if it was naked
Leibfarb mit schönen gülden Stucken	Painted and with golden pieces
Verschnürt war als wer es trucken	That were laced very close
Und glatt an Leib hinan geleimt	And smooth to the body
Hat hüpsch von weitem her gescheint:	And from far appeared very pretty:
Die Brüßt der Königin sah man hangn	The bosom of the queen that hang
Damit sie zierlich thete prangen	Emblazoned and petite
In Händen führt sie einen Stab	In her hands she carried a staff
Das Regiment ich gsehen hab	Decorated with feathers of a Papagai
Von Papengäy Federn gemacht	According to Royal
Nach Königlichem	Ornament and splendor.
Zier und Pracht.	(Trans. KH.)
(Frischlin quoted in Bujok 2004, 18)	

The performance is spectacular concerning gender codes even if we take into account that inversion and playfulness with regard to ethnic otherness and gender were part of the rhetoric of carnivalesque costuming in the early modern period (Christadler 2005). We have learned to read allegoric depictions of America as a seductive woman as an image legitimizing the colonizers' lust for conquest.[3] In the case of Frederick I, however, the case is more complicated: the ruler himself *embodies* America, wearing foreign tattooed skin and foreign feathers, which frame his/her appearance as a demonstration of power. Frischlin emphasizes how Frederic energetically swings himself onto a horse at the end of the performance and—still masked as America—opens the ring race, not showing the lightest trace of weakness. Nothing in the reports and depictions hints towards an ironic performance. Lady America is both attractive *and* powerful.

The framing story of the diplomatic encounter as a whole was that of a diplomatic mission of Lady America. It is documented in the acts of the event. The invitation letter to the other German nobles develops the narrative: it informs the prospective guests that America has come to Europe voluntarily and out of curiosity. The aim of her mission is to maintain good relations with the European courts and to improve knowledge about America in Europe:

... und sie zu wahrer Fortsetzung biß daher gehabter guter Correspondentz zwischen unser allerseits underhabenden Völckern in der Person freundtlich zu besuchen damit nicht allein jnen und jren Eynwohnern unser Gelegenheit desto besser bekandt werde sondern auch wir hingegen augenscheinlich sehen und erfahren was von jhrem rühmlichen Thun und Wesen [uns] mehrmahlen fürkommen ist. (Frischlin quoted in Bujok 2004, 21)

... and to visit them in person for the true continuation of the good correspondence that has existed between all our peoples, so that not only will our lifestyle be better known to them [Europeans] and their residents, but also that we on the other hand will see and learn about their praiseworthy actions and characters and about events there. (Trans. KH.)

This is the reason why the diplomatic host Frederick shows an affirmative, even idealizing identification with America. The male ruler performs as Lady America as he wants to be seen as representing progress and interest in new knowledge. Interestingly, the narrative was taken up enthusiastically by the guests and then spun on in a playful manner. In the letters of reply from noble visitors stored in the files, guests frame their appearance in relation to America's mission. Joachim Carlin von Braunschweig, for instance, replies in his future role of Julius Caesar. He narrates his planned visit as a diplomatic time travel. He writes that he (as Caesar) will gladly visit Stuttgart to fulfill his desire to become acquainted with beautiful America, and because he is curious

---

3   See Michel de Certeau's seminal analysis of Jan van der Straet's allegory of America, which depicts Amerigo Vespucci dressed in full ornat, carrying a flag and navigating instruments an America naked in a hammock (Certeau 1992, xxv—xxvi).

to see how Germany has changed in the last 1,600 years. In this letter, overseas travel and time travel coincide. Frischlin, in turn, extends this diplomatic fiction into the semantics of courtly love: a type of affective language to talk about the (mostly nonsexual) relationship with a noblewoman to prove loyalty to the lady's noble house. In his version, America had informed Caesar about her trip to Germany and Stuttgart, about her participation in the ring race, and had asked him to accompany her as a knight. Caesar is said to have granted her request, having burst into "gantze Lieb" ("full love," Frischlin quoted in Bujok 2004, 23) for her. An overlapping of semantics of sympathy: diplomacy between the German states framed as a courtship spanning across times.[4]

The staging of Frederick I as America was intended to surprise and amuse the visiting nobles and envoys and that was, of course, eminently political: the Protestant sovereign presented himself as self-confidently forward-looking in his identification with the "New World" and its inhabitants. The performance was also pointedly anti-Catholic and anti-Spanish, the identification with the "Indians" was deliberately targeted against the alleged (and de facto) oppression of the inhabitants of the new Catholic territories. On another occasion, Frederick I had a monastery and members of the Jesuit order set ablaze as part of a pyrotechnical spectacle in his Lustgarten (Weber-Karge 1989). That the Jesuit order was the focus of anti-Catholic propaganda is obvious, since the Jesuits were not only present as advisers at the Catholic courts, but also the organizers of the inquisition and therefore an important pillar of the papacy and of Spanish rule in Abya Yala. But they themselves made use of cultural appropriation and masking as part of the missionary methods.

Jesuit Strategies: Accommodation and Regulation

With this background of an identificatory, temporary incorporation of the "Other" in Europe in mind, I will now turn to the missionary methods of the Jesuits in Abya Yala. The Jesuit order (Compañía de Jesus) played a major role in the evangelization of Abya Yala, and for the production of knowledge about indigenous peoples in Europe. It has been argued that the Jesuits might have developed the first global, company-like structure, with a strong headquarters in Rome and independently acting franchises in many corners of the world,

---

4   The event has remained present in museum objects until today: the "Aztec" feather shields that were carried in the parade at the time (as documented in the acts) are still on display at the Landesmuseum Württemberg. https://de.m.wikipedia.org/wiki/Datei:Landesmuseum_W%C3%BCrttemberg_-_Kunstkammer1171.jpg, accessed October 27, 2023.

which were nevertheless linked back to the center via reports and other forms of written communication (Friedrich 2011). Recent research has shown that it was the elaborate channels of communication and the continuous exchange of reports that made the order such an important player of early modern globalization. These communications formed an epistolary empire of letters and reports, deeply embedded in the Catholic sphere of power and domination (Fechner 2015).

The question I want to address first, is why and how mimetic techniques were used to communicate the new faith in Abya Yala, and insofar the evangelization of indigenous peoples favored the transmission of European aesthetics. The Jesuits indeed developed a very efficient and sustainable form of what they called "conquista espiritual." The catchphrase was coined by the chronicler and first provincial of Paraguay Antonio Ruiz de Montoya. The Jesuit strategy consisted—as is quite well known, not least because of the Jesuits own apologetic publications—in "culturalizing" the indigenous people into the new faith. The Jesuits employed a strategy of inculturation that, conversely, meant that they were to accommodate themselves to the symbolic and linguistic systems they encountered. They were to adhere, at least in part, to the cultural norms of their "target groups," that is, to adapt to their way of life. In China, for instance, the Jesuits dressed as Buddhist monks, in Chiquitos—the region of my own research (Harrasser 2021)—they imitated spiritual (shamanistic) practices already in place. Jesuit padres were also the first ones to translate the Bible into native languages and to produce grammars (dictionaries) of the multiple languages they encountered and learned. It would be incorrect to say that physical violence played no role in the mission: there are quite a few testimonies indicating that (and how) duress, coercion, and threat were routinely used by the missionaries; but artistic and communicative means were more important—architecture, images, and especially: theater and music.

Respectively, Cosme and Bartolomé Bueno document a festive event in a Paraguayan mission in the eighteenth century, of course in an idealizing way:

This multitude of nations began to be brought under the rules of society [the Societas Iesu, KH] around the middle of the last [seventeenth, KH] century, by means of presents, persuasion and promises. Through the constancy of the missionaries in their endeavors and exertions, and at the cost of the lives of some of them, these wild beasts were tamed. They managed to make men out of them in order to make them Christians. In the process of reduction ample and regular towns were built ... magnificent temples were erected with beautiful ornaments, in which on festive days one can hear an excellent music of voices and instruments: organs, harps, harpsichords, violins string bases [*violones*], flutes, shawms, etc. (C. & B. Bueno quoted in Waisman 2011, 210)

Central recurring motifs in the reports on the so-called reductions, i.e., Jesuit settlements, are condensed here; and they are interwoven with the mimetic practices I will focus on: the ability of the Jesuits to construct a regulated and productive community, expressed in a musical performance of great virtuosity. Another motif is the formation of the settlements from a "multitude of peoples," that is, from culturally and linguistically diverse indigenous groups that hence-forth were subject to only one law. Another topos is the Jesuit strategy of evan-gelization with "gifts, persuasion, and promises" as an alternative strategy to forced conversion and threat of physical punishment. The idea and rules of the reductions, however, did not originate genuinely from the Jesuits. This form of settlement had already been tried out by other orders, e.g., by the Dominicans in Julí in the Andes (today Puno, Peru), and was desired, even prescribed by the Spanish empire. The reductions were—and this is the important political background—a measure for the Spanish king and his administration to gain an advantage in the ongoing conflict of interests between the Spanish crown and the conquistadores and the capitalist entrepreneurs, the *encomenderos*. As early as in the beginning of the sixteenth century, with the Leyes de Burgos (1512), the Spanish crown prescribed laws to protect indigenous individuals and communities from the most excessive forms of exploitation by the settlers. The conquistadors and colonial entrepreneurs opposed these laws in many places of South America. On the other hand, the *leyes* were meant to produce loyal subjects to the crown. As a consequence, the lives of indigenous people living in the Jesuit settlements were heavily regulated and controlled. In the sixth volume of the Leyes de Indias of 1681, it is then stated that "los Indios" were considered persons and that they could not be enslaved, that Spain was responsible for their protection from slave traders, as well as from exploitation in the *encomienda* and *mita*, the two forced labor systems. Furthermore, the law is supplemented by regulations on the way of life in the "Indian" settle-ments. It is stated that the reductions are

> the most convenient means to instruct the *Indians* in the holy Catholic faith and Christian laws, so that they forget the errors of their ancient rituals and ceremonies and live together policed. Reductions are the solution, so that the *Indians* are gathered in villages, no longer scat-tered and separated by hills and mountains.[5] (Paredes 1681, 6/II, trans. and emphasis KH)

---

5   "Los medios mas convenientes, para que los Indios sean instruidos en la Santa Fé Catolica, y Ley Evangelica, y olvidando los errores de sus antiguos ritos, y ceremo-nias vivan en concierto, y policia, ... resolvieron, que los Indios fuessen reducidos á Pueblos, y no viviessen divididos, y sepearados por las Sierras, y Montes" (trans. KH).

The act of "reducing" was conceived of as an act of gathering heterogeneous indigenous populations scattered throughout the countryside, with the aim of making them manageable and orderly subjects to the law of the king. The new order and the forced "forgetting" of idolatrous practices went hand in hand with *policía* and *concierto*, with government and community. The architectural layout of the settlements operationalized this comprehensive idea of "good government." The settlements were built according to urban patterns, as evidenced by the checkerboard layout of the villages, which was common for colonial urban foundations.[6] The Leyes de Indias envisioned the construction of a church with a door and lock as the first building activity (since the "Indians" were thought to lack awareness of property). Spatial and temporal discipline was considered central to the new order (e.g., Furlong 1962). Village settlements looked like European miniature towns organized around a main square and church. A sundial and a bell tower were erected with the church to fight the imputed indifference to organized work. Legal discipline was considered equally as important: respect for authority, the establishment of a firm social hierarchy, and gender relations. This included the introduction of a new form of family organization, namely, monogamy. Reading and writing were considered prerequisites of "buen policía," of good conduct. Local caciques and important families were given administrative responsibilities (e.g., in local jurisdiction) and played an important role in the local enforcement of Spanish law.

Since the reductions were conceived of as culturalization projects, the aim was to increase material well-being and to practice religion in an aesthetically advanced way. A great deal was invested here: the churches were magnificently decorated, musical instruments were brought to remote places, and workshops were quickly equipped to produce high-quality works of art for the churches, as well as musical instruments (trumpets, violins, even organs) (Waisman 2011, Toelle 2024).

If we take into account that the dominant model of the political economy of colonial biopolitics in many places was the violent enforcement of interests, enslavement, and extraction of bare life, even at the cost of the destruction of human life, the reductions appear as surprisingly early examples of a life promoting, an—in Foucauldian terms—"governmental" mode (Foucault 2004). However, the fact that the Jesuits operated less extractively in the reductions and governed less via coercion does not mean that they did not perform colonial power. Rather, the reductions can be conceived as experiments of a new form of government that combined rational planning, pastoral soul guidance, and

---

6   For the nexus between theatrical/musical practices and urban design see Baker and
     Knighton 2011, especially Baker's introductory essay.

cultural performance. It is important to embed such a Foucauldian reading of the reductions within a broader colonial perspective, as this demonstrates that the colonies provided a testing ground for both extractivist modes of politics that viewed life as a killable resource and life promoting modes of governance that were supported by mimetic techniques and cultural export (Harrasser and Rath 2016). The governmental mode relies heavily on knowledge about the culture and society one intends to transform and to include in the empire.

Ideas of good government as combined with politics of culture are at stake when dealing with the function of music as "softpower" in the Chiquitos region of Bolivia. Music was, as already mentioned, omnipresent in the reductions. It structured days, weeks, and yearly cycles, ecclesiastical celebrations, and commemorations, but it also accompanied the encounter with official visitors. Music was a means to literally incorporate basic attitudes and structures, and it was a tool to create new sensibilities. Anton Sepp and Martin Schmid, two Jesuit musicians, give lively impressions of the elements of music education in the reductions (Schmid 1988, Sepp and Böhm 1696): to incorporate a time structure, to learn to deal with written text as an authority, to exercise patience when copying scores, and, very centrally: to learn physical discipline in order to make controlled use of voice, muscles, extremities, breath, etc., according to Christian ideas of modesty and faithfulness. Music was seen as the royal road to experience the new religion as a conduct of life, which expresses an order of the whole creation as a harmonious cosmos. I also have the impression that music was used decidedly as a community-forming instrument to overcome linguistic differences, if one considers that in a reduction up to ten different languages (in the so-called *parcilidades*) were spoken. I want to stress that the experience of practicing music together operated as the enactment of Christian ideas of the cosmos and of creation in which everybody (or: every body) had their specific place. Musicmaking was employed to produce a sense for the common, a common sense and a hierarchy that connected remote villages with the Emperor in Spain and in heaven.

Imitatio: Jesuit Drag and Becoming Enemy

This brings me to the reactions of those who were to be converted to Jesuit attempts to implement a new faith, a new kind of society and rule. For it is clear that such forms of transmission work both ways, even if they involve hierarchical means of power. A major problem to trace these interactions is, that we do not have too many sources that speak about the indigenous perspective. But that the mission was quite successful, especially viewed in the *longue durée*, is evident: in the majority of areas where the Jesuits were active in the seventeenth and eighteenth century, Christianity remained dominant, even after the Jesuits were expelled from the country in 1767. It is immensely difficult to determine precisely why this is the case, and also, to what an extent the Christian doctrine was incorporated.

One explanation for the Jesuits relative "success" refers to commonalities in beliefs and social norms before the missionaries arrived, so that the new religion was able to "dock in" and produce an accommodated version. Let's look into music and dance. What kind of music and dance did the Jesuits encounter when they came to Chiquitos? Music, dance, and the enjoyment of chicha (corn beer) were part of rituals performed by experts within the communities. The Jesuits called these experts "sorcerers" or "priests"; we nowadays call them shamans. One padre, Juan Patricio Fernández (1729, 293—303), reports the practices of such an expert of the Maniacas community in detail: By exercising physical and spiritual techniques one becomes a *mapono*, a sorcerer/priest: by fasting, by consumption of drugs; by contact with animal spirits, such as bats; and by the illuminating experience of illnesses. The Jesuit talks about the *mapono's*, the shaman's "exercises and extasy" (ibid. 305). This vocabulary is exactly the one that is used for a Jesuit that goes through the famous Ignatic exercises: a Jesuit performing the exercises would fast and meditate, and probably he would flagellate himself with a whip. Also, the *mapono* uses gestures familiar to the European observer. For example, he sprinkles things and people with holy fluids. The Maniacas also organized elaborate "masses" for a "trinity," albeit not for the Christian trinity, but for what the padre calls a "trinity of devils": they report the trias of *Omequeturiqui* (Father), *Urasana* (Son), and *Uropo* (Holy Spirit).

For the ritual, "the temple" is divided in two parts, like a Catholic church. A curtain of twigs and leaves separates the zone where the villagers sing, dance, and drink. Only the shaman is permitted to enter the sacred area behind the curtain. He, like the Jesuit priest, delivers the pleas of the villagers, but he can also fly with the gods; he would fly, for instance, lying in the lap of *Urasanas* mother, an analog to the Holy Virgin. Sometimes, Fernández tells us, the whole building would rise in the air and land again with a big noise. All of this, taken together, results in a scenario that resembles the performances and images of Jesuit Catholicism.

On the other hand, for the Maniacas, the Jesuit padres must have resembled their own holy men: the padres cultivated sexual abstinence, prayer, meditation and spoke with God in an ecstatic manner. And when seen as powerful shamans, they made use of it and used their shamanistic authority. As a consequence, the Jesuit padres were at times feared as powerful magicians, "great shamans" (Griffiths 2006, 191) or "God's sorcerers" (Griffiths 2006, 190). Scholars nowadays therefore call the religious practices of the Jesuits in South America "Christian magic" (Griffiths 2006, 208).

It seems likely to me that, relatively independent of content, there existed shared practices, such as practices that have been called cultural techniques of "mimetic ceremony" (Hanns-Werner Heister and Deborah Singer 2013), such as the techniques of *imitatio christi*, the reenactment of his tortures, as part of the Jesuit exercises; for Chiquitos I have not encountered a clear evidence of it, but among the Guaraní, there is evidence that imitation of godly behavior and divine entities played an important role—especially in ritual anthropophagy that was conceived as a worldly version of the foreseen and a much feared act of devouring the dead by the gods. The Christian rituals around the host, around the devouring of Christ's body, must have resonated with this. The complex of anthropo- and theophagy gives some clues concerning how Guaraní people might have conceived of the padres both as enemies and of culture-bringers. As Eduardo Viveiros de Castro (1992) has pointed out, in Guaraní cosmology the enemy is conceived as the radically other, but in his radical otherness the enemy resembles the Gods; humans and gods are conceived to be of the same substance; and because the enemy and God are structurally similar, missionaries could be feared and worshipped, but when they acted worldly (e. g., when they started to do business, when they had sex), they were killed without much ado.

One of the few ways of becoming immortal during a lifetime was to kill an enemy in order to *become* the enemy. It was necessary to incorporate the enemy to become godlike and not to be eaten by the gods after death. The community participated in the act of incorporation through ritual anthropophagy; Viveiros de Castro documents the incorporation of the enemy by the killer for the Araweté as follows:

> After killing or simply wounding an enemy, the killer dies (*umanun*). As soon as he gets back to the village, he withdraws into his house and lies as if unconscious for several days without eating anything. His belly is full of enemy blood and he vomits continually. This death is not a mere disembodiment, although he must undergo the shamanic *imone* operation; it is a state in which he actually becomes a corpse. ... He feels "as if he is rotting" ... and his bones become soft. (Viveiros de Castro 1992, 240)

After his isolation, after he became the enemy, a ritual with dance and singing is performed. The incorporated enemy now has the function of bringing new songs to the community:

> Thus, the dead enemy is the one who "makes the killer get up" to dance. ... He is literally behind them. ... Indeed, the dead enemy is called the

"song teacher." ... Prompted to rise up by the enemy, the killer gathers around himself all the men for a commemorative dance when he utters the songs that were revealed to him. ... Seen from his good side—his dead side—the enemy is the one who brings music. (Viveiros de Castro 1992, 241)

This type of music is called *Maraka nin*. This translates as "music of the future," "music to be." So the padres, even when conceived as enemies, even when killed, will have brought the music of the future. Divine processes of becoming enemy, via enactment, incorporation or vestment, can therefore be considered as an excess of imitation; an excess of imitation that Glissant and other authors of Neobarocco saw as decisive moment (Glissant 1997, 77) for its South American version. Becoming the Other in one's flesh is of course an extreme form of imitation. At the same time indigenous cultural techniques of becoming the Other (the enemy, the divinity) are mirrored and extended in Christian cultural techniques: both the devouring of the host and performances that include costumes and vestment, e. g., the ritual dressing up of statues of a tortured Jesus, part of the Corpus Christi yearly ceremony.

Resistance: Dressing Up as Priests

Additionally, we can find explicit acts of indigenous resistance that deliberately make use of Jesuit cultural techniques. The already mentioned Antonio Ruiz de Montoya ("conquista espiritual") reports a conspicuous counterappropriation of the Jesuits' musical and theatrical practices. He reports an uprising led by the cacique Miguel Artiguaye in the early seventeenth century that climaxes in an exodus out of a village. The uprising begins with an ecstatic speech by Artiguaye in which he accuses the padres of stealing the people's freedom; moreover, the priests brought not God but the devil. The exodus of 300 villagers is then carried out with great, almost Jesuitical, theatricality: everyone gathers in the plaza, adorned with feathers, bows and arrows, and the whole village leaves with great pomp, accompanied by flutes and drums (Ruiz de Montoya 1639, 135).

Moritz Bach, a German who worked as an administrative officer in Chiquitos that was then already Bolivia, described more worldly appropriations of the Christian repertoire in the 1840s. His protoethnological report appeared in 1843 (that is, 76 years after the expulsion of the order and 244 years after the spectacle at the court of Württemberg). It was written on a trip with the botanist Alcide Dessalines d'Orbigny. Moritz Bach reports, on the one hand, of still very elaborate musical performances in the villages with which the travelers were received, of a mixture of Baroque and indigenous art, of orchestras and ritual dances. But he also tells of satirical plays that were part of the Corpus Christi celebrations:

> In *Barbero*, a boy is carried into the theater to represent *San Juan de Dios*; a light is held under his nose and on his hands, which he blows out and flings away; then he gives absolution with his left hand and with his feet, and finally he pours a gourd of chicha on the barber, who has drunk himself to death and is lying on the floor, whereupon he comes back to life and all those present shout "Miracle! Miracle." (Bach 1843, 57, trans. KH)

It is difficult to say exactly when the satirical plays were adapted for local use (already at the time of the Jesuits or afterwards?). The narrative material comes from European theater of the eighteenth century. In the performance documented, Christian elements—self-sacrifice of Jesus Christ, the host—overlap with indigenous customs: chicha, a drink made from fermented corn, was consumed ceremonially by the Chiquitos, as part of cures or in order to ceremonially seal political agreements. That Saint John performs a chicha baptism to raise a drunken man from the dead is as syncretic as it is audacious: a parodic inflection of Christian notions of life and death in the medium of European theatrical conventions bended by indigenous healing practices. It is all the more remarkable that this disobedience by imagining otherwise made its way on stage as part of the Corpus Christi celebrations. We can conclude that the very theatricality with which the Jesuits proselytized enabled not only an inner but also a public distancing from the Christian religion. This becomes clear, too, in the following episode, also reported by Bach: "In the [play] *San Justo y Pastor*, the two murdered boys of that name are pulled up to heaven with ropes; I once watched them kicking violently and shouting loudly: *Los lazos me cortan, no quiero irme al cielo* [The ropes cut me, I don't want to go to heaven]" (Bach 1843, 57, trans. KH).

Édouard Glissant has argued, that the Baroque arts, especially their versions "abroad in the world," were an immense motor of "rerouting" European rationalism. While modern thought conceptualized nature as something that could be known and reproduced, Baroque techniques turned reproduction into mimicry and knowledge-as-depth into expansion, thereby creating vast patterns of *métissage* that could be used both in hegemonic and antihegemonic manner (Glissant 1997, 77—99). Jesuit drag, the accommodation "method," was appropriated as a tool of satire and—in the case of Artiguaye—for manifest resistance.

Dragging behind the Remnants of Baroque Mimicry

If we—to conclude—take a brief look into the European and Bolivian present, what kind of cultural practices of "dressing up as Indian" do we encounter? In Europe, "dressing up as Indian" is a common carnival-practice both for children and grown-ups. One could say it is the popularized, mass-culture-compatible, residual version of Frederick's corporeal representation of Lady America: idealizing and exotifying an "Other" who has seized to exist, or rather, has never existed, as Lady America was nothing more than an allegory in the flesh of a protestant aristocrat. Deeply embedded in the imaginary of the Global North this type of borrowed plumes for temporary incorporation are the type of one-sided appropriation that "drags behind" both idealization and genozide (in the sense of "everything but the burden," Tate 2023).

Figure 3. Choir and orchestra San Xavier, Festival de Temporada de Música Misional y Teatro Chiquitos 2018 (https://festivaldetemporada.com/coro-y-orquesta-de-san-xavier-listo-para-el-festival-de-temporada-2018/, accessed October 27, 2023).

If we consider festive cultures in the region of Chiquitos today the "bitter, uncontrollable residue" (Glissant 2020, 7) of cultural colonization "dragged behind" becomes more complex and contradictory. We find, on the one hand, a festival for Baroque music, taking place in the renovated mission churches biannually. It is a festival staged for a predominantly white audience from the Americas and Europe. It features musicians from the Global North playing music from the Chiquitos' repertoire and local choirs and orchestras, formed by young people for whom musical education might open a door to higher education, an option that is not available otherwise. For these performances, people from the villages, the former reductions, dress up in the way, the Jesuit padres of the eighteenth century would have wanted them to look like: they wear long, plain, simply ornamented dresses. Their performance enables the *white* audience to meet its own history (Baroque musique, pious Christians) in the rainforest—everything of colonial history but the burden, still, again.

Figure 4. Children representing colonial history, April 23, 2018 Santa Cruz, Bolivia. Photo: Karin Harrasser.

But then, there are other performances, performances that are not fashioned for a *white* public. In 2018 I witnessed a parade of schools from around Santa Cruz (the capital of the province). Pupils from different schools had rehearsed historical scenes to be performed in the street, around the *plaza mayor*. They showed mostly group choreographies, performed in costume. And they all came: children dressed as Jesuit priests or conquistadors, as violin-play-ing church musicians, indigenous students wearing costumes that resemble "Indian-costumes" children would wear in Austria or Germany in carnival. Not only the bitter residues of colonial power are being performed here, but also the remnants of acts of counterappropriation, of wild imitation and of resis-tance—the "uncontrollable" part of that what is dragged along in the popular imaginary. Violence and hope reside side-by-side in the long history of colo-nization.

Figure 5. Children representing colonial history, April 23, 2018 Santa Cruz, Bolivia. Photo: Karin Harrasser.

References

Bach, Moritz. 1843. *Die Jesuiten und ihre Mission Chiquitos in Südamerika: Eine historisch-ethnographische Schilderung.* Edited and with a preface by Georg Ludwig Kriegk. Leipzig: Mittler.

Baker, Geoffrey and Tess Knighton, eds. 2011. *Music and Urban Society in Colonial Latin America.* Cambridge: Cambridge University Press.

Bujok, Elke. 2004. *Neue Welten in europäischen Sammlungen: Africana und Americana in Kunstkammern bis 1670.* Berlin: Reimer.

Certeau, Michel de. 1992. *The Writing of History.* Translated by Tom Conley. New York: Columbia University Press.

Cusicanqui, Silvia Rivera. 2020. *Ch'ixinakax utxiwa: On Decolonising Practices and Discourses.* Translated by Molly Geidel. Hoboken: Wiley.

Christadler, Maike. 2005. "Die Häute der 'Anderen': Indianerkostüme am Württembergischen Hof." *Frauen Kunst Wissenschaft* 40: 18—26.

Fechner, Fabian. 2015. *Entscheidungsprozesse vor Ort: Die Provinzkongregationen der Jesuiten in Paraguay (1608—1762).* Regensburg: Schnell & Steiner.

Fernández, Juan Patricio. 1729. *Erbauliche und Angenehme Geschichten derer Chiquitos, und anderer von den Patribus der Gesellschaft Jesu in Paraquaria Neu-Bekehrter Völcker.* Vienna: Paul Straub.

Foucault, Michel. 2004. *Security, Territory, Population: Lectures at the Collège De France 1977—1978.* New York: Palgrave.

Friedrich, Markus. 2011. *Der lange Arm Roms? Globale Verwaltung und Kommunikation im Jesuitenorden 1540—1772.* Frankfurt am Main: Campus.

Furlong, Guillermo. 1962. *Antonio Sepp S. J. y su 'gobierno temporal' (1732).* Buenos Aires: Ediciones Theoría.

Glissant, Édouard. 1997. *Poetics of Relation.* Translated by Betsy Wing. Ann Arbor: University of Michigan Press.

Glissant, Édouard. 2020. *Introduction to a Poetics of Diversity.* Translated by Celia Britton. Liverpool: Liverpool University Press.

Griffiths, Nicholas. 2006. *Sacred Dialogues: Christianity and Native Religions in the Colonial Americas, 1492—1700.* London: Lulu Enterprises.

Harrasser, Karin and Gudrun Rath. 2016. "Arbeit und die Grenzen des Lebens: Zur Kolonialität und Modernität von Plantage und jesuitischer Reduktion." *Historische Anthropologie* 24, no. 2: 218—240.

Harrasser, Karin. 2021. "Sweet Trap, Dangerous Method: Musical Practice in the Jesuit Reductions of Chiquitos and Moxos in the Eighteenth Century." In *Connect and Divide: The Practice Turn in Media Studies*, edited by Erhard Schüttpelz, Ulrike Bergermann, Monika Dommann, Jeremy Stolow, and Nadine Taha, 209—225. Berlin: Diaphanes.

Heister, Hanns-Werner and Deborah Singer. 2013. "Mimetische Zeremonien und andere gewaltarme Herschaftsmethoden [sic]: Zur Rolle der Musik in den Guaraní-Reduktionen der Jesuiten in Paraguay im 17. und 18. Jahrhundert." *International Review of the Aesthetics and Sociology of Music* 44, no. 2: 213—238.

Recopilación de leyes de los reynos de Las Indias. 1681. Madrid: Julian de Paredes.

Ruiz de Montoya, Antonio. 1989 (originally published 1639). *Conquista espiritual hecha por los religiosos de la Compañía de Jesús en las provincias del Paraguay, Paraná, Uruguay y Tapé.* Reprint. Rosario: Equipo Difusor de Estudios de Historia Iberoamericana.

Schmid, Martin. 1988. *Pater Martin Schmid SJ, 1694—1772: Seine Briefe und sein Wirken.* Edited by Rainald Fischer. Zug: Kalt-Zehnder-Druck.

Sepp, Anton and Anton Böhm. 1696. *Reißbeschreibung: Wie dieselbe aus Hispanien in Paraquariam kommen: Und kurtzer Bericht der denckwürdigsten Sachen selbiger Landschafft, Völckern und Arbeitung der sich alldort befindenten PP Missionariorum.* Nuremberg: In Verlegung Joh. Hoffmanns.

Tate, Greg. 2003. *Everything But the Burden: What White People Are Taking from Black Culture.* New York: Broadway Books.

Toelle, Jutta. 2024. *Mission durch Musik: Stimmen und Klänge in der europäischen Missionierung Hispanoamerikas.* Münster: Waxmann.

Viveiros de Castro, Eduardo. 1992. *From the Enemy's Point of View: Humanity and Divinity in an Amazonian Society.* Translated by Catherine V. Howard. Chicago: The University of Chicago Press.

Waisman, Leonardo J. 2011. "Urban Music in the Wilderness: Ideology and Power in the Jesuit Reducciones, 1609—1747." *Music and Urban Society in Colonial Latin America*, edited by Geoffrey Baker and Tess Knighton, 208—229. Cambridge: Cambridge University Press.

Weber-Karge, Karge. 1989. "... einem irdischen Paradeiß zu vergleichen ...": *Das Neue Lusthaus in Stuttgart; Untersuchungen zu einer Bauaufgabe der deutschen Renaissance.* Sigmaringen: Thorbecke.

Japonist Drag: Performing Entangled Exoticisms in Dance and Theater around 1900

Julia Ostwald

With their appearance at the Parisian World Exhibition in 1900 and their Europe tour from 1901 to 1902, the Japanese theater troupe of Kawakami and Sadayakko Otojirō hit European art and theater circles like a "comet" (Pantzer 2005, xxi), resonating in performances, publications, art, and literature in the years to come.[1] Richard Drain accordingly summarizes the relevance of the company: "[f]or European theatre the century began with the discovery of the Japanese" (Drain 1995, 291). For the first time, as the announcements promised, Kabuki performances by and with "original Japanese people" could be seen in the course of their tour through twelve central and Eastern European countries. Their performances were part of Japonisme—a specific manifestation of Orientalism, which in turn "set the stage for the machinery of exoticism to develop" (Savigliano 1995, 85). According to the Argentinian political theorist and dance historian Marta Savigliano,

> [e]xoticism is a way of establishing order in an unknown world through fantasy … It is the seemingly harmless side of exploitation, cloaked as it is in playfulness and delirium. Exoticism is a practice of representation through which identities are frivolously allocated. It is also a will to power over the unknown, an act of indiscriminately combining fragments, crumbs of knowledge and fantasy in disrespectful, sweeping gestures justified by harmless banality. (Savigliano 1995, 189)

While performing arts and specifically dance around 1900 played a vital role in shaping European fantasies of Orientalized and exoticized bodies in the rather one-directional sense that Savigliano refers to, this article aims at considering the Kawakamis' European tour as a central node from which various

---

1   This includes works by Emil Orlik, Max Reinhardt, Giacomo Puccini's *Madam Butterfly* (1904) or the theoretical texts *Die Schaubühne der Zukunft* (1905) and *Der Tanz* (1906) by Georg Fuchs.

polydirectional lines of resonance emanate to different kinds of exoticisms. Rather than using the term Orientalism, which refers to a European perspective towards "the Orient," I will elaborate on a wider notion of exoticism and ask for its relationship with drag. Accordingly, this article shifts the focus to various forms of exoticism practiced by participants in Japonisme—that is, the Kawakami troupe on the one hand and the Russian dancer Alexander Sakharoff as an artist who can be situated in the wake of Japonisme on the other. In three different case studies, I will trace contradictory manifestations of exoticism and respective gender performances interrelated with cultural and national fantasies. Firstly, I retrace how this relates to the deliberate *self-exoticization* of the Kawakami group during their performances in Europe; secondly, I will turn to Sakharoff as an example for a Japonist *queer exoticization* in modernist European dance; thirdly, I will come back to the Kawakamis as one of the protagonists of a "Westernization" and *straightening* of theater in Japan, who adopted European exoticism for the Japanese stage. A central point of reference in all three examples is Kabuki as a literally queer theater and its specific performative construction of femininity called *onnagata*. *Onnagata* denotes female roles that are performed by specifically trained actors—male and female alike—who inherently trouble binary understandings of gender. A closer look at the dynamic shifts regarding the meaning of *onnagata* in the context of Japonisme—its affirmation, adaptation, or rejection—will not only unravel its changing entanglements with ideas of gender, culture, and nation but will also help to complicate and expand notions of drag.

Short Notes on the Concept of *Onnagata*

According to the abridged narrative widely used today, Kabuki was initially developed as an all-female theater style in the early seventeenth century before becoming an all-male theater after women had been banned from the stage in 1629. Consequently, *onnagata* actors specialized in female roles for life. Though most *onnagata* were male, female *onnagata* also existed, called *onna yakusha* (woman player) (Levy 2010, 246; Isaka 2016, 112—138). Kabuki is translatable as a theater that unites song (*ka*), dance (*bu*), and acting (*ki*). Etymologically, the verb *kabuku* means ""to slant," "to bend," or "to tilt" (Kano 1995, 58), as well as "to lean; to act and/or dress in a peculiar and queer manner" (Isaka 2016, 5). Besides its specific stylized mixture of song, dance, and "exaggerated acting, flamboyant costumes and makeup, and unrealistic stories filled with ghosts" (Isaka 2016, 5—6), Kabuki's queerness is manifested in the concept of *onnagata*. Today's definition of *onnagata* as "men acting as women" became increasingly common since the accelerated Westernization and modernization of Japan in the wake of the Meiji restoration from 1868 onwards[2]—a redefinition that mirrors the modern process of the naturalization of gender. In contrast, *onnagata* in the pre- and early Meiji era rather refers to an ambiguous "labyrinth of gendering" (Isaka 2016, 13) based on the "very presupposition of 'femininity' [being] separable from women's anatomical sex" (Isaka 2016, 7). This historical concept of *onnagata* thus denotes a highly performative understanding of gender in which "women and onnagata, as the doers of femininity, began circulating femininity in the form of reciprocal imitation" (Morinaga 2002, 246). Detached from essentialist bourgeois European ideas of a (gendered) truth beneath the appearance, the femininity of *onnagata* was thought of as second nature, that could be acquired by male *and* female performers through respective techniques (*gei*) (Isaka 2016, 19 and 87—111). Thus, *onnagata* in pre-twentieth-century thought might be understood as a specific practice to perform a femininity that is inextricably linked to masculinity, yet open to performers of all genders, as e.g., Maki Isaka highlights:

> While denoting the role to be performed (i.e., woman), the term "onnagata" inevitably entails connotations regarding the one who performs: male identity, maleness, masculinity, and so on. The concept of the term "onnagata" is ostentatiously composed of the enunciated femininity and the enunciating masculinity. The concept of onnagata thus seems doomed to carry something male-ish about it, but the enunciating masculinity is not directly connected with a male body in and of itself. (Isaka 2016, 112)

Only in the course of the early twentieth century was *onnagata* reconceptualized as a nonnatural "artistic femininity" that is thought to be incompatible with "natural femininity" (Isaka 2016, 17—18 and 141—152), thus leading for the most part to an exclusion of female *onnagata* performers.[3] Modern *onnagata* thus reduces the discrepancy between the performer and the figure performed to the formula of "a male performing a woman." In contrast, the pre-Meiji *onnagata* concept dissolves this discrepancy by attributing greater importance to technique, appearance, and performative figuration than to the subjectivity and

---

2   Meiji Restoration refers to the Japanese revolution of 1868, which marks a forced political, economic, social, and cultural opening of the country towards the "West."

3   Among others, the performative constitution of *onnagata* as well as its modern essentialization resonate in the differentiation of "woman-actor" (*onna yakusha*, a woman performing onnagata such as the famous Ichikawa Kumehachi) from "actress" (a woman performing a woman) (see Isaka 2016, 9). In the 1910s, the first is increasingly supplanted by the second.

identity of the performer. This approach thus opens up iridescent possibilities of performing imitations of imitations of femininity that do not depend on any gendered corporeality beneath an alleged figurative surface. The performances of the Kawakamis in Europe and Japan were part of the historical transition, of Westernizing Japan, that divided *onnagata* femininity into "artificial femininity" and "natural womanness." Accordingly, in what follows I am not interested in any "original" conceptions of *onnagata*, but rather in how it was exploited by different performative practices in Europe and Japan in the early twentieth century.

The Kawakamis' Self-Exoticization

The Kawakamis[4]—that is, the dancer and influential former Geisha Sadayakko and her husband Otojirō—not unknown in Japan upon their arrival in Europe. As a member of the liberal party fighting for democracy Otojirō, under the name Liberty Kid, had already risen to fame in Japan with patriotic and satirical songs in 1890 (Downer 2004, 56). Through an activist amateur group performing Kabuki-style theater, which he founded in response to current political events, his performative work was directly involved in the Japanese nation-building process related to the Meiji restoration. Inspired by a trip to Paris in 1893, during which he attended performances by Sarah Bernhardt and Loie Fuller, Otojirō introduced European aesthetics into Japanese theater. Due to financial hardship and a chance of success as the first "professional" Japanese theater group in the West, in 1899 the Kawakamis accepted the invitation by a Japanese patron to tour through the US; a tour which concluded at the world exhibition in Paris in 1900, where they performed in the theater of the US-American so-called serpentine dancer Loie Fuller. Inspired by this success, from 1901 to 1902 Fuller initiated a second tour through Europe, in which she participated with her solos. Fuller's solo dances with their waving fabrics, on which multicolored light was projected, were seen as the epitome of theatrical technological innovation; accordingly, she was also known as *fée électricité*. In contrast, the Kawakami group presented itself for advertising and marketing purposes as the Kabuki troupe of the nonexistent "Japanese imperial court theater" (Downer 2004, 92—93). By combining Fuller's scenes with those of the Kawakamis, the show not only staged the exoticized binaries of Western progress and alleged Japanese traditionalism, of technology and presumed naturalness (Scholz-Cionca 2016, 53), but also the expanding circuits of globalization.

---

4   When using the name under which the company tours, I always imply the importance of both Sadayakko and Otojirō.

Contrary to the Japanese troupe's claims of traditionalism, their program was anything but authentic; in fact, it provided a stage for Japonisme, the European image of Japanese culture that had been circulating in theater programs throughout Central Europe since the late nineteenth century (Francke 2013). The representation of "Japanese people" was based, among other things, on travel records, images, performances by Japanese acrobats at the world exhibitions, and to a large extent on imagination (Francke 2013; Pantzer 2005, 51). Without being educated Kabuki performers, the Kawakami troupe staged scenes that, in terms of content, aesthetics, and gender performance, were firmly adapted to Western Japonisme. Their program included fragments of Japanese Kabuki pieces such as *The Geisha and the Knight* and *The Shogun*, and japonized pieces of European theater such as *Pygmalion* or a scene from Shakespeare's *The Merchant of Venice*. Text was mostly omitted due to the incomprehensibility of Japanese; plots and characters of traditional Kabuki pieces were regrouped by stringing together melodramatic scenes of love, madness, and death under the premise of maximum effect (Fig. 1). Thus, the bodily appearances staged by the Kawakami troupe were themselves an *imitation*, "already quoted (from pictorial conventions)" of Japonisme (Brandstetter 2003, 256).

Figure 1. *The Geisha and the Knight*, New York, during the US tour, Otojirō on the left, Sadayakko fourth from left. Photo: Byron, *Le Théâtre* 41, Sept. 1900, Bibliothèque Nationale de France.

The performances represented a specific adaptation of Kabuki and *onnagata* to the European audience: by having Sadayakko and other actresses take on female roles, the cast was "straightened" according to European conventions. However, introductory talks, program notes, and press articles highlighted gender ambiguity as a specific "exotic" feature by constantly repeating the narrative that Sadayakko had to substitute a sick male *onnagata* performer, as this exemplary review shows:

> Seit dem XVII. Jahrhundert war es in Japan Frauen verboten, die Bühne zu betreten und Frauenrollen mußten daher stets von Männern dar-gestellt werden. *Sada Yacco*, früher die berühmteste *Geisha* Japans, sah Kawakami spielen und, begeistert von seiner Kunst, wagte sie es, Schauspielerin zu werden. *Kawakami*, der Reformideen des japani-schen Theaters geneigt war, nahm die junge Novizin mit Freuden auf und unterrichtete sie. Eines Tages sprang *Sada Yacco* für einen unwohl gewordenen Frauendarsteller ein, errang einen kolossalen Erfolg und ist seither die *erste* und größte Schauspielerin Japans.[5] (Schwer quoted in Pantzer 2005, 831, italics in the original)

Strictly speaking, Sadayakko and the other female performers did not only appear as actresses who enacted female figures but also as actresses imperson-ating *onnagata* femininity. As I will briefly outline, the perception of Sadayakko, who was hailed as the "Japanese Duse" and "Japanese Sarah Bernhardt," was also imbued with the peculiarly ambiguous femininity of *onnagata*.

Across the board, the reviews emphasized the nondramatic, the synes-thetic intertwining of sonority, physicality, and the "eloquence of the bodies" (Pantzer 2005, 180). It was the voices and the expressiveness of the bodies—especially Sadayakko's—that the reviews focused on. The different prosody and intonation of Japanese brought the sonority of voices to the center (Klankert 2015, 167). Not only the supposed absence of semantic intelligibility led to a discursive feminization of the performers, but also the materiality of their voices and movements. It was said that the actors would talk "hastily, that they stammer, puff, hiss, whisper. The fast facial expressions and all the bodily

---

5   "Since the XVIIth century, women were forbidden to enter the stage in Japan and female roles therefore always had to be played by men. *Sada Yacco*, once the most famous geisha in Japan, saw *Kawakami* perform and, inspired by his art, she dared to become an actress. Kawakami, who was inclined to reform Japanese theater, gladly accepted the young novice and taught her. One day, *Sada Yacco* stood in for a female actor who had become unwell, achieved colossal success and has been Japan's *first* and greatest actress ever since." All translations of sources are by the author.

movements match the manner of speaking" (Pantzer 2005, 832). Repeatedly, falsetto voices were mentioned, contrasting contemporary European ideas of masculine vocality. This staging of femininity culminated in Sadayakko's voice, described by metaphors of birds and flowers. Yet, it resonated not only with stereotypical European constructions of the devout, infantile Geisha (Klankert 2015, 171),[6] but also with the falsetto voice of *onnagata*, as the following contemporary review explains:

> Die Schauspieler, welche Frauenrollen spielen [im jap. Theater, J.O.] sprechen im Diskant; sie machen ihre Sache aber so gut, daß der unbefangene Europäer, der zum ersten Male ein Theater in Japan besucht, oft erst aufmerksam gemacht werden muß, daß alle Rollen von Männern gespielt werden. Sada Yacco ist die erste Japanerin, die mit Männern zugleich Komödie spielt. ... [S]o spricht auch Sada Yacco ihre Rollen—im Diskant: gerade so, wie ein Schauspieler die Rolle sprechen würde. Ein Zeichen, wie die Tradition wirken kann![7] (Japoniscus quoted in Pantzer 2005, 257—258)

In terms of Sadayakko's gestures, contemporary reviews and depictions indicated two opposing qualities: on the one hand, grace and delicateness associated with the image of the devote Geisha; on the other, a fury and an expressive grotesqueness. Especially the latter can be found in numerous images depicting characteristic elements of Kabuki, typically characterized by a lowered center of gravity and bended knees, expressive hand gestures, and broken or twisted lines of the arms. The body axis buckles from the vertical alignment through forward bends of the upper body and side bends of the head, hips, and knees (Fig. 2). In European perceptions, these movements were perceived less as a dance than as a sequence of pictorial single poses (Pantzer 2005, 373), in fact

---

6   Here Klankert makes an analogy to Cio-Cio-Sans's voice in *Madame Butterfly*. The bird-like voice "symbolisiert das Weiblichkeitsbild der Geisha, das sich als europäische Projektion um die Jahrhundertwende in den Künsten herausgebildet und zu einem Stereotyp im europäischen Japan-Diskurs entwickelt hat" ("symbolizes the female image of the Geisha that took shape as European projection in the arts at the turn of the century and developed into a stereotype in the European Japandiscourse"; Klankert 2015, 171).

7   "The actors who play female roles [in Japanese theater] speak in a descant, but they do it so well that the unbiased European who visits a theater in Japan for the first time often has to be made aware that all roles are played by men. Sada Yacco is the first Japanese woman to perform comedy together with men ... [S]o Sada Yacco also speaks her roles in a descant: just as an actor would speak the role. A sign of how tradition can work!"

reflecting the *mie* pose as a characteristic pausing of the movements in Kabuki as a heightened expression of emotion at the climax of a sequence (Zorn 2013).

Figure 2. Celso Hermínio: *Sada Yacco* (1902), published in *A Parodía* 126/3(1902), Lisbon, Photo: BLX-Hemeroteca Municipal de Lisboa.

Especially Sadayakko's madness and death scenes were discussed in reviews, where her portrayal was, however, overlayed with the European image of the femme fatale and the figure of Salome typical for that time (Brandstetter 2003, 259). Simultaneously, audiences were kept aware of the fact that Sadayakko modernized Japanese theater by being a "female actress" performing female figures instead of former "male women"[8] (Hevesi in Pantzer 2005, 601).

European perceptions of Sadayakko's performance in particular, and of the Kawakami troupe in general, were thus characterized by a deep uncertainty about how and as what they should be placed or identified, an uncertainty that applied equally to questions of gender performance, cultural "authenticity," artistic discipline, and temporal positioning. According to Peter Pantzer, who collected contemporary reviews of the tour across German-speaking countries, "[f]inding the right perspective, making a correct judgment was indeed not easy when you had to choose between drama and circus, pantomime and play, museum exhibition and cabinet of curiosities"[9] (Pantzer 2005, LXVII, trans. J. O.). Introductory talks and the press emphasized the distance between "original" Kabuki and the Kawakami troupe's aesthetics and had the effect that the actual performances were haunted by the European "knowledge" about how a Kabuki performance would actually be performed. Thus, the Kawakami troupe was even accused of fraud given that this "European-Japanese" theater (Sazanami in Pantzer 2005, XXV) claiming to be original, was not to be found in Japan. Yet, it was exactly this uncertainty that opened up a spectral variety of ascriptions. While the judgment of the troupe's aesthetics was based on the paradigmatic exoticist entanglement of effeminacy, naturalness, and "primitivity"—thereby missing its high level of aesthetic stylization—some understood its presumed "primitivity" as lagging behind a supposedly progressive Europe.[10] Other saw the Europeanized adaptations of traditional Kabuki, particularly in terms of the straightened cast, as reflecting an ostensibly emancipated and therefore progressive Europe (Fournier 1900) or even its supposed "blossoming of feminism"[11] (Pantzer 2005, XXXV). Theater reformer Edward Gordon Craig, in a deeply misogynist article entitled "Sada Yacco" (1921, 261—266), contrarily called the actress a threat to the "naturally" "masculine theatre" (1921, 266) of Japan. Conversely, for avant-garde author and theater theoretician Georg Fuchs, the staged "primitivity" of Japonist theater and Kabuki signified the

---

8   In the German original: "Schauspielerinnen weiblichen Geschlechts …. Früher gab es Frauen männlichen Geschlechts."

9   In the German original: "Den rechten Blickwinkel zu finden, ein Urteil korrekt zu treffen, war in der Tat nicht leicht, wenn man zwischen Drama und Zirkus, Pantomime und Theaterstück, musealer Ausstellung und Kuriositäten-Kabinett zu schwanken meinte."

10   As one of numerous examples a review by Bruno Petzold: "this is a type of naturalism as it can only emerge from a people, that … has not yet lost its primitivity, and close proximity with nature, which still … relates to the flowers and the beasts" (in Pantzer 2005, 62).

11   In the German original: "Blütetage des Feminismus."

aesthetic ideal of the *future* theater of Europe with synesthesia and physicality at its center (Fuchs 1905).

By performing Japonisme, the Kawakami troupe practiced a firm self-exoticization. According to Savigliano, self-exoticization has a certain amount of agency; however, it is limited by an unequal distribution of power between performers and spectators. Although the Kawakamis' performances clearly operated in the framework of exoticism as described by Savigliano, their self-exoticization still did not entirely fit into an economy of cultural ascriptions and unequivocably distributed risks. Also, the extensive feminization of the Kawakami group, which can be read with Edward Said (1978) as a paradigmatic discursive operation of Orientalism aiming to distinguish supposedly progressive (masculine) Europe from "effeminate" and "regressive" non-Europeans, seems too one-sided in the case of the Kawakamis. Rather, the selling point of the group's bewildering work was not only that the performance was based on reciprocal imitations of artistic cultural practices (the Kawakamis quoting from European theater, from Japanese Kabuki, *and* from Japonisme, which in turn quotes from Kabuki and other Japanese arts), but more that this mimetic circuit was presented by supposedly "original" Japanese Kabuki performers. The Kawakamis rather very consciously modeled the imagination of their European audiences by deliberately staging and discursively framing Japonist phantasmas. Instead of clear-cut power relations as suggested by Savigliano or Said in the exoticist and Orientalist context, the troupe's self-exoticization hints at complex interactions in which active and passive roles cannot be ascribed so easily.

Alexander Sakharoff's Queer Exoticism

The exuberant nonbinary gender performances of dancer Alexander Sakharoff in the early years of the twentieth century can be read in the context of performative Japonisme as introduced to Europe by the Kawakamis. Born to a Jewish family in Mariupol, then part of the Tsarist empire, in 1886, Sakharoff studied painting in Paris and moved to Munich in 1905 where he became part of the circle of artists associated with the Neue Künstlervereinigung (the predecessor of the expressionist group Der Blaue Reiter). He started to take lessons in ballet and acrobatics and was involved in costume balls. In 1910, he made his debut as one of the first male solo acts within the context of modern dance. However, his work eluded the canonized lineages of modern dance by explicitly drawing from various references, such as circus techniques and acrobatics (Sakharoff 1922, n. p.). During the interwar period, together with his dance and life partner Clotilde van Derp, he toured with great success through Europe, North and

South America, and Asia, including Japan. Patricia Veroli describes Sakharoff as a "bridge figure" (Veroli 2002, 171) between Western and Eastern Europe, who connected heterogeneous lines of Russian, French, and German symbolism. Thus, Sakharoff "was exposed to various influences, and filtered them in a way that it has heretofore been possible to know and understand only in parts" (Veroli 2002, 171). Sakharoff's dances in exuberant costumes (designed by the dancer) were equally characterized by exoticist elements and diverse historical references to European antiquity, the Renaissance, and particularly the Baroque. Similar to Vaclav Nijinsky and the Ballets Russes, whose "archaic, exotic or 'Oriental'" aesthetics created a distance that made ambivalent stagings of the male body possible (Burt 2022, 58), Sakharoff's dances raise the question of how his radical disruption of heteronormative gender performances interacted with his exoticist aesthetics. While dance scholar Lucia Ruprecht described Sakharoff's dances in general and his "Baroque" solos (such as his impersonation of Sun King Louis IVX in *Pavane Royal*) in particular, with the term "gestural drag" (2019, 169—192), aligning the "intermittent temporality" (177) of his practice with theories of the baroque body and current queer theories of temporal drag, I would like to suggest to take a look at Sakharoff's work from the perspective of Japonisme and related *onnagata* performativity. In other words, I read his solos as a queer exoticism in which a nonbinary performance of gender is linked to a bewildering performance of cultural fragments with a specific affinity to the past.

Formative for Sakharoff's dance concept was the close friendship with the expressionist Munich-based Russian painter couple Alexej Jawlensky and Marianne Werefkin, both members of Neue Künstlervereinigung Munich. They were collectors of Japanese art, theater masks, and woodcuts of theatrical and dance scenes, which they studied intensively. Werefkin and Jawlensky not only portrayed the dancer in a Japonist style in feminized postures and with a whitened face, but they also introduced him to Japanese/Japonist aesthetics (Fäthke 2011). Jawlensky accordingly described their close exchange as follows:

> For several years we were always together and he [Sakharoff] came to see us almost every day. The years of our friendship were very interesting … We discussed all of his training as a dancer. I always watched him dance. He also loved and understood my art very well. (Jawlensky quoted in Stamm 2002, 17)[12]

---

12   In addition, two years before his debut, Sakharoff experimented with Wassily Kandinsky on a synesthetic theater. Georg Fuchs's writings *Die Schaubühne der Zukunft* (1905) and *Der Tanz* (1906), both inspired by attending performances by the Kawakamis, provided the theoretical background for this.

Figure 3. Alexander Sakharoff in a dance pose inspired by Italian Renaissance. Photo: Heinrich Hoffmann (around 1912), Deutsches Tanzarchiv Köln [56013].

Figure 4. Sakharoff in a version of *Pavane Royale* (around 1919). Photo: Hanns Holdt, Deutsches Tanzarchiv Köln [56014].

Yet, in his stagings Sakharoff by no means referred back to "the Japanese" in terms of motifs, but adopted fragments of Japonisme into his "reenactments" (Ruprecht 2019, 175) of historical as well as exoticist dances such as *Dance of the Baroque Bacchus, Pavane Royal, Chinoiserie, Poème nègre* (danced by Clotilde Sakharoff) or *Golliwog's Cake Walk*. Among other things, the heavy white face makeup that Sakharoff wore in almost all of his dances is striking. It resonated not only with Baroque makeup traditions but also with the white makeup mask of the *onnagata* in Kabuki. Dance scholar Gabriele Brandstetter has furthermore pointed to the Japonist shaping of Sakharoff's specific modeling of postures and movements, which include the upper body bowed forward or sideways, poses with a bent standing and striking leg, the vertical body axis buckled out of alignment in several places, and expressive hand and arm gestures (Brandstetter 1997, 154—158; also Veroli 2002, 186) (Fig. 3—4). While in historical Baroque dance, the body is aligned vertically, striving upwards with a high center of gravity, Sakharoff's body is specifically broken into several axes with a slightly lowered center. It is this significant breaking of his postures and movements with the "vertical masculinity" (Veroli 2002, 204) of classical ballet and baroque dance that is imbued with echoes of Japonisme, more specifically the performativity of *onnagata*.

In his work, Sakharoff aimed for gender fluidity when claiming that the only suitable gender for the art of dance is "the young man as a being that ... unites the possibility of both sexes in himself"[13] (Sacharoff 2002a). He argumentatively associated this quest with feminized male figures: initially with the ephebe of Greek antiquity (Sacharoff 2002a), and, shortly thereafter, with various androgynous figures such as Louis XIV, or the "feverish clown with which he parodied the cakewalk ... or the Renaissance angels with wings made of real feathers" (Veroli 2002, 187). In a time that was marked by "sexual antagonism" and "a battle *within* the sexes" (Showalter in Veroli 2002, 175), and in which homosexuality became a key issue, Sakharoff's performances raised highly ambivalent reactions. Reviews expressed the pressurization of contemporary heteronormative ideas, responding to it with admiration and rejection; they accused him of feminization and partly expressing homophobia. As an example, the expressionist writer Friedrich Markus Huebner emphasized Sakharoff's particular performance of dual gender ("Doppelgeschlechtlichkeit") in which he recognized a "confusingly" liberating effect:

---

13   In the German original: "der Jüngling als ein Wesen, das noch ... gleichsam die Möglichkeiten der beiden Geschlechter in sich vereinigt."

Sacharoff verwirrt. Er verwirrt uns Heutige. ... Er öffnet die Schleusen-
tore des Anarchischen. Er stellt dar und glorifiziert das "Charakterlose."
... Es ist gleichgültig, wie Sacharoff seine einzelne Programmnummer
nennt. Es ist auch gleichgültig, an welche historischen Ideen er seine
Gewandungen anähnelt. Zuletzt ist gleichgültig, die Musik welches
Komponisten er als Teppich seines Schreitens, Beugens, Betens
benutzt. Das immer wieder und vor allen Dingen Außerordentliche ist,
daß die Zertrenntheit der Geschlechter, das Vasallensein des Mannes,
des Weibes an ihren beziehentlichen Charakter, daß der Dualismus
der Begehrungen in Sacharoff sich synthetisiert und nun zu einer
einzigen, charakterologisch nicht mehr faßbaren Geste der zwiefach
geschlechtlichen Nacktheit wird. ... Die Statue des Ich ist zerbrochen,
und aus allen Poren dieser hermaphroditischen Figur flackert der Aus-
druck geglückter, erwünschter, gesteigerter Erlösung von der Enge
des einsartigen Selbst. (Huebner 1914, n. p.)[14]

The influential French critic André Levinson similarly described Sakharoff as
a performer whose dances were defined more by "affectation" and "equivocation" than by their topics, titles, or costumes: "This equivocation persists in all
his dances, which, although differentiated by costume, are the same, whether
they are called Pavane, Rigaudon or Cake-Walk"[15] (Levinson 1929, 426). While
Ruprecht aligns Sakharoff's gender performance with baroque burlesque
Ballet de Cour in which dancing "en travestie" constituted a form of "majestic
drag" (Franko 2003, see also Franko 2015), I would argue that the gender-re-
lated incomprehensibility of his gestures, which seems to have permeated all
of Sakharoff's performances, reached beyond baroque concepts. His performative approach was rather characterized by an entanglement of gendered

---

14   "Sakharoff confuses. He confuses us contemporaries. ... He opens the floodgates of
the anarchic. He portrays and glorifies the 'characterless' ... . It doesn't matter what
Sacharoff calls his individual program number. It also doesn't matter which historical ideas he chooses to resemble in his costumes. Finally, it doesn't matter which
composer's music he uses as a carpet for his striding, bending, and praying. What is
always and above all extraordinary is that the separation of the sexes, the vassalage
of man and woman to their relational character, that the dualism of desires is synthe-
sized in Sacharoff and now becomes a single, characterologically no longer compre-
hensible gesture of twofold sexual nakedness ... The statue of the ego is broken, and
from every pore of this hermaphroditic figure flickers the expression of successful,
desired, heightened redemption from the narrowness of the one-like self."
15   In the French original: "Cette équivoque persiste dans toutes ses danses qui, dif-
férenciées par le costume, n'en font qu'une seule, qu'elle s'intitule pavane, rigaudon
ou cake-walk."

and cultural—or better—exoticist matters respectively connected to specific (queer) temporalities. Though Sakharoff was part of European exoticism and its colonial and racist implications, his artistic work might be called a queer exoticism that to a certain degree, was bending exoticism itself.

As an example, I would like to come back to his aforementioned solo *Golliwog's Cake Walk* to the music of Claude Debussy.[16] It premiered in 1913, as part of a program in which Sakharoff also performed Baroque-influenced solos. The racist Golliwog doll, inspired by minstrel shows and designed by the illustrator Florence Upton in 1895—a grotesquely exaggerated, childlike, Black figure in a suit[17]—bears no resemblance to Sakharoff's staging: a photo of the solo (Fig. 5) rather shows an Orientalized figure in a doll-like, elongated pose with spread-eagled arms and legs on demi-pointe. The figure wears a blue wig (as a hand-colored version of the image shows) and an Oriental costume—"a marvel of feathers and long fringes" (Veroli 1992, 85)—with puffy pants covered in ornaments. The face is whitened and heavily made up.

Figure 5. *Golliwog's Cake Walk*. Photo: Hanns Holdt, (n. d.), Deutsches Tanzarchiv Köln [12166].

---

16   Described by Brenda Dixon-Gottschild as "another example of whites copying blacks copying whites" (1997, 26), this partner dance was a parody of white social dances by African American slaves. It later became an essential part of the minstrel show, and from about 1900 until World War I a popular white social dance in Europe and the United States.

17   See, for example, Brown 2008, 66.

Figure 6. *Golliwog's Cake Walk*, from "Alexandre et Clotilde Sakharoff: biographie: documents iconographiques" (n. d.), Bibliothèque nationale de France [FRBNF39511909].

The movements are moreover "described as febrile and spirited, and brought off with an extraordinary disarticulation of the limbs, a sense of lightness, and a mastery of the body even when it was held in the most unusual positions" (Veroli 2002, 206). They at best show only traces of the eponymous cakewalk (Fig. 6). Characteristics such as leaning backward, high prances, arms stretched forward, and a low center of gravity can only be found as residues in Sakharoff's dance in exaggerated backbends and poses suggestive of swinging arms. The bent forward upper body, poses on demi-pointe with the legs partly parallel, partly turned out with mostly bent knees and highly stylized hand gestures, rather evoke eclectic associations that meld cakewalk with baroque, Japonist, and vaguely "Oriental" facets of movement. Sakharoff's mocking stylization of the cakewalk eluded both hegemonic masculinity and exotic illusions of original cultures. It is not without an ironic undertone (von Delius in Peter/Stamm 2002, 49) that Sakharoff deliberately juggled codified signs of present and past cultures, races, genders, and sexualities. Through the heterogeneity of costume and makeup, gestures, and poses as a "laboratory of symbols" (Veroli 2002, 192), he overburdened the body with signs and thereby withdrew from any stable attributions. Sakharoff's cakewalk and other solos did not follow the binary logic of a masquerade, either in the sense of a gendered cross-dressing or as ethnic drag (Sieg 2002). Correspondingly, he demanded "independence from the laws of representation [Abbildlichkeit]"[18] (Sacharoff 2002b, 220). Sakharoff rather seemed to invoke the notion of reminiscence, as coined by Mark Franko when reflecting on Japanese Butoh dancer Kazuo Ohno and his performance *Suiren* ("Water Lilies").[19] Ohno's drag "speaks of disparate sexes in one body without invoking paradox or inviting us to delude ourselves about the 'truth'" (Franko 1992, 603). With a reference to Roland Barthes' thoughts on Japanese puppet theater Bunraku, Franko further states:

> Attempting to transcend the double bind of doxa and paradoxa (whether male and female, heterosexuality and homosexuality, or dress and its crossing) Ohno may be in search of just such a third term, "which is not a synthesis but a translation: everything comes back, but it comes back as fiction". (Franko 1992, 603)

Franko's conclusion that this "fictive body as third term assumes roles non-parasitically, *through reminiscence rather than polemical masquerade*" (Franko 1992, 603, italics J.O.), also applies to Sakharoff's embodiments: they were no imitation of, but fragments that echo gendered and cultured gestures without evoking any kind of origin. In this sense, Émile Vuillermoz calls Sakharoff a "master of an invisible ballet" (1933, 48), "who never dances alone" as he "evokes the living and the dead" (47). When Sakharoff quoted disparate fractions of

---

18   In the German original: "Unabhängigkeit von den Gesetzen der Abbildlichkeit."

19   The Japanese dance form Butoh draws from traditions of Kabuki and Noh as well as from European modern expressionist dance (see, among others, Fraleigh 2010). The title of Ohno's performance refers to Claude Monet's paintings of water lilies, which were created in the context of Japonisme. Against this backdrop, the solo addresses gendered and cultural transfers.

current and outdated European and non-European performative practices in order to transpose them into nonbinary "reinventions of dance styles," he created, as Veroli put it, "an ivory-tower world, removed from time and from social and national transformations" (Veroli 2002, 192).

Yet, this removal can as well be understood as a parodist commentary on heteronormative standards of masculinity and the logic of exoticism of his time. If exoticism creates a representative order and allocates social roles "through fantasy" (Savigliano 1995, 189), Sakharoff's solos such as *Golliwog's Cake Walk* withdraw from exoticist representations. He rather refers to exoticism by queering and exposing it as a work of fantasy itself.

While Sakharoff worked with elements associated with drag performance such as opulent costumes, wigs, and overall effeminate modeling of postures, he simultaneously withdrew from logics of drag such as the "destabilizing gesture," "exploitation of the opposition of construction and essence," or "the assertation 'that appearance is an illusion'" (Garber 1997, 152). Sakharoff's "decentralized gender" (Veroli 2002, 192) rather *invented* fictional figurations of in-between genders and cultures without stressing the discrepancy between performer and performed. Insofar as he was not operating within any binary logic, his aesthetics bore similarities to the concept of *onnagata* as a performative and technically achieved femininity independent of the performing subject. The notion of *gei* that is central to Kabuki (and Japanese arts in general) as an "acquired artistic technique implanted into one's body via repeated, longtime, physical cultivation" (Isaka 2016, 103) is echoed in the importance that Sakharoff ascribes to the continued bodily practice fueled by a variety of techniques: "Our dances are worked out in every detail and sometimes many years pass before they are actually to our satisfaction. ... The true dancer must be an artist—he must learn technique (most importantly breathing)" (Sacharoff 1932, see also Sakharoff 1922). Many reviews emphasize Sakharoff's "intellectual, frantically ambitious technique, which consciously depicted every pose down to the last detail"[20] (Brandenburg 1921, 121–122) leading to artificiality and stylization (Levinson 1929, 278). The concept of work that stands out in Sakharoff's approach is that of a body that has been worked through by various techniques, and which appears in changing figurations without impersonating a stable figure. Thus, work—to again return to Franko's thoughts about Butoh dancer Kazuo Ohno's drag—also forms a theoretical perspective. Referring to Roland Barthes' observation that in the historical Japanese puppet play Bunraku (a predecessor of Kabuki and Butoh) work "is substituted for interiority"

---

20 In the German original: "eine intellektuale, krampfhaft ehrgeizige Technik, die jede Pose höchst bewußt bis ins Einzelne durchbildete."

(Barthes 1976, 45), Franko proposes work as a category that goes beyond issues of subjectivization and dichotomies such as interiority and expression, authenticity and masquerade. As such, it is "a third term for theatrical theory: neither subjectivism nor alienation" (Franko 1992, 602). Sakharoff's elaborated gestures of an in-between gender that simultaneously echo various cultural fragments, among them Japonist elements of his time, are an example of such a work. A work that is not a gendered or ethnic cross-dressing, but a "through-dressing" (Franko 1992, 604) and a through-gesturing that queers exoticism's quest for representation.

Dragging Exoticism onto the Japanese Stage

As a third example of references to *onnagata* in the early twentieth century, I will follow the Kawakamis back to Japan, where shortly after their European tour they became the most committed innovators of theater in the so-called Shinpa style (also Shimpa), meaning New School drama.[21] Shinpa's central effort to Westernize Japanese theater by overcoming Kabuki and "replacing *onnagata* with actresses" (Kano 1995, 6) is part of theater reforms that played a decisive role in Japan's forced opening up to the West and its striving "to display [its] legitimacy as an advanced nation, one that could not only avoid colonization by nations such as the United States, Britain, Germany, and France but one that would eventually become a colonial power itself" (Kano 1995, 6). Thus, the fierce contemporary debates around Kabuki and New School Shinpa, *onnagata* and actresses—as women acting like women (Kano 1995, 58)—reflect broader societal struggles for a "modern, civilized and masculine Japan" (Kano 1995, 95). The supposedly traditional, archaic, feminine, and Eastern Kabuki is not only placed in a binary opposition to this new nation's ideals, but theater should "become a school in which spectators would learn how to be subjects of such a nation" (Kano 1995, 95). While the Japonist Kabuki program of the Kawakamis in Europe was therefore viewed extremely critically in Japan (Kano 1995, 92), the tour simultaneously afforded the troupe the authority to claim themselves as experts in Western theater. Thus, Kawakami called his idealized theater style *seigeki*, "straight theater." The term not only refers to a focus on spoken word drama, but to an encompassing "straightening" of all theatrical means according to Kawakami's association of *seigeki* with a "correct" or "pure" performance of Western drama (Kano 1995, 59, also 57—84). Among other things, "straight

---

21   Shinpa as New School drama is historically largely replaced in the 1910s by Shingeki as New Theater, that actually detaches itself from all residues of "old school" Kabuki theater (see, among others, Kano 1995, 58).

theater" included the adaptation of Western plays and the primacy of dialogues over song and dance, as well as the "straight" assignment of roles in terms of essentializing gender. Even more, "straight" theater meant a masculinization of "resources, and time [that] would be allocated rationally and efficiently, and … in which masculine subjects would enact masculine scenes to educate others to act masculine" (Kano 1995, 76—77). Rejecting Kabuki and its performative femininity of *onnagata* (male and female alike) as "'queer' and abjected" (Kano 1995, 59), the "natural" femininity of the modern actress was turned center stage. Sadayakko, described as a "Western lady" (Kano 1995, 91) upon her return from Europe, epitomized this new model of a Japanese actress.

However, the Westernization of theater that Kawakami intended was not as pure as he claimed. Rather, it was a case of reverse exoticism that dragged the logic of Western exoticism onto the Japanese stage, as Kawakami's Shinpa adaptation of the Shakespeare play *Othello* in 1903, among others, showed.[22] *Othello* was staged as one of the first "straight" and at the same time "colonial plays" (Kano 1995, 12) followed by *The Merchant of Venice* and *Hamlet* in the same year.[23] After their successful experimentations with self-exoticizing performances of alleged Kabuki in Europe, the Kawakamis now claimed to be the only Japanese to have studied and to "authentically" perform Shakespeare.[24] Contrary to an advertisement poster that showed figures in historical European dresses, including Othello with a blackened face and hands in front of Greek columns, Kawakami's actual staging was "an extract of Shakespeare's play" with "one-tenth the length" (Osanai in Liu 2007, 413) of the original. It moved the setting to present-day Tokyo and Taiwan. Here, Othello, performed by Otojirō, was called Washirō, a colonial general in Taiwan—an island Japan had just colonized in 1895. Washirō, a character transferring Othello into the Japanese context, appeared as a member of burakumin, "a traditional outcaste group

---

22 The reason why Kawakami chose *Othello* was the "fact that it has few strong female parts in comparison with Shakespeare's other plays, many of which include important active roles for women" (Yasuko 2016, 488).

23 There is a longer history of performances of Shakespeare in Japan reaching back to the mid-nineteenth century. Strikingly, Shakespeare is often performed in Kabuki adaptations. For the specific affinity between Kabuki and Shakespeare in terms of gender-bending performances, see Pronko 1967 and Brandon 1999.

24 A text in incorrect English on the advertisement poster states: "Othello, to be produced by Mr. Kawakami and Madam Sada Yacco, is the adaptation from Shakespeare's play of which they have seen the performance in Europe where they have engaged with their troupe previous year, and learned the art of the acting much differing from our conventional. No foreigner ever had such a good opportunity as this time to see Shakespeare's drama in its almost original form in Japan" (quoted in Liu 2007, 420).

in Japanese society" (Yasuko 2016, 488). In the play, he is sent to Taiwan to put down local uprisings. Through the performance of military masculinity, he strives to be accepted as a full Japanese citizen. A stage shot (Fig. 7) shows male actors as male figures in contemporary Japanese and Chinese uniforms and suits. Otojirō/Washirō stands in the center in blackface, transferring its pejorative uses in the West to the Japanese context. The actors epitomize the notion of a straightened theater in strikingly erect poses, without tilted torsos, the arms and heads in line with the upper body, only moving in a small range of bodily space. Yet, two energetically sitting figures, each with a helping assistant in lunges behind their backs, recall the importance of acrobatic fight scenes, which Kawakami takes from his Japonist Kabuki performances into his straight theater. Another image shows Sadayakko as Desdemona, here named Tomone, wearing a traditional Japanese dress, hairstyle, and makeup in a similar "straight" posture. In an image of her as Oriye (the Japanized Ophelia) in the *Hamlet* production of the same year (Fig. 8), however, she can be seen dressed in Western style, performing the madness scene with a strikingly motionless body, which completely contrasts her madness dances in Kabuki style for which she became famous in Europe.

Figure 7. Stage shot of *Othello* (1903), Kawakami Otojirō standing in the middle, property of the Tsubouchi Memorial Theater Museum, Waseda University Tokyo, No. F01-25994.

Figure 8. Sadayakko as Oriye (Ophelia) in *Hamlet* (1903), property of the Tsubouchi Memorial Theater Museum, Waseda University Tokyo, No. F64-00678.

Thus, as Kano puts it, the "definition of [the modern Japanese] actress involves more than a woman performing" (Kano 1995, 32). Her identity is rather formed in comparison to a range of preceding models of performative femininity such as "the male *onnagata* ... and his performances in Kabuki, New School, and New Theater productions, the Western actress, the *onna yakusha* (woman player) who appeared in Kabuki and New School, and, finally, the New School actress" (Levy 2010, 232—33). Finally, there were also male *onnagata* in Kawakami's productions (Ortolani 1995, 237), so the different types of performers of femininity were not mutually exclusive but competed in a mimetic circle for the greater "naturalness" and the representation of psychological interiority.[25] However, it is important to note that Kawakami introduced explicit scenes of cross-dressing and ethnic drag in various productions.[26] That is, while "straight theater"

---

25 It was not uncommon in contemporary discourse to see (male) *onnagata* as the better performers of the manly "modern woman," because of the alleged exaggerated femininity of Japanese women, as contemporary critic Osanai Kaoru, among others, notes: "I believe that the onnagata, a man by birth, is much more suited to the modern woman than today's Japanese actresses, who have terribly little of the manly element in them" (quoted in Levy 2010, 239). So there is a "hierarchy of cultural legitimacy" in which "it is the Western actress who stands unchallenged at the top of the totem pole, with the onnagata and the Japanese actress battling it out for second place" (Levy 2010, 238).

26 For example, in *Dumb Travel* and *Around the World in Seventy Days* (see Kano 1995, 95—104).

paved the way for the gradual essentialist replacement of *onnagata* by "natural" actresses, the importance of cross-dressings as inversion increased.

To come back to the straightening of *Othello* in terms of aesthetic means, dance and song were not erased but ascribed to the group of indigenous Taiwanese rebels. In their appearance at the beginning of act IV, they sang folk songs and "hopped and leapt about screaming some sort of incantation" (Yasuko 2016, 489). The Kawakami's Shakespeare adaptations can be said to have drawn on exoticism in two ways: on the one hand, the staging of Shakespeare itself was perceived as exotic in the Japanese context with "the most exotic elements of all: the translated text and the modern actress" (Levy 2010, 202); on the other, his concession to the audience's affinity for dance and song was reframed according to an exoticist logic by assigning it to the exoticized Taiwanese "Others." This might be called a reversed exoticism that adopted the Western theatrical means as exotic spectacle and in which actors play "at being 'Western' colonial masters who subject indigenous peoples in colonies to their rule" (Yasuko 2016, 489). Yet, the actors of this abridged version of the "original" Shakespearean *Othello* in the guise of contemporary Japanese and Taiwanese did not perform ethnic drag in the sense of Sieg (2002) as "the performance of 'race' as a masquerade" or "a ritual of inversion" (2). The show followed much more the dramaturgy of exoticism as a mimetic strategy to become similar, but not equal—the desire to become a more refined Japanese West, as Kano puts it:

> It is the drag against the full identification with the West, the impossibility of a perfect passing as Western, that came to be understood to be Japanese qualities. And to a certain extent, it is these Japanese peculiarities, now understood to be Japanese essences, that are later made to serve as the basis of postmodern performance genres such as butō and underground theater. (Kano 1995, 170)

Nevertheless, contrary to their claims, the Kawakami's straight theater in many ways exhibited this impossible and undesired entirely "passing as Western." Their productions, which distort binaries such as original/adaptation, Japanese/European, feminine/masculine, *onnagata*-actress, constantly teetered on the edge of comedy (e. g., see Brandon 1999, 37), as, for example, in the perception of *Othello* as a "travesty of the worst kind" (Levy 2010, 210) by some of his contemporaries, or in the explicit parody of Washirō's masculinity in *New Othello* (1906) (Kano 1995, 108).

Closing Thoughts: Dragging and Exoticism

The Kawakamis' European tour in 1902 can be described as a point of crystallization from which various entanglements between Japanese and European dance and theater modernisms radiated outward. In a time of deep societal changes in Japan and Europe, the three case studies show complex and contradictory migrations of gendered and cultured stagings of bodies that revolve around the performative femininity of *onnagata* as a central point of reference. In research on Kabuki, the term "drag" is rarely used because, in its widespread binary understanding as an inversion of gender or cross-dressing, it does not seem appropriate to the complex mimetic processes of *onnagata* (Mezur 2005, 256). However, through *onnagata*, the notion of drag might become more complicated. Within the Japonist framework that I have sketched out, drag could be understood in an expanded sense: as a variety of performative practices that are not limited to the category of gender but inextricably linked to particularly situated ideas of culture and nation, as the notions of *self-exoticization, queer exoticism,* or *reversed exoticism* suggest. Furthermore, these practices do not operate in simple binary oppositions as crossings in terms of gender or ethnicity. Much in line with the idea of a performative femininity in *onnagata* that does not refer to the subjectivity of the performer, even in the proclaimed "straight" productions of the Kawakamis in Japan, different performative models of femininity exist without contradiction next to each other.

Within the Japonist framework, all three examples point to the alliance of exoticist draggings with commodifications.[27] However, while neither the Kawakamis nor Sakharoff were detached from colonial exoticism, they also revealed its deeply fictional constitution by deliberately performing exoticism with an ironic component or even taking a parodistic turn. In the case of the Kawakamis, their performances in Europe questioned seemingly clear-cut power relations of exoticism while also reproducing them on the Japanese stage. Their work on straightening Japanese theater finally led to the marginalization of the ambiguity of *onnagata* while simultaneously introducing scenes of drag as an inversion. In the case of Sakharoff, exoticism was related to a queer modernity. Eventually, his practice might also have pointed to the possibility of detaching the exotic from the colonialist and redefining it, as his French contemporary Victor Segalen has put it: "as the ability to conceive otherwise" (Segalen 2002, 19). In this sense, drag could refer to a work in which cultural sediments are layered and rearranged to create an exuberant body that explodes the exotic from within.

---

27   See Köppert in this volume on commodification and ethnic drag.

References

Barthes, Roland. 1976. "The Dolls of Bunraku." Translated by David Savran. *Diacritics* 6, no. 4: 44—47.

Brandenburg, Hans. 1921. *Der moderne Tanz.* Munich: Georg Müller.

Brandon, James R. 1999. "Kabuki and Shakespeare: Balancing Yin and Yang." TDR *The Drama Review* 43, no. 2: 15—53.

Brandstetter, Gabriele. 1997. "Die Inszenierung der Fläche: Ornament und Relief im Theaterkonzept der Ballets Russes." In *Spiegelungen: Die Ballets Russes und die Künste,* edited by Claudia Jeschke, Ursel Berger, and Birgit Zeidler, 147—164. Berlin: Vorwerk.

Brandstetter, Gabriele. 2003. "'Blumenhaft und schlächterhaft': Japanische Körperbilder in Europa; Rezeption, Projektion, Fiktion in Texten und Bildern der Zwanziger Jahre." In *Ostasienrezeption im Schatten der Weltkriege: Universalismus und Nationalismus,* edited by Walter Gebhard, 247—266. Munich: Iudicum.

Brown, Jayna. 2008. *Babylon Girls: Black Women Performers and the Shaping of the Modern.* Durham, NC: Duke University Press.

Burt, Ramsay. 2022 (originally published 1995). *The Male Dancer: Bodies, Spectacle, Sexualities.* New York: Routledge.

Craig, Edward Gordon. 1921. "Sada Yacco." In *The Theatre Advancing,* 261—266. London: Constable.

Downer, Lesley. 2004. *Madame Sadayakko: The Geisha Who Seduced the West.* London: Review Press.

Delius, Rudolf von. 2002 (originally published 1913). "Alexander Sacharoff." In *Die Sacharoffs: Zwei Tänzer aus dem Umkreis des Blauen Reiters/Two Dancers within the 'Blaue Reiter' Circle,* edited by Frank-Manuel Peter and Rainer Stamm, 49. Cologne: Wienand.

Drain, Richard. 1995. *Twentieth Century Theatre: A Sourcebook.* New York: Routledge.

Fäthke, Bernd. 2011. "Von Werefkins und Jawlenskys Faible für die japanische Kunst." In *"Diese zärtlichen, geistvollen Phantasien": Die Maler des "Blauen Reiter" und Japan,* edited by Brigitte Salmen, 103—132. Murnau: Schloßmuseum.

Fournier, Louis. 1900. *Kawakami and Sada Yacco.* Paris: Brentano's.

Francke, Daniela, ed. 2013. *Im Rausch der Kirschblüten: Japans Theater und sein Einfluss auf Europas Bühnenwelten.* Vienna: Brandstätter.

Franko, Mark. 1992. "Where He Danced: Cocteau's Barbette and Ohno's Water Lilies." Special Issue "Performance" PMLA 107, no. 3: 594—607.

Franko, Mark. 2003. "Majestic Drag: Monarchical Performativity and the King's Body Theatrical." TDR *The Drama Review* 47, no. 2: 71—87.

Franko, Mark. 2015. *Dance as Text: Ideologies of the Baroque Body*. New York: Oxford University Press.

Fraleigh, Sondra. 2010. *Butoh: Metamorphic Dance and Global Alchemy*. Urbana: University of Illinois Press.

Fuchs, Georg. 1905. *Die Schaubühne der Zukunft*. Berlin: Schuster & Loeffler.

Fuchs, Georg. 1906. *Der Tanz*. Stuttgart: Strecker & Schröder.

Garber, Marjorie. 1997. *Vested Interests: Cross-dressing and Cultural Anxiety*. New York: Routledge.

Gottschild, Brenda Dixon. 1997. *Digging the Africanist Presence in American Performance: Dance and Other Contexts*. Westport, CT: Greenwood Press.

Huebner, Friedrich Markus. 1914. "Alexander Sacharoff." *Phoebus: Monatsschrift für Ästhetik und Kritik des Theaters* 1, no. 3: 101—104. https://www.sk-kultur.de/tanz/sacharoff/seiten/text_4.html. Accessed August 30, 2024.

Isaka, Maki. 2016. *Onnagata: A Labyrinth of Gendering in Kabuki Theater*. Seattle: University of Washington Press.

Kano, Ayako. 1995. *Acting Like a Woman in Modern Japan: Gender, Theater, and Nationalism*. New York: Palgrave.

Klankert, Tanja. 2015. "Das Echo der Gastspiele von Otojirō Kawakami, Sadayakko und ihrer Truppe in den deutschsprachigen Printmedien." In *Sound and Performance: Positionen—Methoden—Analysen; Thurnauer Schriften zum Musiktheater*, edited by Wolf-Dieter Ernst, Anno Mungen, Nora Niethammer, and Berenika Szymanski-Düll, 159—173. Würzburg: Königshausen & Neumann.

Levinson, André. 1929. *La Danse D'Aujourd'Hui*. Paris: Edition Duchartre et Vanbuggenhout.

Levy, Indra. 2010. *Sirens of the Western Shore: The Westernesque Femme Fatale, Translation, and Vernacular Style in Modern Japanese Literature*. New York: Columbia University Press.

Liu, Siyuan. 2007. "Adaptation as Appropriation: Staging Western Drama in the First Western-Style Theatres in Japan and China." *Theatre Journal* 59, no. 3: 411—429.

Mezur, Katherine. 1995. *Beautiful Boys/Outlaw Bodies: Devising Kabuki Female-Likeness*. New York: Palgrave Macmillan.

Morinaga, Maki. 2002. "The Gender of Onnagata as the Imitating Imitated: Its Historicity, Performativity, and Involvement in the Circulation of Femininity." *Positions* 10, no. 2: 245—284.

Ortolani, Benito. 1995. *The Japanese Theatre: From Shamanistic Ritual to Contemporary Pluralism*. Princeton: Princeton University Press.

Pantzer, Peter, ed. 2005. *Japanischer Theaterhimmel über Europas Bühnen: Kawakami Otojirō, Sadayakko und ihre Truppe auf Tournee durch Mittel- und Osteuropa 1901—1902*. Munich: Iudicium Verlag.

Pronko, Leonard Cabell. 1967. *Theater East and West: Perspectives Toward a Total Theater.* Berkeley: University of California Press.

Ruprecht, Lucia. 2019. *Gestural Imaginaries: Dance and Cultural Theory in the Early Twentieth Century.* New York: Oxford University Press.

Sacharoff, Alexander. 2002a (originally published 1910). "Bemerkungen über den Tanz." In *Die Sacharoffs: Zwei Tänzer aus dem Umkreis des Blauen Reiters/ Two Dancers within the 'Blaue Reiter' Circle,* edited by Frank-Manuel Peter and Rainer Stamm, 46. Cologne: Wienand.

Sacharoff, Alexander. 2002b. "Spiritualität." In *Die Sacharoffs: Zwei Tänzer aus dem Umkreis des Blauen Reiters/Two Dancers within the 'Blaue Reiter' Circle,* edited by Frank-Manuel Peter and Rainer Stamm, 220—21. Cologne: Wienand.

Sacharoff, Alexander. 1932. "How I Arrange My Dances." Typescript. Salzburg: Derra de Moroda Dance Archives, image collection, folder 4.

Said, Edward. 1978. *Orientalism.* New York: Pantheon Books.

Sakharoff, Alexandre. 1922. "Mes Maîtres." In *Clotilde et Alexandre Sakharoff,* edited by Maurice de Brunoff. Paris: n. p.

Savigliano, Marta E. 1995. *Tango and the Political Economy of Passion.* Boulder: Westview Press.

Scholz-Cionca, Stanca. 2016. "Japanesque Shows for Western Markets: Loïe Fuller and Japanese Theatre Tours Through Europe (1900—1908)." *Journal of Global Theatre History* 1, no. 1: 46—61.

Segalen, Victor. 2002 (originally published 1955). *Essay on Exoticism: An Aesthetics of Diversity.* Translated and edited by Yaël Rachel Schlick. Durham, NC: Duke University Press.

Sieg, Katrin. 2002. *Ethnic Drag: Performing Race, Nation, Sexuality in West Germany.* Ann Arbor: University of Michigan Press.

Stamm, Rainer. 2002. "Alexander Sacharoff: Dance and the Fine Arts." In *Die Sacharoffs: Zwei Tänzer aus dem Umkreis des Blauen Reiters/Two Dancers within the 'Blaue Reiter' Circle,* edited by Frank-Manuel Peter and Rainer Stamm, 11—45. Cologne: Wienand.

Veroli, Patrizia. 1992. "Archives of the Dance: Between Art and Fashion; Alexandre Sakharoff's Theatre Designs." *Dance Research: The Journal of the Society for Dance Research* 10, no. 1: 78—93.

Veroli, Patrizia. 2002. "The Mirror and the Hieroglyph. Alexander Sacharoff and Dance Modernism." In *Die Sacharoffs: Zwei Tänzer aus dem Umkreis des Blauen Reiters/Two Dancers within the 'Blaue Reiter' Circle,* edited by Frank-Manuel Peter and Rainer Stamm, 169—217. Cologne: Wienand.

Vuillermoz, Émile. 1933. *Clotilde et Alexandre Sakharoff.* Lausanne: Editions Centrales.

Yasuko, Ikeuchi. 2016. "Colonial Othello in Taiwan." In *A History of Japanese Theatre*, edited by Jonah Salz, 488—489. Cambridge: Cambridge University Press.

Zorn, Bettina. 2013. "Das traditionelle Theater Japans." In *Im Rausch der Kirschblüten: Japans Theater und sein Einfluss auf Europas Bühnenwelten*, edited by Daniela Francke, 35—50. Vienna: Brandstätter.

EPILOGUE

nora chipaumire in conversation with Jay Pather

When I was asked to invite an artist for a talk at the 2022 Facing Drag conference, it was absolutely clear that nora chipaumire would be that artist, someone who has located her work in issues of social justice consistently while at the same time pushing boundaries of form. Her work challenges status quo through the use of fertile approaches to performativity, what one can term within the contexts discussed in this book as dragging. chipaumire's choreographic work explores with a fierce intensity the body as performative of race and gender. Her film Afro Promo #1 King Lady (2016) is described by chipaumire as "an Afro-feminist manifesto beautifying bodies to claim the right to life," as a statement around magnifying beauty in response to the negation of and invisibilizing of Black bodies. In portrait of myself as my ~~father~~ (2015)—performed in a boxing ring, chipaumire embodies a specific critique of hypermasculinity and emasculation. It is these methodologies of dragging in chipaumire's work and particularly their relationship to an ongoing challenge with coloniality that I wanted to bring attention to in our talk.

Jay Pather

JP: Thank you nora for taking this time to reflect on your performance work within this provocative framing of Facing Drag set up by the University for Music and Performing Arts Vienna. Let's begin by thinking through an early film of yours *Afro Promo #1 King Lady*.

nc: In *Afro Promo #1 King Lady*, I wanted to figure out how we could create a superhero that was promoting Africanness as well as Blackness as ways of being. I appeared as King Lady, because I am a lion (laughs)—operating from an animist point of view. The lion is the king. And I am a woman when it suits me … When I made this work, in 2016, the Marvel movie *Black Panther* and the like with Black superheroes, that made any sense to me, had not come out, so I made my own.

JP: There is a hyper quality to this piece as in a lot of your work. You are dragging. You expect us to pierce through your use of typologies and to reflect on your obsession with stereotypes.

nc: There is a lot of hype around Black bodies! I create a hyper space around African Black bodies. My method of dragging or of augmenting the body expands it so that it becomes hypervisible in a specific way.

When I moved to the United States, I could pass for whatever Black there was anywhere. But since I am African, I was also interested in ways in which I could distinguish myself from just this flattening of Black skin, while always aware of not hijacking another's experience as my own, or for my own benefit. However, I am born and raised in Zimbabwe. The animist way of being is something that is truly a part of my DNA. And in this realm of animism, the question of gender is also very hyper. So in some ways, the expansion of the body in *Afro Promo #1 King Lady* is informed by animist thought and the current discourse on animism. It explores what the body is capable of and how it is able to change form. So, when I say I am a lion, the possibility of being one, of transforming, exists in the right circumstances and with enough alcohol (laughs) and the right kind of sound. To shapeshift into that beast is very much what my clan is after … I come from these spectacular ways of imagining the body.

The question of gender may be boring to an extent. In *Afro Promo #1 King Lady*, however, I was like let me beef this up. I was interested in working on how masculinity is viewed. In the instances of both, my performance *portrait of myself as my ~~father~~* and my film *Afro Promo #1 King Lady*, the performer obviously read as male appears with this big old bow and stuff and in very pretty colors. I am in less pretty colors. But I have the longest penis (uh, that I'm wearing). It is kind of dragging on the floor. I also augmented my shoulders with these pads from American football—dragging along the stereotype of the loudness and hypervisibility of the Black male body, especially when it is read as an American body. But I am not American. I am, in fact, African. So this work is trying to put together stereotypes of the African as the animist and of the hypervisible Black, the North American, specifically African American. In the US everybody talks about the radical Black space. What is radical? What is Black? I am African, not only Black. Black is also a drag for me. In this new world we take that on and it has become part of everybody, not just Black bodies. Everybody seems to be Black to the extent that they're listening to Elvis Presley.

JP: With regard to hypervisibility: in your acclaimed opera *Nehanda* (2022) opacity is preeminent.

Figures 1 (p. 221) and 2 (p. 223). *Nehanda* (2022) by nora chipaumire, presented at Espace Cardin during the Festival d'Automne in Paris, France. Photo: Laurent Philippe.

nc: Hypervisibility and opacity are similar, really. They do the same awesome work to inspire questions. *Nehanda* conjures up the great female spirit of Zimbabwe. But when we perform we all show up in regular dress. So in fact we are dragged in many ways. You would expect that in a work like *Nehanda*, we would show up in our tribal outfits, but we did not. We showed up in our township outfits, in regular clothes. We looked like we were just hanging out, not doing that particular historical or traditional work. But it was the spirit of Nehanda that I intended to rise—slightly obscured, no visual cues help you to understand that.

In the talk after the performance in Amsterdam, the moderator complained about not getting all those things that they expect to see in Europe, when a work is so-called from Africa. The people on stage looked like they could be just from down the street. And then they were doing what should have been opera. We created a series of false expectations. I think that is similar to drag and similar to being hypervisibilized. It is just approached differently. In *Nehanda* you're supposed to open your ears and you don't have much guidance, with anything more than that.

JP: Well, let us talk about the dexterity of dragging at the colonial encounter, the double consciousness that emerges in the minds of colonized peoples who now are forced to take on a whole other culture. And what emerges is multiplicity and sophistication. This, for example in the use of kilts, seems to be a backdrop of *Nehanda*.

nc: When the British were marching north from South Africa they had drummers who were Scottish, dressed in their kilts. It is said, the native combatants who were waiting to fight these invaders thought they were women. Since they would not fight women they would let the British army come close until it was too late. The kilts have remained as part of the memorialization of a misreading of the body.

The flair and the swag within which the kilt is worn in that part of the world is heck of a cool thing, also in my own family ... My grandmother was the first to really encounter white people—colonization. So, you know, it's only three generations removed. And looking at the kilts: I have always been very curious, about the way we defend Western dress. Several years ago, there were some guys who thought, oh, let's do a political act and put on some animal skins and stand in the middle of the city center in Harare. They were quickly arrested for indecency and have never been heard of again. Which is very scary.

I was also very intrigued by the way women are encouraged to wear the *durag*, the cloth tied around the head to cover exposed hair, which seems to me to come from the "downstairs" population, you know, like in the English houses with their upstairs and downstairs. The workers, the keepers of the house are downstairs, and they're the ones who cover their heads, they're not supposed to be sexy. They're supposed to have aprons, it's functional, but the upstairs people, they show off their hair. And here we are, all are covered women of a certain age. It is the norm. These are very recent acquisitions of a cultural language. But they are so much a part of who we are.

JP: I am interested in the shapeshifting in your works such as *portrait of myself as my father*. This performance considers the African male through the lens of capitalism, Christianity, colonialism and liberation struggles, and how these political and cultural traditions impact the African family and society on a global scale.

nc: I think, people like me who were born in a colonial situation and came through the colonial education system actually understand the specific difficulty with family relations. We are consciously aware of what is wrong on a minute-by-minute basis. And that fact is that the men in my own family all die young through alcoholism or any kind of disease—whatever, you name it. In my work, I was very curious to understand: what is this kind of constant destruction of the family and its genderedness. At the very end of this work, I carry my father on my back since I pretty much surrendered to this as a lifelong work. I have to carry my father, or at least the carcass of my father, who could be every Black man, because without the ability to carry him, which also means the ability to forgive him, we all would be dead. In my work, I wanted to find a way to deal with what ails our families when somebody is absent.

In Senegal, we were performing this work in many Western spaces. The work is loud. It encompasses many languages, whether it's Wolof from Senegal, or Patois from Jamaica, or sometimes Shona and English, accompanied by inaudible mumblings. In Saint-Louis, pretty much by half an hour into the work, all the white people had left. The work was too much for them. It smelled bad. It was too loud. Because whenever we transgressed the boxing ring, we actually talked to people. And the rest of the public started to talk back to us, which is the most beautiful thing about any kind of living act in Africa. It becomes a conversation. In Senegal, it became a congress. It was a conference where everybody who stayed could pretty much have their say. Those who didn't like it left. The young Black Africans stayed till the end. What should have been an hour-and-a-half performance became a four-hour piece—an event that would not stop. It went to the point where it is not about putting on an act. In this moment, we were alive and so was my father, because to say his name within that event was to make him live.

JP: However, it is not just about carrying your father at the end. By the end, there is a sense of you refusing to perform and to objectify your own body.

nc: I want to go back to the fact of knowing the conundrum that is the African Black experience. Or I would even be more specific as to the Zimbabwean Shona experience. One can't escape. I make work that calls me or demands me to do it. Even though I have done my own *Rite of Spring*, I quoted Stravinsky making it about me and about being consumed, you know, which is how I feel. If I am on the subway, on the street, anywhere in the world, I am always looked at.

So, how to hyperextend that lookingness in my performative work, so that you really have nowhere to look but the thing implicating myself. As an aside, I am often mistaken for something other. If I could get paid for the number of times I am called *sir!* I start to almost enjoy it, you know, like, oh, I could pass. I could pass because this person is paying so little attention, which is also hurtful in a way. Of course, I draw the line at male customs officials patting me down. I'm like, oops, can I get a woman to do that?

So, my work is to bring that feeling in this moment with the public. And I will speak collectively because everyone in the team is asked to really go far. That means allowing yourself to go into spaces that are fragile. To bring to consciousness a specific rigor and a surrender.

JP. Lindy-Lee Prince[1] talks about the tension between drag as a perpetuation of heteronormative definitions of gender and drag queen performances as acts of subversion and transgression. You are working with an external kind of visuality with one of the performers: Pieter van Heerden, who is a white South African actor, reads as cis male and very often gets singled out in an artist conversation afterwards even excluding you! There is a nod here towards what can be seen as kind of an obvious form of drag.

nc: Well, Pieter is a tall Afrikaner dude and somehow he makes the fifteen Black people disappear! In *Nehanda* he has no clothes on except for an Elizabethan wire skirt. He is Elizabeth. He is Empire. He is Cecil John Rhodes. I wonder if it could be called indigenizing the white settlers in drag. Pieter is tasked to arouse compassion in the native African. I'm coming at it from a very Zimbabwean attitude: we have not recovered from colonization and we have not had any reconciliation meetings, and we probably will not. How could this white body carry this? And I think because Pieter surrenders to the pain and to the obtuseness, perhaps even the joy of being absolutely naked with just this wire skirt. Plus, the nudity is such an affront to the Shona sensibilities.

Yet, Pieter is also taking on this power of empire, of Elizabeth, the Queen. He gets singled out because he surrenders totally. Perhaps he sacrifices himself, which white South Africans kind of do really well. We witness Pieter hurt himself to maybe say the thing that hasn't really been said: that, you know, we're fucking sorry and we're criminals, and this shit should have never happened.

---

1   Lindy-Lee Prince, "Creating Personas, Performing Selves—Gazing Beyond the Masks of Drag and Neo-burlesque Performance," thesis presented for the degree of doctor of philosophy in the Department of Social Anthropology, University of Cape Town, 2021.

JP: I am interested in the tension in your work between what is quite obviously dragging, a kind of dragging the past along, and this very contemporary, very present burning, being vulnerable in the present.

nc: I think history isn't in the past. It's in our bodies. And on the daily exchanges with Pieter as a South African and me being Zimbabwean we talk about other Africans in South Africa. That is the continued dialogue we have—that is because of the past, but we have to deal with it now, and we have to figure out how to be human and how to care for each other.

JP: Could you maybe expand a little on how *Nehanda* works? Also, with regard to the use of orality?

nc: I am working with an archive of the Shona *Bira* ceremony. The instruments, the guitars, the drums help this mirroring of the call on ancestral spirits for intervention, central to the *Bira*. The guitars push the language of this mirroring into another sphere altogether and the drums are there to remind us of the quantum physics held in the drumming culture. The voice is throat singing—it is vibrato. The language is primarily Shona with some English in it, thinking through what court arguments could be because the text is built from a colonial court case that really happened, commencing in March 1898. It is called Elizabeth or the Queen versus Nehanda and actually appears in case law. I used it to think through the voice about: what is law, what is jurisprudence, what is jurisdiction? The arguments are all sung approaching something that Puccini or Wagner could never think of. However, since there is no talking and it's all sung, it is still opera. And I dare anyone to challenge that. It is all told in song. It ticks all the boxes for opera. And it is 5.5 hours long ...

JP: That qualifies already.

nc: Well, it is actually very short because in my work I was thinking of Zimbabwean songs which are all night long rituals, which I describe as revolutionary parties. They go on from sunset to sunrise. So that is longer than 5.5 hours. The initial proposition was to do an all night long piece. Of course, nothing has prepared the European culture industry as it exists for such a work. I mean, unless it's Wagner's *Ring* cycle. Then people can sit there for days and weeks. But when it comes from southern Africa, calls itself an opera and is a 5.5-hours long work in a language the audience does not understand ... as if everybody in Europe understands Italian.

I would say, it should be taken as an opera that, instead of some archaic work, defines what opera should be today. My opera is a legal court case. It is about reparations, about restitutions. It demands a return of all the dead bodies. Because the African people of whom we speak—the people who were involved in this court case: their bodies remain in London's Natural History Museum today. So this work is not just about "the spirits," but a provocation to think around how canned bodies can be brought to rest. And until they do not rest, we cannot rest.

JP: Your work has been described as disruptive by commentators. However, the disruption had been already there. It is a violent context that you are speaking to. So, it's not like you are disrupting what is already profoundly disrupted.

nc: I am here because of a disruption. We are here because of a disruption. The disruption has already happened. The work that we do is to bring us to a conversation, but definitely not a disruption. I think, when people say that it stems from a Eurocentric lens of what an operatic work looks like. You know, how the performers move, how the audience is positioned ... I am not aspiring to appropriate a specific use of space, a use of gesture, a use of the body, a use of the public. I am thinking of this work as a congress, an *indaba*, in which everyone has a space to speak. It is always better when the public does speak and engage with what is happening. My desire is to do that kind of work that provokes the public to either get up or talk back.

JP: I think that is a good point to open this discussion to other delegates. Chris?

Chris Standfest: Thank you very much, nora. I would be interested in who you create your work for?

nc: I lived in so many different spaces. But when I am in my village, where people really don't care about what is happening in the urban spaces, there is just that. And that is real too. Zimbabwe is so massive that there is an urban elite, there is a township elite, and then there is a rural reality. And I am blessed to have the possibility to be in all those spaces. Or maybe not blessed. Maybe that's the curse.

This art thing we talk about—dance, whatever—was not designed for a person like me, an African girl. I come from a working, poor family, so I have no bourgeois thing, you know—no urban thing either. Being the first person in my family to go to university, I am inserting myself as the first public. But I would really prefer if my grandmother understood it. I am not saying other people cannot understand my work, of course. Thinking beings will get something, but the fact that me and mine were never supposed to come into spaces like this is an important reckoning for me, and something that perhaps allows me to keep this burning fragility that raises the question of if I am even allowed to be in here. And then there's the question of who or what am I, if I *am* in here. So that may answer your question to whom I am speaking, to what public. I am not excluding anyone, but I am really zoning in on: what would my mother say? What would my grandmother say to all my nephews in the village? Could they recognize themselves in my work? They would understand the language, whether it is the gestures, the subversion or the sonic interruption. I would not need to translate. The people who are asking for translations are generally the gatekeepers: *Black girl from Zimbabwe, well, explain to us what you are doing?* My work, however, has to be complete in and of itself. I should not need to translate. Perhaps it is time that the world understands that an African body can speak or act and we are not obliged to translate.

Zimitri Erasmus: Thank you, nora. When I was watching your work and listening to you and Jay, I thought of call-and-response rituals. And just linking this to the previous question on who do you do your work for: Could you give us a sense of ways in which the audience responded? I am asking this because you were saying any thinking, and I would add, feeling, being, would not need translation, right? The layers of communication in your performances are so multiple that there is a window for almost anyone to respond. But it depends on ways of knowing that enable response or provoke withdrawal. You say that you are the first public, but you are also calling, aren't you?

nc: You are quite right: when I say, I am my first public, I mean people like me. People like me, not just me. Sometimes I am the only person in the room to carry this dilemma of being looked at or of being the first in one's clan to speak English ...

I think your obligation, once you buy a ticket, is to stay through the course. You are obliged at least to think with the artist. Also if it becomes uncomfortable, if it feels like: this is not for me. I think, if people buy a ticket, they have already made a contract. They have agreed to spend time with this thing. However, privilege works like: oh, I don't have to sit through this because it doesn't affect me. You can leave, when you are challenged in the way you relate to the world, because you are privileged.

JP: What are you inviting to be present in your work?

nc: Presence is a good word instead of representation to describe my work, the methods, the process, the practice. We really work physically, in a daily research mode, stressing the body to a point where we can be totally in surrender to what the gesture needs to be. Training the body emotionally and mentally, so that we can do this every day. For many in the team, the ancestors are always present. So they are having to negotiate that hyperspace of owning their physical body, but also surrendering their physical body in different moments of the work. Presence. You're there. Yeah.

JP: I just want to end by thanking you for the sheer exhaustion of being that shapeshifter, because you gave us everything from the hyper drag, from the evocation of drag in its most accessible common form to undoing dragging in a spectacular way.

Acknowledgments

Facing Drag emerged from a series of international conferences and lectures on gender at the University of Music and Performing Arts Vienna (mdw) starting during the challenging period of the COVID-19 pandemic, between 2022 and 2024. In contrast to recent political regressions and calls for defunding the humanities—gender and decolonial studies in particular—the publication of this volume coincides with a hopeful and future-oriented development: the founding of the International Research Center Gender and Performativity (ICGP) at mdw in 2025. We would like to express our heartfelt thanks to all contributors to the event series—this includes not only the authors featured in this volume but also those whose contributions and presence shaped the intellectual landscape of the event series and our Facing Drag research network: Nadia Davids, Diedrich Diederichsen, Stephan Geene, Fatima Naqvi, Mamela Nyamza, and meLê Yamomo. Our gratitude extends to the audience, to our colleagues and, in particular, to the students whose engagement, questions, and critical insights were essential to the depth and dynamism of the discussions. Special thanks go to the former gender studies team—Mariama Diagne, Silke Felber, Susanna Hufsky, and Julia Ostwald—whose dedication made both the events and the editing of this volume possible.

The volume accompanies Eveln Annuß's book on *Dirty Dragging*, cofunded by the German Research Foundation, DFG (Heisenberg project *Demarcations and Performative Transpositions*), and the FU Berlin. We are deeply grateful for the generous financial and institutional support provided by mdw's Rectorate, its Research Support Office, and the university's publishing house, mdwPress (very special thanks also to Max Bergmann and to Kathrin Heinrich for their stunning professionalism and cordial assistance). Without this backing, the realization of *Facing Drag* would not have been possible. We wish to give our special thanks to Rector Ulrike Sych, whose unwavering support enabled us to pursue our work. Our sincere appreciation also goes to Vice Rector for Organizational Development Gerda Müller for championing structural support for gender research as well as to Head of Research Support Therese Kaufmann for her crucial involvement in realizing both the event series and this volume—also to the Stabsstelle Gleichstellung, Gender und Diversität, especially to Andrea Ellmeier and Ulli Maier; the Institute for Cultural Management and

Gender Studies (IKM), in particular to its head Dagmar Abfalter; and all our mdw colleagues for their support of our endeavor. Moreover, we cordially thank the current ICGP-team—Philipp Hohmann, Thari Jungen, Kyra Schmied, Marina Rauchenbacher, Karo Spöring as well as Michael Thomas Taylor for revising the manuscript, Oliver Brentzel for the cover design—against all odds, and Marion Bräuer for graphics.

Postscript

"We ask you ... to ensure that there is no visual similarity to the iconic logo of the brand ... belonging to our client." The original design for the cover by Oliver Brentzel, reflecting on practices of quoting without quotation marks, was scrapped just before printing and on what we schlepp along involuntarily—another casualty of today's crackdown on queering, the bureaucratic misuse of copyright law, and institutional preemptive obedience. Keep on Dragging ...

Biographies

Evelyn Annuß, Professor of Gender Studies, heads the International Research Center Gender and Performativity (IGCP) at the University of Music and Performing Arts Vienna. Her work is dedicated to the flight lines of aesthetics, theories of performativity, and the critique of politics. As a cultural studies scholar of theatre and literature, she focuses, among other things, on political spectacles—their historicity and mediality—in the context of National Socialism, colonial racisms, and processes of (re-)fascization. Her new book *Dirty Dragging. Performative Transpositions* is being published simultaneously in German and in English by mdwPress.

Sam Ehrentraut is a research associate and a doctoral candidate in the FWF project *Dramaturgies after Postdramatic Theater* at the Department of Theater, Film, and Media Studies at the University of Vienna. He is also affiliated with the Cluster of Excellence *Temporal Communities* (Free University of Berlin), where he organizes collaborative formats that bring academic and artistic perspectives into dialogue. His research focuses on performative dynamics of time-based media, media ontologies, and aesthetic concepts in the field of trans studies.

Nanna Heidenreich is a media and cultural studies scholar and a curator for film/video/interventions. She is currently Professor of Transcultural Studies at the University of Applied Arts in Vienna, after positions in universities, art and film schools in Düsseldorf, Köln, Hildesheim and Braunschweig. As a curator, she has worked with Forum Expanded / International Filmfestival Berlin (Berlinale) and HKW (Berlin) among others. Her work focuses on critical migration studies, postcolonial media theory, image politics and queer cinema. Current research areas are age/rage, the relation of fascism and aesthetics, and so called "alien species". She lives in Berlin and Vienna.

Elaine Frantz is a historian of violence in the nineteenth and twentieth century United States. Her work focuses on particular historical conflicts characterized by systemic violence, and considers the function and results of this violence, and how contemporaries—perpetrators, victims, witnesses, and the broader public—themselves described and responded to these acts of violence. She has published books on the reconstruction-era Ku Klux Klan and on nineteenth-century male drinking culture, and is now finishing a book on policing in Pittsburgh, with the working title: *"Just a Copper": Policing Pittsburgh 1869—1934.*

Aurélie Godet is a Full Professor of U.S. History at Nantes Université, France, and a junior fellow of the Institut Universitaire de France for the 2023—2028 period. After working on the history and ascendency of conservative movements and ideas in the United States between 2005 and 2014, she pivoted to a new research topic in 2015: the history of festive practices in the Atlantic world from the sixteenth century to the contemporary period. She recently completed a manuscript titled *Betwixt Fear and Hardship: Joy in French Colonial Louisiana, 1682–1769*, and currently sits on the editorial board of the online, peer-reviewed *Journal of Festive Studies*, which she cofounded in 2019.

Katrin Köppert is an art and media scholar. Her work focuses on media theories of digital colonialism, critical theories of computation, post-/decolonial media theories of the Anthropocene at the intersection of art, design, and visual cultures, digital memory studies, queer media aesthetics. She currently holds the professorship for media theory at the Institute for Music and Media Studies at Humboldt University in Berlin and is a Junior Professor of Art History/Popular Cultures at the Academy of Fine Arts in Leipzig. She has recently published the co-edited book *digital:gender—de:mapping affect* (Spector Books, 2025) and is now writing a book on *Computational Blackface*.

Karin Harrasser is the director of ifk International Research Center for Cultural Studies in Vienna and a Professor of Cultural Theory at the University of Arts Linz. In addition to her academic activities, she has been involved in various artistic and curatorial projects, e. g. at Tanzquartier Wien or with MAPA Teatro and the Colombian Truth Commission in Bogotá. Her research currently focuses on asymmetrical cultural transfers between Europe and South America and on modes and histories of cultural violence. Recent books: *Surazo. Monika und Hans Ertl: Eine deutsche Geschichte in Bolivien* (2022), translated into Spanish and Brazilian, and *Gegenentkommen* (2023).

Julia Ostwald is a dance scholar and postdoctoral researcher in the ERC-project OLFAC. *Exploring the Intervening Performativity of Smell* at the University of Arts Linz (AT). Situated at the intersections of dance theory, performance studies, and cultural history, her research focuses on the entanglements of sensual perceptions, aesthetics, and (body-)politics in the context of dance and choreography. Julia previously worked as a senior scientist in gender studies at mdw-University of Music and Performing Arts Vienna and as a project assistant at the doctoral school gender_transcultural at Salzburg University.

nora chipaumire was born in 1965 in what was then known as Umtali, Rhodesia (now Mutare, Zimbabwe). She is a product of colonial education for black native Africans—known as group B schooling—and is invested in knowledge acquisition and sharing outside of prescribed parameters.

Jay Pather is a choreographer, curator, and dance scholar. He is the director of the Siwela Sonke Dance Theatre and served as Associate Professor at the University of Cape Town's Centre for Theatre, Dance and Performance. He directs the Institute for Creative Arts and curates major public-art and live-art events such as the Infecting the City Festival and the Afrovibes Festival. His work combines performance, site-specific interventions and interdisciplinary arts practice to explore post-coloniality, spatial justice, and urban embodiment.

Raz Weiner (Dr.) is a scholar of performance studies, politics, and embodiment. His work focuses on traditions, archives and contemporary forms of colonialism, racialization and queerness, the production of bodies and knowledge, and the co-constitution of human societies and digital worlds. Before becoming a guest lecturer (2024) and research fellow (2023) at mdw, he was based in the School of Politics and IR at Queen Mary University in London (2020—2022) and the Faculty of Architecture and Town Planning at The Technion in Haifa (2021—2023).

About mdwPress

The Open Access University Press of the mdw

mdwPress is the open access academic publisher of the mdw – University of Music and Performing Arts Vienna. With this press, the mdw aims to increase the visibility of its research in all its diversity. Free from commercial motives, mdwPress makes research results freely accessible and reusable for the interested public.

The quality and academic freedom of mdwPress are ensured by an academic board whose regularly rotating internal and external members are characterized by distinguished academic achievements. Each proposal for a publication project, including a suggestion for the peer review procedure of the entire manuscript, is discussed and determined by this board.

mdwPress is open to all academic publication formats, including journals and innovative formats, and welcomes inter- and transdisciplinarity. Where necessary, mdwPress relies on external partnerships.

About This Volume

This volume is the outcome of international conferences and a concomitant lecture series between 2022 and 2024, among them the transdisciplinary conference "Facing Drag in Performing Arts and Popular Culture" organized by Evelyn Annuß, Silke Felber and Julia Ostwald at the mdw in June 2022. It is supported by open access funding from the mdw. After the project proposal was accepted by the scientific advisory board of mdwPress, the volume underwent an independent, international double-blind peer review by two reviewers. The mdwPress advisory board agreed with the positive reviews and accepted the book for publication.

GPSR Authorized Representative: Easy Access System Europe, Mustamäe tee
50, 10621 Tallinn, Estonia, gpsr.requests@easproject.com

www.ingramcontent.com/pod-product-compliance
Lightning Source LLC
Chambersburg PA
CBHW061730120626
46550CB00005B/1759